The transpersonal

At present there is no book that deals with the whole range of approaches to the transpersonal in counselling and psychotherapy. The transpersonal approach has become of much more interest recently because of the impact of Ken Wilber's work. His map of psychospiritual development has been very influential. Psychology and spirituality are now linked in a very convincing way, where one grows out of the other, distinct but connected.

John Rowan has maintained an interest in the transpersonal for the past twenty years, and his many successful books reveal a transpersonal concern. This is the first time, however, he has devoted an entire book to the subject. The book is unique in providing the first comprehensive account of the transpersonal as it applies to psychotherapy and counselling. Rowan shows where the idea comes from, how it has developed, how it can be used. The book is intensely practical and refers back constantly to what the psychotherapist or counsellor actually does in the area of the transpersonal. At the same time it is theoretically rich and deals with some of the most contentious issues with which the transpersonal practitioner has to contend.

The transpersonal will be of interest to counsellors, therapists and psychologists who are currently working without any concept of the transpersonal and thus doing an injustice to the complexity of the whole human being.

John Rowan is a Chartered Psychologist, qualified psychotherapist (AHPP) and accredited counsellor (BAC). He is author of a number of successful books, including *Ordinary ecstasy: Humanistic psychology in action* (2nd edition, 1988) and *Subpersonalities: The people inside us* (1990), both published by Routledge.

Other titles by John Rowan from ROUTLEDGE

The reality game
A guide to humanistic counselling and therapy

The horned god
Feminism and men as wounding and healing

Ordinary ecstasy
Humanistic psychology in action, second edition

Subpersonalities
The people inside us

The transpersonal

Psychotherapy and counselling

John Rowan

London and New York

First published in 1993
by Routledge
11 New Fetter Lane, London EC4P 4EE

Simultaneously published in the USA and Canada
by Routledge
29 West 35th Street, New York, NY 10001

Typeset in Bembo by Michael Mepham, Frome, Somerset
Printed in Great Britain by
Biddles Ltd, Guildford and King's Lynn

British Library Cataloguing in Publication Data
A catalogue record for this book is available from the British Library.

Library of Congress Cataloging-in-Publication Data
Rowan, John
  The transpersonal : psychotherapy and counselling / John Rowan.
  p.   cm.
  Includes bibliographical references and index.
  1. Transpersonal psychotherapy.   I. Title.
  RC489.T75R68   1993
  616.89'14—dc20   92–15268
                                                                 CIP

ISBN 0–415–05361–7
     0–415–05362–5 (pbk)

This book is dedicated to Cernunnos and my Shakti

Contents

Figures

Introduction

This book is for everyone who is interested in psychotherapy or counselling, whether as a practitioner, as a student or as a client. Some people prefer the word consulter, some people use the word patient, but in this book the word client is used.

This book is about the transpersonal. It will be two or three chapters on before it becomes completely clear what that means. It seems that we have to try various paths to lead up to it, all based in personal experience. We can at least say that it seems to be something to do with spirituality, and that spirituality and religion are not the same thing.

Let me speak personally at this point. For years I kept myself in a state of ambiguity and vagueness about spirituality. I agreed willingly that it made sense to talk about altered states of consciousness, such as ecstasy and peak experiences, and I even explored some of them through meditation and LSD as well as through counselling and group work. I even agreed that some of my experiences were like some of the experiences related by some of the mystics, along the lines which Pahnke's research (1971) made famous. But I resolutely shut my eyes to any possibility that I might have to go further into the same realm as had been opened up by such experiences – that seemed to mean aspiring to sainthood, which meant being perfect. I would have to shine. Maybe I would have to levitate, or heal people, or have visions, or walk on water – the list of possible demands seemed endless and absurd. I had given lectures about the Jonah complex (Maslow 1973) and the repression of the sublime (Haronian 1974) – both about how we run away from our higher possibilities because to own up to them would be too challenging – but all at once I realized that I was suffering from these syndromes myself.

Admitting that I was a spiritual being, I found, was a bit like admitting that I was in love: there was the same scary sense of commitment, of risk-taking, of stepping over a line, of taking on a big responsibility. There was the same sense of not being able to see the end of the line – partly I knew, but partly I couldn't know, what I was getting into.

I had been in the growth movement for about ten years when these ideas really hit me. This had meant an enormous amount of self-exploration and self-discovery through group and individual work. I had worked through my Oedipal material, my birth material, my good and bad breast material and so on and so forth, and felt, rightly or wrongly, that I had gained what the human potential movement promised – that I was a fully functioning person. But still I held back from this new material.

If we once admit that we are spiritual beings, then the whole game takes another turn. Instead of patching wrecks, or even realizing potentials, we are dismantling the barriers which are keeping us away from the divine. That which separates us from our spiritual centre has to be questioned, seen through and transformed.

Psychotherapy is about a person daring to open up to what is inside. The methods of spirituality (transpersonal therapy, image work, meditation and prayer) I now see also as daring to open up to what is inside. We can, as it were, use the same internal gestures which we found useful in therapy, to go further into this deeper level. There is a good discussion of all this in one of the first books which ever came out in this area, Boorstein's (1980) excellent compilation of selected papers.

But of course this means that psychotherapy is already a spiritual exercise. Simply paying attention to what is really going on inside us (as opposed to what should be going on or what we would like to be going on) could be seen as a spiritual act. Thomas Oden (1972) pointed out how similar the pietism of Jewish and Protestant sects in the 17th and 18th centuries was to the practice in encounter groups. It is just a question of acknowledging that, and being prepared to go further in the same direction.

PSYCHOTHERAPY AS BRIDGE

So perhaps we could think of psychotherapy as being connected to spirituality. The simplest way this could happen is for it to be a bridge leading us into the spiritual realm. If we think of psychotherapy as a bridge between psychology and spirituality, this may be a good starting-point. What could we mean by this?

At one end of this bridge psychotherapy is firmly supported on the ground of conversation, research evidence, the body, the physico-chemical and all the rest of it. There are clear connections with psychology, perhaps spelt out most firmly by the personal construct people, the cognitive therapy people and the behaviour modification people. There is every prospect of even more of these connections being made in the future – more and more specialized forms of psychotherapy have learned journals now, and Janov (1977) has written on the neurology of therapy.

From this well-established base psychotherapy arches out into space, and the other end of the bridge seems to be hidden in mist. What we are aiming at in therapy has been very variously described: the healthy person; the whole person; the fully functioning person; self-actualization; individuation; making the unconscious conscious, and so on. The concepts are vague and very open-ended, and a long journey seems quite often to be involved; it is hard to know whether one has arrived at the end of it. As one reaches the end of one span of the bridge, more spans become visible, further along the bridge.

People who have ventured out further along this bridge include the Jungians; the psychosynthesis people; the transpersonal people; the Osho people; some of the biofeedback people such as Maxwell Cade; some of the primal integration people; some of the holistic health people, and so on. Nearly all of these are very cagey about talking of the other end of the bridge: come a little further, they say, and we shall find what we shall find.

It seems pretty clear to me now that what is at the other end is spirituality. In other words, to reach the end of the bridge means facing and exploring the numinous, the holy, the divine.

Of course, this can be a very scary challenge. Meeting the divine is not a matter to be taken lightly. It means reopening a whole lot of doors, and perhaps a whole lot of wounds, which many of us thought we had closed for ever.

But the point is, we have begun to do this already. Every time we have a breakthrough in therapy, a point where we say 'Ah!' (not 'Aha!' which is close but different), it means experiencing something spiritual. Sometimes it may be experienced as inside ourselves: this is the typical experience of contacting the real self. Sometimes it may be experienced as outside ourselves: this is the typical experience of contacting the transpersonal self. Sometimes it may be experienced as a total letting-go: this is the typical experience of contacting the divine, which may be known as energy, as nature, as god or goddess, as pure being, as the void, or whatever.

Within each of these experiences of breakthrough there are depths and differences – we shall attempt to construct a map of them in a later chapter. But what they all have in common is that they represent an opportunity – which may be accepted or rejected – of acknowledging that we are spiritual beings, that we do have to recognize the realm of the divine.

At a transformational management conference I went to, a group of us came up with the notion that a radical political question to ask was – *What is the balance of good stuff and garbage in your life? In this conference? In the transformational network? In Britain? In society at large?* If we now see the good stuff as that which enables us to get close to that in us which is divine, and the garbage as that which separates us from that, we can see that this is not only a radical political question, it is a radical spiritual question too.

The word spiritual has a daunting ring to many of us, certainly to me, because of the childhood memories of formal religion which it may bring up. For me, this was all about trying to live up to impossible ideals which I had had no hand in setting up. It made me feel bad more often than it made me feel good. Guilt and hypocrisy seemed to go together hand in hand in religion.

But now I know it doesn't have to be religious in that sense. The breakthroughs I made in therapy were liberating, not confining. And the breakthroughs I have made in spirituality have also been liberating – more about discovering what I was really about than discovering new demands or commandments.

Inevitably at some point we shall have to open up all the thorny questions of what our model of the divine is going to be. I have ventured a long way into this area myself, but it is not something which needs to be dealt with at the beginning. My tendency as an intellectual is to look in all the books, but as a wise Buddhist once said: the big book is the self. We can discover a surprising amount just by opening up more and more; the books can come when they come, and so can the individual teacher.

There was even a discovery about this – there is a saying which many people have repeated, that when the student is ready the teacher will arrive. At first I understood this to mean that when I was ready I would meet some wonderful person who would guide me along the way. But now I see that it can just as well mean that each person I meet, each event in my life, can be my teacher; I will only be able to see this when my readiness is there.

I found I had a great fear of the complications of spirituality – was I going to have to sort out the whole intricate web of occultism, spirits, theosophy, healing, astrology, the Tarot, the Kabbala, and all that? (We shall see later that the answer to this is No.) Was I going to have to examine the claims of the Buddha, the Tao, Tantra, Yoga, Sufism, gnosticism, Christianism, Judaism, Islam, the Goddess and all the rest? (We shall see that the answer to this too is No.) But this is not all that different from the fear of the person who comes to psychotherapy for the first time, faced with the numerous schools and techniques and conflicting claims of that field. And the same advice applies: go one step at a time; find what suits you; stay with it as long as it works; keep trying seriously and with commitment, and you will achieve whatever there is to be achieved.

It seems to me that spirituality is not as scary as I thought at first it was going to be. It has been very good for me to cross the bridge. Now I am coming back to say that it is OK to go further. And about the middle of the bridge there is a fascinating area called the imaginal world, which enables some amazing new things to happen in therapy. So it's useful as well as good in itself.

Psychotherapy as the three-faced goddess, then: one face looking back to childhood and the repressions and hangups of the past; one face looking into the present, the existential now; and the other face looking forward to spirituality and the divine. Something fundamentally ambiguous and hard to contain. Something much more risky and dangerous than we had supposed. Something much more deep and wonderful than we had ever imagined.

SOME POSITIONS

Many people talk of levels of consciousness, or states of consciousness, but here I want to use the concept of positions. This then does not raise all the awkward challenges, which we shall be looking at later on, as to whether there really are higher or lower levels in these matters.

All counsellors and psychotherapists work from more than one position at a time. Some people think of this as the ability to work on the conscious and the unconscious at the same time. This is a very common, though by no means universal, way of dividing up the world of consciousness. All those who espouse psychoanalysis do so, as do all those whose schools stem directly from Freud or Jung. So it has acquired some respectability, at least amongst those who look to Freud or Jung as exemplars. A rather similar position is held by Mahrer (1989a), who speaks of operating potentials of the person, of which we are or can be consciously aware, and deeper potentials which are not available to consciousness in the same direct way.

Some think of it as working from the position of the body and the position of the mind. Reich and the Reichians and neo-Reichians, of whom Lowen (1976) is perhaps the best known, have emphasized this position, and have gone into the ways in which we can work directly with the body in our attempts to move the mind.

Some talk of operating from an intellectual position and an emotional one. This is popular among the followers of Carl Rogers, the person-centred school. They emphasize the way in which we have to work on an emotional level if we want an empathic relationship with another person.

It is not enough to listen to the words, we have to listen to the feelings which lie behind or within the words. In psychoanalysis, some talk of listening with the third ear, and this is a similar idea.

Some talk of working at the three positions of body, mind and spirit. As we shall see later, this in fact opens up a whole extra realm with its own laws and its own structures. To take this third step opens up the possibility of working in a transpersonal way.

What we shall be looking at in this book is the position of the transpersonal. The view being put forward here is that this is a position at which all counsellors and psychotherapists work some of the time, though they may be unaware of it, and may not think of it in those terms. It will be argued that just as we speak prose without necessarily giving it that label, so also do we communicate from a transpersonal position without necessarily calling it that.

What is this transpersonal position? There are three reasons why it is difficult to give a quick definition of it.

1   It is not an ego function, and the language in which we write books is an ego function. So the language in which we write books, which we might call ordinary language, essentially deals with ego functions of one kind and another. Ordinary language, then, misses something essential about it, and hence falsifies it to some degree.

2   It has to do with spirituality, and our culture has a curious attitude to spirituality, either dismissing it altogether as a primitive misunderstanding, or regarding it as something very religious and very special, the domain of the priest or the saint. We may be very aware of fakers and frauds claiming to be spiritual in their efforts to exploit people. In any case it is not for us, as ordinary people, as counsellors, therapists or psychologists.

3   When we first come across it for ourselves as an actual experience, it usually seems to us holy and ultimate, and it seems then something of a desecration to try to talk about it in everyday terms. Yet we know that many other things which seemed to us quite superhuman and marvellous when we first came across them do later tend to seem more ordinary.

In spite of these drawbacks, it seems that it must be worthwhile to attempt at least a first approximation to a definition of the transpersonal. The most succinct version I have come across comes from Stanislav Grof. He says that transpersonal experiences can be defined as:

experiences involving an expansion or extension of consciousness beyond the usual ego boundaries and beyond the limitations of time and/or space.

(Grof 1979, p. 155)

This at least puts us into the right general area. Just as paying attention to the intellectual content of a person's discourse puts us into one realm of consciousness, and paying attention to the emotional content of that person's discourse puts us into another realm of consciousness, and paying attention to the unconscious aspects of a person's discourse and actions puts us into another realm of consciousness, now we are saying that there are other realms, of which the transpersonal is one. Frances Vaughan puts it very well when she says:

> The transpersonal perspective holds that a large spectrum of altered states of consciousness exist, that some are potentially useful and functionally specific (i.e. possessing some functions not available in the usual state but lacking others) and that some of these are true 'higher' states. Higher is here used in Tart's (1973, 1975a) sense of possessing all the properties and potentials of lower states, plus some additional ones. Furthermore, a wide range of literature from a variety of cultures and growth disciplines attests to the attainability of these higher states.
>
> (Walsh and Vaughan 1980, p. 11)

This talk of 'higher' states may make us nervous, but they are not higher in the sense of being unattainable or requiring great dedication to attain. They are potentially present in all of us, and have to with things like intuition, creativity, imagination and the like. They are part of being human, and even children may have access to them (Cohen and Phipps 1979).

THE PRE/TRANS FALLACY

A useful distinction has been made between what is transpersonal and what is prepersonal. The transpersonal goes beyond the personal (the limited, the ego-bound, the everyday world of ordinary discourse); the prepersonal has not yet reached the personal, and is more limited than the personal. Wilber (1983b) says that to confuse these two is to commit the pre/trans fallacy. Yet the confusion is very common. Someone who is firmly fixed in the middle position (the personal, the everyday consciousness, consensus reality, what Wilber calls the Mental Ego position) may very often see anything other than that as inferior to that. For example, someone who is wedded to the model of there being just the conscious and the unconscious minds will tend to see the transpersonal as just another example of material from the unconscious, and therefore as essentially prepersonal. Someone who only distinguishes between the intellectual and the emotional may see the transpersonal as just another part of the emotional realm, and misjudge it in that way.

Someone who is firmly fixed at the ego-bound personal position and wants to steer clear of both the prepersonal and the transpersonal is committed (though perhaps not aware of the fact) to Aristotelian logic. Anything which goes outside Aristotelian logic (A is A, A is not not-A, nothing can be A and not-A at the same time), it seems to such a person, must be irrational. It is true that someone may not have reached an understanding of Aristotelian logic, and may be irrational in that sense; that would be an example of the prepersonal, not of the transpersonal. If someone, or a group of people, were to deny Aristotelian logic by preferring something more primitive or less demanding, such as magical thinking or tribal thinking, this would be prepersonal, and Wilber (1981b) has a long discussion of this in historical terms.

The transpersonal, on the other hand, goes beyond Aristotelian logic, and starts to be interested in dialectical logic, process logic, many-valued logic, fuzzy logic and so forth – all sorts of variations which show that Aristotelian logic is a choice, not an inevitable law of thought. (The Boolean logic which underlies most computer programs is based on the Aristotelian model.) When we are working from the transpersonal position it makes sense to say that A is never simply A, and that if it were it could never change. It is only because A is not simply A that it has within it the potentiality for change. To a psychotherapist or counsellor, this is meat and drink, or one of the basic facts of life. If Jane or Andrew were simply Jane or Andrew, they would be stuck with themselves for ever, and could never emerge from their stuck place. Perhaps not every therapist realizes that they are denying Aristotelian logic every time they work for real change with a client, but this is one of the many instances of where we are working transpersonally without even realizing it.

This book is dealing with something of direct relevance to counsellors and therapists, not with the whole history of spirituality. Many of the people we have talked about in this book have been influenced by Eastern religion, paganism, Christianism, existentialism, etc., but this is not what we are about here. We are concerned with the theory and practice of the transpersonal, understood as a particular modern approach to spirituality, in relation to counselling and psychotherapy.

ONE-TWO-THREE-INFINITY

There is a tendency which one can observe in this field to go in for what I have called the 'one-two-three-infinity' definition of spirituality, which seems to me dangerously inadequate. In this version we say that there is the body and its sensations (one), the emotions and feelings and desires (two), the intellect and its thoughts (three), and everything else is a sort of mystical oneness called spirituality (infinity).

This kind of thinking is very common with New Age people, with EST (or Forum, as it is now called), with the Guru Maharaj-Ji, with Transcendental Meditation, with some aspects of Zen Buddhism, with the Enlightenment Intensive, with Rajneesh (or Osho) and many others who should know better. The dangers of it have been discussed very well by Richard Anthony and his colleagues in their discussion of cults, where they warn against one-step enlightenment as a snare and a delusion. They call this a unilevel approach, and they have a number of arguments against it, all based on bitter experience and history.

> In practice, unilevel groups fail to be effective catalysts for spiritual transformation because of two characteristic flaws that cause them to confuse transcendent and mundane experience. First, they are overly literal and 'definitive' in their interpretation of language and texts, with too little appreciation of symbolic and metaphoric levels of meaning. This is the problem of *univocality*. Second, they harbour the attitude that the value as well as the proof of spiritual transformation lies in predictable, observable consequences in the mundane sphere. This is the problem of *consequentialism*. Univocality and consequentialism are closely linked and tend to occur together. They are the defining features of the unilevel category.
>
> (Anthony *et al.* 1987, p. 41)

They do not mean, of course, that consequences are of no account, merely that to link them too closely to transpersonal experiences makes the everyday consciousness the judge of the transpersonal consciousness – a tempting but inappropriate and unsafe move.

What I am talking about here, on the other hand, is what Anthony and his colleagues call a multilevel approach, which they consider to be much safer and less likely to lead to dogmatism and unreality and danger.

It seems to me that there are several quite separate and distinct experiences which can rightly be called spiritual, some of them much more accessible and common than others. In transpersonal practice we begin to explore these experiences and have them for ourselves.

cage and tells me to follow him. I am the first one to get off the bus, and I follow a female officer into the jail. She tells me to turn around and face the wall. She removes my shackles, and pats me down aggressively. I don't have to look down to know that my ankles are sore and red, and that my wrists are scratched up from the handcuffs.

After giving a deputy my name, I am told to sit and wait. There are about fifteen chairs, two phones, and a tiny television hanging on a wall. Once again, I am the only female, but these men are wearing dark blue, not red, like the men from the bus. And none of them look Hispanic. One guy is not even wearing a uniform—he wears dirty jeans and a faded t-shirt instead. He is clearly drunk. I guess that's the reason he's here. Another guy is scratching himself, picking on his pimples, and talking to himself. Then an officer brings in a woman who sits two seats away from me. My pleasant surprise to finally see a woman is killed by the stench coming from her. Her hair is very dirty, and she doesn't seem to be in her right mind, either. She has an awful sunburn and she's picking at her skin, peeling it and throwing it to the floor. Every now and then a few officers pass by and say hello to her. I think it's safe to assume she's a regular. Why are the mentally ill jailed?

I am thirsty, hungry, and tired of sitting on this plastic chair. Then I hear somebody say that it's already after four o'clock in the afternoon and that we've missed dinner. This means that we will not get anything to eat or drink for the rest of the day. I don't know how long I must wait here; no one will tell me anything. I sit in a chair for a few hours, glancing at the television every now and then without really being able to focus on the shows. Finally, when I can't hold it anymore, I use the bathroom and drink some water from the faucet. I wait a couple of more hours. So far, everything I thought I knew from movies about jails has been wrong.

It's after midnight. I never thought I would look forward to sleeping in a jail bunk, but I'm exhausted. Why aren't they taking me to a

WHAT THE TRANSPERSONAL IS NOT

Sometimes it helps to set some boundaries to a concept, so that we can tell more easily what it is not. Here are some of these boundaries, which are helpful, I believe, in defining the transpersonal.

The transpersonal is not the extrapersonal

A distinction has been drawn by Alyce Green and Elmer Green (1986) between the extrapersonal and the transpersonal. This is very similar to the distinction made by Wilber (1980), and also used by Grof (1988), between the Lower Subtle and the Higher Subtle. It is very much like the distinction made by Marc–Alain Descamps (1990) between the horizontal transpersonal and the vertical transpersonal, but I find this language a bit confusing. (We shall be looking at these terms in more detail in later chapters.) The essential differences are laid out below.

Extrapersonal	Transpersonal
Spoon-bending	Higher self
Levitation	Deep self (Starhawk)
Extra-sensory perception	Inner teacher
Dowsing	Transpersonal self (psychosynthesis)
Working with crystals	High archetypes (Jung)
Clairvoyance	The soul (Hillman)
Telepathy	The superconscious (psychosynthesis)
Radionics	Creativity (surrendered self type)
Radiesthesia	Some peak experiences
Blindsight	Intuition (surrendered self type)
Fire-walking	Some healing
Bloodless skin-piercing	Some near-death experiences
Out-of-body experiences	Upper chakras
Paranormal generally	Subtle energy systems
Fakirism	Guidance self (Whitmont)
Mind over matter	The Self
The psychic	Transfigured self (Heron)

Green and Green (1986) suggest that the basic distinction is that in the transpersonal there is something divine, whereas the extrapersonal is basically nondivine. This may be a tricky way of making the distinction, because how can anything be nondivine, strictly speaking? But I think it can be helpful in pointing in the right direction.

In the past this distinction between the extrapersonal and the transpersonal has not been drawn so clearly, and Jung's notion of the collective unconscious includes both. Work with past-life experiences is sometimes closer to one and sometimes to the other. But Stan Grof (1988) finds the distinction useful in his work, which is, as far as I can see, quite close to my own. The fullest description of it is to be found in Wilber (1980), and we shall be returning to this in later chapters. Enough for the moment to say that the extrapersonal and the transpersonal are not the same thing. This is just one expression of the general point made earlier about the inadequacy of the one-two-three-infinity definition of spirituality.

The transpersonal is not the same as the right brain

There is a lot of interest these days in the two halves of the brain, and it is often said that our civilization neglects the right brain and overstresses the left brain. Book after book comes out attributing more and more marvellous characteristics to the right brain, and we are told that we have to cultivate the right brain more if we are to be whole people.

There may be something in this, and there is no wish here to pour cold water on the whole idea, but it is important to make the point that to locate the transpersonal in the right brain is a mistake. It is a mistake because it necessarily lumps the transpersonal with the prepersonal.

Everyone who writes about the two hemispheres of the brain seems to agree that the left brain is the one to do with the categories of formal thought (what we have been calling the mental ego and Aristotelian logic). This means that everything else has to be located in the right brain. But as we have seen, this puts in one place two things which are very different – the prepersonal (which has not yet got to the position of formal logic, or which finds it too hard and denies it), and the transpersonal (which goes beyond the ordinary categories of thought and finds them insufficient or inappropriate for its work). To confuse these two things seems misleading and unhelpful. To ask where exactly in the brain the transpersonal is located seems to require another fallacy in any case – the fallacy of misplaced concreteness, where we try to make a process into a thing: it would be like asking where goodness is located in the brain, or honesty, or trust.

The transpersonal is not the New Age

There is a good deal of interest these days in the New Age, and in my travels I have seen whole sections of bookshops, and even whole bookshops, devoted to it. But the general attitude of the New Age seems to be undiscriminating, and even to be against the whole idea of discrimination.

As I look over the shelves of the New Age section in the bookshop, the only thing I can find in common between the books and equipment on show is that they are all suitable for gullible people. There is a complete mixture of the good, the bad and the ugly.

If there is anything else in common, it seems to be devotion to the positive at all costs. One must believe anything, accept anything, not question or deny anything. There is even a book which says in its title that we cannot afford the luxury of even one negative thought. This is to take a one-sided position which cannot be justified, and which is certainly nothing to do with the transpersonal, or with spirituality in any genuine sense.

The transpersonal is not religion

The most general use of the word 'religion' is to mean an organization of some kind. We speak of the Christian religion, and mean the churches and chapels which publish the holy books and promulgate the holy doctrines. We speak of the Muslim religion, and mean the whole organization ranging from the most simplistic fundamentalism to the most sublime Sufism, expressed again in books, art works, rituals, pilgrimages and so forth. We speak of Judaism, and mean the whole way in which this is expressed in society, whether fundamentalist, orthodox, liberal, Hasidic or whatever. But the transpersonal is to do with personal experience, which may or may not be expressed in religious terminology. And if it is expressed in some religious way, it is just as likely to be some little-known religion such as paganism, animism, polytheism or pantheism, as one of the better-known and better-organized religions. In other words, the transpersonal is a realm of personal discovery, not something which one joins.

This point is well put and elaborated by Joseph Fabry, who has this to say about it:

> To maintain or restore health, we must consider all three dimensions. The spirit, like the body and the psyche, is part of every person, not just the religiously inclined. The spiritual dimension, which Frankl calls the
> → *noös*, contains such uniquely human attributes as our will to meaning, our goal orientation, our creativity, our imagination, our intuition, our faith, our vision of what we can become, our capacity to love beyond the psychophysiological, our capacity to listen to our conscience beyond the dictates of the superego, our sense of humour. It also contains our

self-detachment or ability to step outside and look at ourselves, and our self-transcendence or ability to reach out to people we love and causes in which we believe. In the area of the spirit we are not driven; we are the drivers, the decision-makers.

(Fabry 1980, p. 81)

This is a very good preliminary statement about the transpersonal, and takes us a little nearer again towards understanding it.

It is not really important in this introduction to give a hard-and-fast definition of the transpersonal. It will be more fruitful to give, as it were, an ostensive definition all the way through the book, to keep on saying – here is one more aspect of the transpersonal. In one way the transpersonal is one of the outposts of psychology. But perhaps a useful phrase to keep in mind is that the transpersonal is the shallows of mysticism. As such, it is accessible to all.

THE TRANSPERSONAL IN EVERYDAY LIFE

It is important to realize that the transpersonal is very familiar to us already. If it were something strange and new, it would hardly warrant talking about except by the few who are interested in such things. But if it is very common, it would make much more sense to say that all practitioners could take an interest.

Inner voices

Many of us have had the experience of hearing a voice (perhaps coming from inside us, perhaps coming from somewhere outside us), warning us, giving us hints or hunches, giving us information and so forth. We speak of 'the still small voice of conscience'. Sometimes it may seem like an actual voice, and at other times it may seem like a vaguer felt sense of some inner communication.

The whole idea of a vocation depends upon this sense of hearing a calling. In its original use it actually means to be addressed by a voice. Gandhi, among many others, relied a great deal on his inner voice, both in his spiritual and in his political work (Chatterjee 1984).

Some contemporary research on this was carried out by Myrtle Heery (1989), who found that subjective reports of inner voice experiences could be divided into three categories:

1   Inner voice experience as a fragmented part of the self.

2   Inner voice experiences characterized by dialogue providing guidance for growth of the individual.
3   Inner voice experiences where channels opened toward and beyond a higher self.

The first of these is not necessarily transpersonal at all, but rather tends to come under the heading of subpersonalities. As I have written at length elsewhere (Rowan 1990), many subpersonalities are well within the normal range of variation. We do not need to invoke the transpersonal to account for most of them.

The second category is much more likely to relate to the transpersonal, particularly in the form of the archetype of the transpersonal self. One's inner voice, one's inner sense, can be a real guide to what direction to take in life choices.

The third category, Heery found, was confined to people who had practised some form of meditation on a regular basis. So this seems to go further than the normal kinds of access to the transpersonal which we are talking about here.

It seems, then, that the experience of a voice can be less than transpersonal, can be genuinely transpersonal, or go further than the forms of the transpersonal we are examining in the present text.

Intuition

It used to be thought that there was such a thing as 'women's intuition', but the more this has been investigated over the years, the more it has become evident that intuition is not peculiar to one gender.

It seems clear that there are several different types of intuition, which are really rather different from one another. Let us look at six of them, recognizing that there may well be more. Each of them seems to entail a different notion of the self, such that we cannot have that form of intuition until we have developed to that level of the self. In all of them we may be faced with unusual ways of discovery or prediction.

The child self

This is a level of consciousness where fantasy and reality are not always too well distinguished. Fantasies may be very vivid and emotional, and the person may come to conclusions about what is going on in the real world which are really more to do with private fantasies. But the young child may be very perceptive, knowing that something is wrong without knowing exactly what it is.

At the earlier stages there may be no external implementation of such fantasies, but later they may express themselves in the form of play. Such play may take permanent expression sometimes in the form of paintings, models, constructions or even writing. Other people form part of this fantasy, part of this play, and we do not make much distinction between what is to do with them and what is to do with us. The classic example is the young child who always knows what the baby is trying to say.

Intuition may become very intense at this level, because there are few inhibitions due to knowing what must logically be the case; there is a wider sense of possibility than we have later. It is possible to get back into this level of intuition by lowering our barriers and being childlike, and many creative people use this method.

The magical self

At this level we use intuition to deny our loneliness and isolation. It has to do with the denial of separateness to ward off fear and anxiety. It consists of techniques, often of a ritual kind, which give or restore connection and communication with others. These are tied up with a group, and it is the needs of the group which are the key to intuition at this level. This happens a lot in close families. What the intuitive person does is, as it were, to tune in to the group, and to realize its fears (and answers to them) in concrete form. Sometimes trance is used for this purpose – a trance in which the individual becomes more part of the group and can speak out in terms of the group's obsessions. Cases of apparent possession or poltergeist phenomena may be expressions of this level of being. This is the *participation mystique* which is found in primitive tribes and still in certain communities such as some of those in Sicily, for example. In our own culture the production of good graffiti, spellbinding speeches, popular music, popular badges and successful advertising may occasionally take this form.

The role-playing self

At this level intuition is turned towards being used or exploited, in order to give the person a niche in society. Intuition is used to get social rewards of one kind and another. The whole emphasis seems to be on problem-solving. Fantasy for its own sake is disapproved of and suppressed. There may be a notion of intuition as regression back to the unconscious, in the service of the ego. Or it may be seen as psychic, sensitive, an unusual skill.

But more usually, intuition is regarded as something which is fully tamed and at the service of society. Many scientific discoveries come from this level of intuition. There is a lot of emphasis on techniques, amounting eventually to a technology of intuition which can be packaged and sold for a price. Intuition is simply another skill to be learned, another role to be played.

The autonomous self

At this level intuition is seen as the expression of the most central self. It is something which can be fully identified with and in that sense owned – 'I am my intuition'. At first, the emphasis on problem-solving may be kept, but often this gives way to a more spontaneous approach. This means that we can see this as the beginning of a transpersonal approach to intuition. It is as it were on the borderline between the everyday world of the previous self, and the fully transpersonal world of the one next to be described. There may sometimes be a negativistic tinge to it, and one may say in effect – 'Who needs the plodding old intellect?' But more often it seems to go with an independence which is not attached to being positive or negative. Often here it is associated with creativity. There may still be a use of techniques (such as the *rapport* approach of NLP), but usually these techniques are self-invented or put together in an idiosyncratic way from existing materials. And in any case the person at this level will improvise in any real situation which may come up. The person can respond with fresh, brand-new insights to people who present themselves.

The surrendered self

At this level intuition is essentially seen as coming from a source other than the self. Action has to be taken to open oneself up to this source, which may be experienced as internal or external; but once this decision to open up has been taken, the rest is acceptance rather than doing. The source may be conceptualized as inspiration, as the Muse, as an archetype, as a goddess or whatever. At this stage one can tune in to this guidance, which may be very helpful in situations of 'go' or 'no go', and be receptive to specific energies. There may be an experience of being a channel for this Otherness. There may or may not be an interest in problem-solving. There is often some selection of problems for solving – some problems are not worth solving, or might do harm if solved. There is a sense of wanting to be worthy of being used in this way. This is what we find at the subtle level, the transpersonal position proper.

The intuitive self

Beyond this there is a further stage, where the person has fully digested the Otherness, and identified with it – entered into a concrete unity with it, through meditation and/or prayer. At this stage the person may say, perhaps – 'I am intuition. Intuition has overcome the me-ness of me. I'm not interested in solving problems – I can't even see any problems.' This would be something like illumination, or transcendence. This is quite clearly transpersonal, but beyond the level at which we are really interested in this book. It is an interesting exercise, however, to try approaching any problem in the spirit of seeing that there is no problem. This may enable us sometimes to see the whole thing quite differently and act more constructively.

Further thoughts

It seems to me that this analysis makes it a lot easier to explain why there should be so much disagreement about intuition, when people get together to talk about it. If people are coming from such widely different levels of consciousness, it is no wonder they fall out. Such differences in basic assumptions can run very deep, and be very hard to perceive.

Of course it is tempting, but I think indefensible, to fudge these issues by saying something like – 'I am not just at one of these levels – I flit about amongst them'. I do not really believe in this butterfly notion of the self – such remarks are usually self-defensive and self-deceiving. Of course, having got to one level, one still has access to the earlier levels; but from a lower level, one does not necessarily have access to the higher levels. Each level is nested within the one next door, as it were. In the terms mentioned already, Child and Magical are prepersonal stages, Role-playing and Autonomous are personal stages, and Surrendered and Intuitive are transpersonal stages of development

After recognizing these different approaches, it would seem absurd to now ask – 'Yes, but what is intuition really?' It would seem to say about intuition, as Hegel says about God, that – 'The idea which a person has of [That] will correspond with that person's idea of self, and of freedom.'

Like so many things, intuition differs depending on where we are in our psychospiritual development – this is something we shall take up in detail later. At the earlier levels, intuition, like emotion, tends to be a chancy thing, which comes and goes according to no particularly evident rule. It just comes in a flash, and goes away again – we have no means by which to hold on to it.

At the autonomous level, intuition begins to be more regular and dependable, and it becomes the main way in which we perceive things. Wilber (1980) talks about 'vision-logic' at this stage, and we are using symbols and images much more now, instead of relying on words all the time. There is a sense that we don't need to know how or why we intuit things, any more than we have to know how we see the sunset, or how we lift our arm.

It is at the surrendered level that intuition comes into its own, and becomes our main way of relating to other people. At this level we can tune in to it at will, and either bring it in or switch it off, just as we can close our eyes or open them, or listen to something or switch off. This has to do with relaxing our definition of where we begin and end, and with opening up the level of soul.

There seem to be at least three different experiences within intuition: the first of these is a feeling which might be expressed in the words – 'I know but I don't know why'. This is what we often call a hunch. At the earlier levels this is uncomfortable, as if we had no right to know things without proper evidence to back them up. We often distrust these intuitions as being fantasy or imagination, which, of course, sometimes they are. But in the process of further development we learn to separate those we can trust from those that are fantasies, simply by using this faculty much more often. It is of course very useful for a therapist to have access to this.

A second type could be expressed in the words – 'I have a sense it is right' – this 'sense' comes into the superconscious (which we shall be talking about in detail), and is to do with rightness and choice. This again can come at any stage, but it is only at the transpersonal stage that we can choose to tune in to it at will. This means that we have to tune in to the most holistic, largest vision we may have, quite intentionally. Without a connection to this 'larger picture' it is too easy be a prey to illusions. If we hold our connection to our higher or transpersonal self, then we can trust that our intuitions are in line with ultimate good.

The third type can be stated in the words – 'It came to me in a flash' – these intuitions may be very minor and chancy at the earlier stages, as mentioned above, but at the autonomous stage and beyond they may include major insights, sometimes glimpses of what seems like an intuitive plan at the highest level.

At the levels earlier than the autonomous, intuition of all types may be accessed directly or through great music, works of art or even in the most unexpected and strange ways. But at the later stages it is more a question of choice.

Goldberg (1983) has a good discussion of many of these matters at greater length. In all these cases, the message may be more or less ambiguous. As in the pronouncements of the Delphic oracle, the intuition may give only part of the picture, leaving the rest to be filled in by some other means. At other times there is little doubt about the completeness of its message, for it enters consciousness with enough light to make itself felt in an unambiguous way.

Creativity

Creativity is like intuition. It can be found on six levels, in just the same way as we have seen for intuition, and again we could say that it is only the later levels which we should call truly transpersonal. It is sometimes said, both of creativity and of intuition, that it is an activity of the superconscious, but we now have reason to believe that this is not always so. It is hard to regard the earlier forms of creativity, belonging to the child self, the magical self or the role-playing self, as truly transpersonal.

Harman and Rheingold (1984) certainly say this, suggesting that we think in terms of creativity as a spectrum of activities – some in the middle of the spectrum and easily visible and classifiable as creativity proper, some in the infra-red and of the nature of automatic reactions which turn out to be uniquely appropriate to a situation, and some in the ultra-violet, truly spiritual experiences with a touch of the divine about them. It is these latter which we can regard as coming from the superconscious – a term used by Assagioli which we shall be examining in the next chapter.

The way to access this particular aspect of creativity is well stated by Rudyard Kipling, who tells us that his Daemon (creative spirit) helped him to write *The Jungle Book*. He says: 'Note here. When your Daemon is in charge, do not try to think consciously. Drift, wait, and obey' (Quoted in Harman and Rheingold 1984, p. 34). The way I sometimes put it in workshops I lead is to say – 'Close your eyes. Repeat the problem three times to yourself [by this time in the workshop we have clarified the problem a great deal], and go into a place of not-knowing. Wait for the answer to emerge. It may come as a sentence, as an image, as a sound, smell or taste, or in some other way; just wait and let it come.'

It often helps to start an exercise like this in a relaxed state, and many books (e.g. West 1975, Feinstein and Krippner 1988, Harman and Rheingold 1984) have instructions on how to reach such a state. This is quite different from the kind of instructions which hypnotists use, as outlined very fully in Karle and Boys (1987).

Once having got into the relaxed state, a little more elaborate instruction for getting into the creative place can be found in Shorr (1983). He asks the person to imagine that there are three gates to pass through, one after the other. With the question, problem or issue in mind, pass through the first gate, find out what may be there; go through the second gate, find out what may be there; and then go through the third gate, find out what may be there and report on what they see, do and feel. Some people need to go through a fourth gate before they get what they need.

One can of course get even more elaborate. An excellent exercise which I have used many times is to ask a client to become very small and wander around inside their own body, giving a running commentary as they do so, looking for the creative place. After a while, if they have not already found it, I suggest that they are now at the entrance, trying to look inside. Then they are inside the creative place, and noticing what they see, what they feel there. Then someone is coming towards them, someone who lives in that creative place all the time. What does this person look like? The person comes closer and can be seen more clearly. Perhaps this person has a name, but I do not insist on this. And now I suggest that the client becomes this creative person, and takes on that person's name and identity. Now the creative person writes down ten answers to the question, problem or issue which the client brought in. Then I ask the client to come back and discuss the whole event.

This brings us close to channelling, and of course people at this level of creativity often say things like – 'I was just the channel, it was not me doing it.' Luckily this whole area has now been covered extremely well in the book by Jon Klimo (1988), who suggests that 80 per cent or so of channelling is quite ordinary stuff from the lower or middle unconscious (Assagioli's terms again), some is from the paranormal (what we have now called the extrapersonal), but that some is from the superconscious, the transpersonal.

We can also say that at the very highest level we may come into the realm of those spiritual experiences where we suddenly see that there is no problem. Suddenly the problem disappears, because we see the whole situation quite differently. It is rare, however, to see this in the ordinary counselling or psychotherapy situation.

Peak experiences

One of the key ideas which has made the idea of the transpersonal more acceptable is the notion of the peak experience. If the statistics are right (Hay 1990) well over half of the people reading this book will have had at least one peak experience in their lives.

The great writer about peak experiences is of course Abraham Maslow, who in various books over the years has explained what they are and how they feel and what they mean. Here is a typical example, taken from the Hay book just mentioned:

> I was walking across a field turning my head to admire the Western sky and looking at a line of pine trees appearing as black velvet against a pink backdrop, turning to duck egg blue/green overhead, as the sun set. Then it happened. It was as if a switch marked 'ego' was suddenly switched off. Consciousness expanded to include, *be*, the previously observed. 'I' was the sunset and there was no 'I' experiencing 'it'. No more observer and observed. At the same time – eternity was 'born'. There was no past, no future, just an eternal now... then I returned completely to normal consciousness finding myself still walking across the field, in time, with a memory.
>
> (Hay 1990, p. 50)

It can be seen how this fits with the definition of 'transpersonal' which we noted from Grof.

So it is often through peak experiences that we get glimpses of the world of soul or spirit. In that sense they could also be described as 'peek' experiences. We can then either ignore them or make much of them, take them as meaningful or meaningless, be proud or ashamed of them, treat them in any way we wish. But they are hard to forget.

And this brings us in touch with a very important point. As mentioned earlier, we grow, in our psychospiritual development, up from the prepersonal through the personal to the transpersonal. At various staging points along the way we change our notion of the self, and see the world differently in consequence. But we can have glimpses of what is ahead at any stage. The peak experience is just one example of such a glimpse, which may come at any point. Now it is very important to understand this idea of a glimpse, and Anthony and his colleagues help us again:

> The term 'glimpse experience', which we are introducing in this volume, is intended specifically to be a counter-inflationary term, emphasizing that the great majority of mystical or transpersonal experiences are only temporary glimpses beyond mundane ego-consciousness and do not involve true transformation to a more transcendent, encompassing state... Glimpse experience... can be pro-transformative and can foster spiritual development in many ways, provided there is an aware-

ness that the glimpse is relative and not absolute, initiatory and not conclusive, temporary and not permanent.

(Anthony *et al.* 1987, p. 188)

It is difficult to get the right balance between overvaluing the transpersonal and undervaluing it. As we go through this book, we shall be continually coming back to the question of exactly what status it has, and just how special it may be. In a fascinating paper, Davis, Lockwood and Wright (1991) found that the most common reasons why people often did not report or even refer to their own peak experiences were: that they were special, intimate and personal experiences which they wanted to keep for themselves; that they might be devalued or put down; and that they were too difficult to describe in words.

The person who has done most to put the peak experience on the map is Abraham Maslow, so let us see that he says about them.

All peak experiences may be fruitfully understood as completions-of-the-act... or as the Gestalt psychologists' closure, or on the paradigm of the Reichian type of complete orgasm, or as total discharge, catharsis, culmination, climax, consummation, emptying or finishing.

(Maslow 1968, p. 111)

Most of us have had a number of peak experiences, although we haven't always labelled them as such. One's reactions while watching a beautiful sunset or listening to an especially moving piece of music can lead to peak experiences. According to Maslow, peak experiences tend to be triggered by intense, inspiring occurrences. 'It looks as if any experience of real excellence, or real perfection... tends to produce a peak experience' (Maslow 1973, p. 175). The lives of most people are filled with long periods of relative inattentiveness, lack of involvement or even boredom. In contrast, in their broadest sense, peak experiences are those moments when we become deeply involved in, excited by and absorbed in the world.

This can happen through very natural experiences, if we will let it happen. Tanzer (1967) found that childbirth could be a potent source of peak experiences, if the mother allowed it to be, and ways were found of teaching mothers how to have such experiences. Instead of having a painful and distressing time, these mothers often had 'a great and mystical experience, a religious experience if you wish – an illumination, a revelation, an insight' (Maslow 1973, p. 183).

It can happen in sport, in dance, in all kinds of body activities. But it can also happen in intellectual activities. Maslow talked with many great scientists about their work, and came to the conclusion that peak experiences were very important for the most creative type of scientist:

> He lives for the moments of glory when a problem solves itself, when suddenly through a microscope he sees things in a very different way, the moments of revelation, of illumination, insight, understanding, ecstasy. These are vital for him.
>
> (Maslow 1973, p. 185)

Of course, we have to allow this to happen. Maslow (1970) points out that it is quite possible to push these experiences away, to deny them, to ignore them. I remember reading an article in some publication of the Secular Society which described someone's camping holiday. One day in the late afternoon, he cycled over the top of a hill and saw a village in the valley below. At that moment the clouds opened, and a ray of sunshine hit the church and illuminated it. The whole village seemed lit up in a most extraordinary way, and gave shape to the whole valley. The author said that for a moment he was tempted to experience a feeling of awe, but he quickly decided that it was more profitable to think about his plans for where to stay the night. This is what Maslow calls a nonpeaker.

The most powerful peak experiences are relatively rare. They have been portrayed by poets as moments of ecstasy, by the religious as deep mystical experiences. For Maslow, the highest peaks include 'feelings of limitless horizons opening to the vision, the feeling of being simultaneously more powerful and also more helpless than one ever was before, the feeling of great ecstasy and wonder and awe, the loss of placing in time and space...' (Maslow 1970, p. 164). This now ties in with our understanding of the transpersonal. We can say that a peak experience of this latter kind may give us a glimpse at least of the transpersonal realm.

There can be peak experiences in psychotherapy, usually but not always associated with catharsis. Here is one example of such an event:

> In midsession, this 25-year-old single woman, after ventilating and experiencing numbness and tingling of her extremities, suddenly displayed signs of fear, crying out in horror, with her body attempting to move backward and away. Her hands attempted to cover her face and eyes, as though she did not want to see. When asked to report her experience, she described herself as being on the brink of a dark abyss, a black void which she felt was threatening and dangerous. She tried in vain to escape, to move away, but felt trapped, there being no place for her to go where she would not be faced with this darkness. While describing this phenomenon, she was asked if this was a familiar place

for her; she admitted to a feeling of familiarity with the *sense* of the experience, but not with the details. It was as though she knew that she always existed on the brink of this void, and she could describe many of her compulsive ways of avoiding it. Maintaining voice contact with the body worker, she was encouraged to examine that darkness and void as thoroughly as possible; this she did, descending slowly and carefully, as though climbing down a steep rock wall. When she reached an impasse where she could no longer find anything to hold onto, she was encouraged to have faith in herself and to jump. After a hesitant pause, she did so. Her face, wracked with fear and tension, suddenly shone with pleasure and brightness. Breathlessly, she reported herself flying, feeling free and expansive, full of pleasure about herself, her depths, and her heights.

(Wong and McKeen 1980, p. 306)

This seems quite a clear example of a peak experience, and it can be seen here how the action of the therapist, enabling and facilitating the experience, was of the utmost importance. Maslow went on to say that there could be plateau experiences, representing a new and more profound way of viewing and experiencing the world. This involves a fundamental change in attitude, a change that affects one's entire point of view and creates a new appreciation and intensified awareness of the world. It is important to realize, however, that this is not a settled permanent state – we still want to be able to have much more ordinary experience as well – but rather a state which we can call on at any moment, in case of need.

The question has been raised as to whether peak experiences can be had to order, as it were, in an intentional way. One of the group leaders in the 1970s used to promise a peak experience if you went on one of his weekends. It is easy to laugh at this, but how about the question of using LSD, mescalin, psilocybin or other hallucinogenic drugs? Pahnke (1971) conducted an experiment using psilocybin along these lines. It was carefully arranged as a double-blind experiment, where matched pairs of volunteers were given tablets before a Good Friday service. Half of these people were given psilocybin, and half were given a placebo (actually nicotinic acid). Nobody knew which member of the pair had been given which drug until the codes were translated later. The results were striking: eight out of the ten young men who had the hallucinogenic drug had mystical experiences, as assessed by an instrument derived from classic literature on mysticism. None of the control group had anything like the same depth of experience.

Interestingly enough a paper was published twenty-five years later which was based on interviews with those who had taken part. It was found that the mystical experiences were still remembered, still valued, and had had a marked effect on the person's life.

> Each of the psilocybin subjects felt that the experience had significantly affected his life in a positive way and expressed appreciation for having participated in the experiment. Most of the effects discussed in the long-term follow-up interviews centered around enhanced appreciation of life and of nature, deepened sense of joy, deepened commitment to the Christian ministry or to whatever other vocations the subjects chose, enhanced appreciation of unusual experiences and emotions, increased tolerance of other religious systems, deepened equanimity in the face of difficult life crises, and greater solidarity and identification with foreign peoples, minorities, women and nature.
>
> (Doblin 1991, p. 14)

This is a remarkable finding, and suggests that the panicky banning of all responsible research with such drugs was a mistake.

Equally powerful results may come out of near-death experiences. John Wren-Lewis describes a near-death experience which he had in Thailand, which resulted in a state of consciousness described like this:

> I simply entered – or rather, *was* – a timeless, spaceless void which in some indescribable way was total aliveness – an almost palpable blackness that was yet somehow radiant. Trying to find words for it afterwards, I recalled the mysterious line of Henry Vaughan's poem *The Night*: 'There is in God (some say) a deep and dazzling darkness'.
>
> (Wren-Lewis 1991, p. 5)

In his case, too, this did not go away. It seemed to be a state which resided somewhere at the back of his head, and could be called on at any moment.

> The sense of awe-full wonder has at the same time a feeling of utter obviousness and ordinariness, as if the marvel of 'everything-coming-into-being-continuously-from-the-Great-Dark' were no more and no less than 'just the way things are'. From this perspective, the term *altered* state of consciousness would be a complete misnomer, for the state is one of complete normality. It seems, rather, as if my earlier state, so-called 'ordinary' human consciousness, represents the real alteration – a deviation from the plain norm, a kind of blinkered or clouded condition wherein the bodymind has the absurd illusion that it is somehow a separate individual entity over against everything else.
>
> (Wren-Lewis 1991, p. 6)

This now begins to sound like an advanced spiritual stage of development, rather than the lower levels which we shall be mostly concerned with here, because there are no symbols or images to speak of.

I suspect that the reason why the experience of Wren-Lewis was so profound and long-lasting was because of the excellent preparations he had already put in, in terms of self-development and self-awareness. (He had done group work, therapy, meditation and prayer.) As Hegel puts it – rather well, I think:

> This process followed by self-producing Spirit, this path taken by it, includes distinct moments; but the path is not as yet the goal, and Spirit does not reach the goal without having traversed the path. It is not originally at the goal; even what is most perfect must traverse the path to the goal in order to attain it.
>
> (Hegel 1974, Vol. 1, p. 75)

It seems to be true that traumatic experiences can provide the final push to a process which is hanging fire. This is perhaps why catharsis is used in so many therapies, ancient and modern. I had an example in my own work with a client recently, where he had been doing quite well over a period of some months, but could not seem to get any further. He was in a car accident, where he nearly died, and afterwards he felt quite different, as if he knew who he was and what he was about. It was the breakthrough we had been waiting for, and it worked admirably. We parted company soon after that, so I do not know how long it lasted.

What also seems to be the case is that if a person has a spiritual experience of some kind and is not prepared for it, it can still act as a glimpse of something ahead, which can act as an inspiration to persevere on the path. What I would warn against is the idea that one can skip stages willy-nilly. In particular, I think there is a frequent attempt to skip from the role-playing stage to the surrendered stage, without going through the autonomous stage. What this does is to produce 'spiritual' people who have not dealt with their own personal nastiness in therapy, and are therefore quite dangerous. In the case of Wren-Lewis, he had done a good deal of work on himself, and therefore the dangers of inflation were reduced considerably. Also, in terms of the points made in *Spiritual Choices*, he was related to a religious discipline which taught him certain lessons about humility, as all the great religions do at their best. Some of the people with glimpses or with real deep spiritual experiences do not have this discipline, and again the dangers of spiritual inflation are very real in such cases.

There is a radical shift when we move from one state of spiritual awareness to another. My feeling at the moment is, however, that every breakthrough of this kind feels like the final one. I think this is the reason why there is so much bad feeling between spiritual masters: each thinks the other has not had this really truly final experience, but has had something lesser. This is quite analogous to the bad feeling between psychotherapists, where each thinks that the other had not really had the most important insight or breakthrough.

There is a diagram of this in Chapter 5, showing how we progress step by step, learning more and more, up to a certain point, where we suddenly drop through into a wholly different state. My strong belief is that ALL breakthroughs are like this: it ALWAYS feels as if we are dropping into something wholly other, where none of the previous learnings or rules apply. And therefore we have to be very watchful NOT to assume too much about any one breakthrough, as if it were full and final and all-consuming. Or perhaps Kant's maxim could be adapted, where he said something like 'Want happiness for other people, duty for yourself'. Here it would be – 'Respect other people's breakthroughs, be cautious about your own.'

The dangers and difficulties of such experiences, when they come too suddenly or too forcefully, are outlined in a later chapter.

Part I

The opening up of the transpersonal

Chapter 1

Some pioneers

Let us look now at where this field has come from. This will help in getting our bearings by reference to some familiar landmarks. If we try to understand these experiences, we are in good company. Over the years, many eminent people have made contributions to our understanding of what they are all about.

WILLIAM JAMES

One of the earliest and most important of these was William James. He made a special study of the freedom of the will, and came to the conclusion that two steps were important: firstly acknowledging that our own choices are creative; and secondly acknowledging equally that sometimes we have to surrender our will. For the first, consider this quotation:

> Suppose, for instance, that you are climbing a mountain, and have worked yourself into a position from which the only escape is by a terrible leap. Have faith that you can successfully make it, and your feet are nerved to its accomplishment. But mistrust yourself, and think of all the sweet things you have heard the scientists say of *maybes*, and you will hesitate so long that, at last, all unstrung and trembling, and launching yourself in a moment of despair, you roll in the abyss. In such a case (and it belongs to an enormous class), the part of wisdom as well as of courage is to *believe what is in the line of your needs*, for only by such belief is the need fulfilled. Refuse to believe, and you shall indeed be right, for you shall irretrievably perish. But believe, and again you shall be right, for you shall save yourself. You make one or the other of two possible universes true by your trust or mistrust.
>
> (James 1896, p. 59)

That is at the level of the personal. But now James moves on to the transpersonal, and here he tells us that there are rare times when instead of striving to strengthen will, we must be prepared to put it aside, to surrender it. When we want to go further in our own development, particularly in the transpersonal area, we cannot do it by an act of will. The intention to go onwards has to be there – 'Walk on!', as the Zen Buddhists say – and this can bring us close to the complete unification aspired after, but 'it seems that the very last step must be left to other forces and performed without the help of our own will' (James 1901, p. 170).

James recognized the existence of a spiritual self, as well as a material self and a social self. He saw it as more inner, more subjective, more dynamic. He experimented with nitrous oxide (laughing gas) as a way of opening up his consciousness, and spoke of 'the tremendously exciting sense of an intense metaphysical illumination' (James 1969, p. 359). But although drugs like this can open up a sense of the mystical, this sense often fades away again. It takes more than that to make such experiences a real possession and a real part of our identity. We saw earlier that the right set and setting can make a big difference to this. But James went on to achieve his own mystical experiences, and eventually came to the conclusion that: 'there is a continuum of cosmic consciousness, against which our individuality builds but accidental fences, and into which our several minds plunge as into a mother-sea or reservoir' (James in Murphy and Ballou 1960, p. 324).

He spoke of the higher self (what we are calling the transpersonal self), and said: 'He becomes conscious that this higher part is conterminous and continuous with a MORE of the same quality, which is operative in the universe outside him, and which he can keep in working touch with, and in a fashion get on board and save himself when all his lower being has gone to pieces in the wreck' (James 1901, p. 384). So he was always interested in the practical aspects of spiritual experience, and how it actually worked in daily life. However, he never used the actual term 'transpersonal'.

DANE RUDHYAR

Not well known outside his own circle, Dane Rudhyar was a writer, philosopher and astrologer who specialized in a more spiritual approach, using many of Jung's ideas and contributing much of his own.

'Instead of impersonal,' writes Rudhyar, who started using the term in 1929, 'let us use another word more telling – transpersonal. A personal type of behaviour (or feeling, or thought) is one rooted in the substantive and conditioned form of the personality. A transpersonal form of behaviour is one starting from the universal unconditioned Self in Man and using the personality merely as an instrument' (Rudhyar 1975, p. 117).

Elsewhere Rudhyar speaks of his own use of the word in contradistinction to the usage of some others. They use it to mean any state of being or consciousness beyond the personal level. He does not. His own view is this:

> I have used the term since 1930 to represent action which takes place *through* a person, but which originates in a centre of activity existing beyond the level of personhood. Such action makes use of human individuals to bring to focus currents of spiritual energy, supramental ideas, or realizations for the purpose of bringing about, assisting, or guiding transformative processes.
>
> (Rudhyar 1983, p. 219)

This again is not quite the same thing as what we today mean by the word, and so we have to say that Rudhyar, while being well worth listening to, is not exactly an exemplar of what we most want to talk about here.

CARL GUSTAV JUNG

Jung and those who followed after him have made an enormous contribution to this field, particularly in the area of myths and symbols. Jung's conception of the collective unconscious enabled him to tune in to the mythopoetic level inside himself and other people, and to see connections which other people had never suspected. He made respectable, so to speak, a whole range of experience which had been excluded as being crazy or weird. And he drew attention to the existence of symbol systems (such as alchemy, astrology and the Tarot) not as freakish survivals from a superstitious past, but as accurate portrayals of our inner life today. He trusted very much to his own experience and followed it, and Radmila Moacanin reminds us that: 'All of Jung's discoveries were accompanied by dreams or synchronistic events that either pointed the way or gave him confirmation that he was proceeding in the right direction' (Moacanin 1986, p. 39). This gives all his work, no matter how apparently abstract, a personal quality which we now see as very valuable.

Jung seems to have been the first person to have used the word 'transpersonal', though what he meant by it is not quite what we mean today. In his essay *The Structure of the Unconscious*, published in France in 1916, Jung says:

> the collective psyche comprises... that portion [of the mental functions]

which is firmly established, is acquired by heredity, and exists everywhere; whose activity is, as it were, automatic; and which is in
consequence transpersonal or impersonal.

(Jung, Vol. 7, par. 454)

It is clear that here he is identifying the transpersonal with the collective
unconscious. This becomes even clearer in the fifth edition, published in
1943 (he revised this essay several times), where he says:

We have to distinguish between a personal unconscious and an impersonal or transpersonal unconscious. We speak of the latter also as the
collective unconscious, because it is detached from anything personal
and is entirely universal.

(Jung, Vol. 7, par. 103)

From this we can see that although Jung was the first to use it, he was not
the first to create its present meaning.

It must be said that Jung has made huge contributions to our understanding of the whole transpersonal area, particularly on the question of
symbols. But it also has to be said that he cruelly limited himself by his
insistence that he was an empirical scientist, and that everything he talked
about could be contained within psychology. This meant that he had to
cram everything spiritual somehow into the collective unconscious. This
is a kind of reductionism, where Jung is forced by his own logic into saying
that the spiritual is nothing but the psychological.

As Demaris Wehr points out, this has the curious effect of turning
Jungian psychology into a religion, while at the same time denying that it
is any such thing.

With the archetype as the governing concept, analytical psychology is
a religion that transcends and embraces the religions of the world... Jung
founded his psychoreligion on the authority of experience, which in his
case and that of his patients was numinous and transformative.

(Wehr 1988, pp. 94–5)

Jung is confusing different levels within the spiritual realm, and reducing
them all to different aspects of the collective unconscious.

Later Jungians are clearer about this, and James Hillman in particular
has come out strongly in favour of the idea that Jungians should stick to
the soul, and steer clear of the spirit. He will talk happily about gods,
because they belong to the level of soul, being multiple, like all symbols;
but he will not talk about God in the monotheistic sense, regarding that
as beyond his concerns: 'Within the affliction is a complex, within the

complex an archetype, which in turn refers to a God' (Hillman 1975, p. 104). Note that he says 'a God', not 'God', as Jung might have done. Hillman has a polytheistic vision, which is very much a part of the transpersonal level as it is understood today.

> Polytheistic psychology does not focus upon such constructs as identity, unity, centeredness, integration – terms that have entered psychology from its monotheistic background. Instead, a polytheistic psychology favours differentiating, elaborating, particularizing, complicating, affirming and preserving. The emphasis is less upon changing what is there into something better (transformation and improvement) and more on deepening what is there into itself (individualizing and soul-making).
>
> (Hillman 1981, p. 124)

But this is considerably different from what Jung himself was saying. Jung was monotheistic in Hillman's sense of the word. And as such, he never really understood Eastern philosophy or Eastern religion. As Coward (1985) noted, Jung never really understood or embraced Yoga, and refused to talk about the top two chakras. He never understood or accepted the concept of *samadhi*, still less the idea that there were several different levels of *samadhi* to be experienced.

This means that we shall have to disagree in part with the following statement of Jolande Jacobi:

> Jungian psychotherapy is not an analytical procedure in the usual sense of the term, although it adheres strictly to the relevant findings of science and medicine. It is a *Heilsweg* in the two-fold sense of the German word: a way of healing and a way of salvation... It has all the instruments needed to relieve the trifling psychic disturbances that may be the starting-point of a neurosis, or to deal successfully with the gravest and most complicated developments of psychic disease. But in addition it knows the way and has the means to lead the individual to his 'salvation', to the knowledge and fulfilment of his own personality, which have always been the aim of spiritual striving.
>
> (Jacobi 1962, p. 59)

We can now see that she is right in saying that Jungian psychotherapy is a way of healing as well as a therapy in the ordinary sense – this is part of what the transpersonal level involves and entails. She is wrong, however, in saying that it is a path to salvation. That is more to do with the world of spirit, the monotheistic level, which the Jungian approach cannot deal with. Nor can any of the transpersonal methods we shall be meeting in this book lead to salvation. (See Chapter 5.)

We cannot leave a discussion of Jung without remarking on his racism and sexism. Both of these were of course very common, almost universal, at the time when Jung started his career, but they are serious stumbling-blocks for the student today. Farhad Dalal says: 'He *explicitly* equates: (1) The modern black with the prehistoric human; (2) The modern black conscious with the white unconscious; and (3) The modern black adult with the white child' (Dalal 1988, p. 263). This is of course offensive to blacks, who find it hard to overlook such consistent and strongly expressed prejudice, put over in the light of theory and clinical validity. Jung thought that blacks were inferior, not just different.

Similarly, Demaris Wehr shows how Jung's idea of women is hopelessly tangled up with his view of the *anima*. This is also the case for Edward Whitmont (1969), who does exactly the same thing:

> One is struck by Whitmont's choice of the words 'the world of the absolutely other' to describe women... To apply it to women suggests, once again, that the anima projection renders men incapable of perceiving the humanness of women. Like Jung's, Whitmont's description of the anima reveals men's fear of real women and of the 'feminine' within themselves... Jung and Whitmont elevate men's fear of women to the level of symbol and mythologize it, rather than challenging the fear itself.
>
> (Wehr 1988, p. 110)

Wehr concludes that Jung's psychology intersects with sexism at the point where men desire, consciously or unconsciously, to avoid their own bodies with all their imperfections, and their own passions, with all their vulnerability.

So although Jung was a great pioneer and trailblazer, particularly in the area of myth and symbol, he cannot be relied on as a trustworthy guide through the world of the transpersonal.

ARCHETYPES

One idea which he did contribute, however, has been taken up and used a great deal, and we need to look at it carefully to see what it has to offer. This is the notion of an archetype. It is not an easy concept to get hold of, and some of the explanations given seem to me seriously flawed, as for example that they are of the nature of biological instincts. Let us see if we can come to grips with it, first of all by looking at the views of one of the best modern interpreters of Jung, Andrew Samuels:

[Jung] found that imagery fell into patterns, that these patterns were reminiscent of myth, legend and fairytale, and that the imaginal material did not originate in perceptions, memory or conscious experience. The images seemed to Jung to reflect universal human modes of experience and behaviour. Jung designated these *primordial images*, using this term from 1912 onwards, in spite of numerous changes and modifications in the theory... To universality and collectivity must be added two further factors – depth and autonomy...

By 1917 Jung was speaking of the collective unconscious expressing itself in the form of *dominants*, special nodal points around which imagery clustered... The important thing to note in the move from primordial image to dominant is that the innate structure, whatever it is is called, is regarded as more and more powerful, to the point where it becomes actor rather than acted upon. There is a shift in Jung's view of the balance of power between pre-existing structure and personal experience...

In 1919 Jung introduced the term *archetype*... The archetype is seen as a purely formal, skeletal concept, which is then fleshed out with imagery, ideas, motifs and so on. The archetypal pattern is inherited but the content is variable, subject to environmental and historical changes... Archetypal themes can be detected even if contents vary greatly; the arguments over cultural transmission are bypassed...

From 1946 onwards, Jung continued to make a sharp distinction between archetype and archetypal image. He refers to the archetype *an sich* (as such), an unknowable nucleus that 'never was conscious and never will be... it was, and still is, only interpreted' (CW 9i, para 266)... Jung's catchprase for archetypal patterns was that they are 'biological norms of psychic activity' (CW 9i, para 309n)...

The baby's apprehension of his experience is structured by innate archetypal forms which force him to reach out and search for corresponding elements in the environment... In this context, Jung refers to the archetype as 'a system of readiness for action' (CW 9i, para 199).

(Samuels 1985, pp. 24–7)

This seems to state it pretty clearly, but already we have trouble with the phrase 'biological norms of psychic activity'. This suggests that they are of the nature of drives or instincts, and these are outmoded concepts in psychology today. However, if we look on Rupert Sheldrake's (1988) idea of morphic resonance as a biological norm, this might make more sense, and certainly June Singer (1990) seems to think so. But before we settle for this, let us look at another view:

One more word we need to introduce is *archetype*. The curious difficulty of explaining just what archetypes are suggests something specific to them. That is, they tend to be metaphors rather than things. We find ourselves less able to say what an archetype is literally and more inclined to describe them in images. We cen't seem to touch one or point to one, and rather speak of what they are like. Archetypes throw us into an imaginative style of discourse. In fact, it is precisely as metaphors that Jung – who reintroduced the ancient idea of archetype into modern psychology – writes of them insisting upon their indefinability... Let us then imagine archetypes as the *deepest patterns of psychic functioning*, the roots of the soul governing the perspectives we have of ourselves and the world. They are the axiomatic, self-evident images to which psychic life and our theories about it ever return...

But one thing is absolutely essential to the notion of archetypes: their emotional possessive effect, their bedazzlement of consciousness so that it becomes blind to its own stance. By setting up a universe which tends to hold everything we do, see, and say in the sway of its cosmos, an archetype is best comparable with a god. And gods, religions sometimes say, are less accessible to the senses and to the intellect than they are to the imaginative vision and emotion of the soul.

(Hillman 1989, pp. 23–4)

This is really quite a different view, and one which comes closer to the general orientation of the present work. We do not look for biological explanations, which perhaps could be seen as a reductionist way of going on, but rather trust to the mythopoetic mind itself as its own explanation. Singer (1990) speaks of 'the archetypal matrix in which we are all embedded', and this is perhaps more like it – archetypes are not things which we have, but more like a sort of home in which we partake. But let us have another view:

The word archetype is well chosen, for *typos* means something that makes an imprint. And so arche-types mean the ancient, primordial types that are impressed on the psyche as a result of the age-long experience of life that man and the animals before him have passed through. The collective unconscious is composed of, or contains, these archetypes, patterns of psychic energy, of life energy, much as the structure of the universe, so far as we know, consists of energies which we can neither explore directly nor define exactly. Jung has compared them to the axis systems of crystals, which determine the form and structure of the crystal even while the salt is in solution and therefore consists not of crystals but of molecules or dissociated atoms.

Consequently, while the term archetype refers to a very real fact, anything we say about it must necessarily be quite tentative. We are on much safer ground when we begin to examine the forms in which the archetypes manifest themselves... [They] can appear also in the patterns of continuous action that we call mythologems. For example, the hero has a typical history and a typical task to perform; the encounter of anima and animus leads to a drama that repeats itself over and over again in real life as well as in fiction.

These mythologems are the subject of mythology, of legends, of folklore and fairy tale, and significantly enough the same themes repeat themselves in history and are to be met with as well in all significant drama and epic. They also form the theme of fantasy, whether this is the basis of great art or the idle occupation of an empty hour, and they appear in dreams and in the products of active imagination.

(Harding 1965, pp. 136–7)

This fills out the picture somewhat, and helps us to see how useful this concept can be in the actual process of psychotherapy. We shall see in the next chapter how important the processes of active imagination and the imaginal world really are in this field. And one of the most important aspects of this is the way in which archetypes can be personalized:

Archetypes are preexistent, or latent, internally determined patterns of being and behaving, of perceiving and responding. These patterns are contained in a collective unconscious – that part of the unconscious that is not individual, but universal or shared. These patterns can be described in a personalized way, as gods and goddesses; their myths are archetypal stories. They evoke feelings and images, and touch on themes that are universal and part of our human inheritance. They ring true to our shared human experience; so they seem vaguely familiar even when heard for the first time... Myths from Greece that go back over 3,000 years stay alive, are told and retold, because the gods and goddesses speak to us truths about human nature. Learning about these Greek gods can help men understand better who or what is acting deep within their psyches.

(Bolen 1989, pp. 6–7)

But it is not only gods and goddesses who can be perceived and treated in this way: there are many archetypes, and today there are a number of writers who are treating them as important. For example, Moore and Gillette (1990) have written at length about the importance of the four archetypes King, Warrior, Magician and Lover for understanding men, the maturity in men. Carol Pearson (1991) has given us a great deal of information and help in tackling twelve archetypes: the Innocent, the Orphan, the Seeker, the Lover, the Warrior, the Caregiver, the Destroyer, the Creator, the Magician, the Ruler, the Sage and the Fool. She has even devised a questionnaire which enables people to discover which archetypes are dominant in their lives at a given moment, and which archetypes have something to do with the Shadow – that aspect of ourselves which we like least and may disown altogether.

All in all, we may say that in the archetypes we have one of the major concepts which are of use in the transpersonal area, and no matter what our reservations about some aspects of Jung himself, this is one very solid contribution he has made.

ROBERTO ASSAGIOLI

It seems that the honour of first using the word 'transpersonal' in relation to psychotherapy has to go to Roberto Assagioli (1975). He introduced his system of psychosynthesis, which in some ways follows Jung and in some ways goes further, in the years after 1910, and opened up his Institute in Italy in 1926. In 1927 the Institute published a book in English called *A new method of treatment – Psychosynthesis*. In 1934 an article entitled 'Dynamic psychology and psychosynthesis' appeared in the British *Hibbert Journal*, and this contained Assagioli's 'egg diagram' which mentions the 'Higher Self'. This higher self was later called the Transpersonal Self. But the essential feature can easily be seen in Figure 1.1: the Higher Unconscious (sometimes called the Superconscious) is not the same as the Collective Unconscious.

In other words, it was Assagioli who first made the distinction between the collective unconscious and the transpersonal. The collective unconscious is something much wider and more inclusive, and Assagioli wanted to distinguish between the archaic and primitive contents of the collective unconscious and the superconscious contents of the same. In the terms we have been using so far, the archaic archetypes are prepersonal, while the superconscious archetypes are transpersonal. To say that all archetypes are transpersonal is to make for a confusion, and for the commission of the pre/trans fallacy.

> In reality, there exists not only a difference but an actual antagonism
> between these two conceptions of 'archetypes' and from this confusion

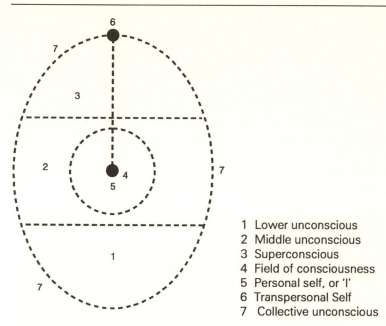

1 Lower unconscious
2 Middle unconscious
3 Superconscious
4 Field of consciousness
5 Personal self, or 'I'
6 Transpersonal Self
7 Collective unconscious

Figure 1.1   The Assagioli egg diagram of the human psyche.
Source: Rowan (1988a), p. 94.

between them arise various debatable consequences, debatable at the
theoretical level and liable to be harmful in therapy.

(Assagioli 1967, p. 8)

Here Assagioli is distinguishing between the prepersonal and the transpersonal contents of the collective unconscious: at the other end of the scale
Assagioli distinguishes between the superconscious activities (the transpersonal) and the Spirit (often now called the Self with a capital S) which goes
beyond the superconscious.

To have a true experience of the Self, however, it is necessary to
disidentify also with the superconscious. This is very difficult because
superconscious states can be so joyous and meaningful that we easily
become attached to and identified with them.

(Whitmore 1991, p. 116)

Here we are in an area which Jung could not touch. This then enables
Assagioli to distinguish between different kinds of mystical experiences.
Savikalpa samadhi is the ecstatic experience of the archetypes, which may

at this level be god-forms (Aphrodite, Cernunnos, etc.) or experiences of the higher self (inner teacher, etc.) or communion with saints (Mary, Luke, etc.) or power animals (as in shamanism) or spirit guides (as in channelling, etc.) or high archetypes (as we saw in the previous section) – all these symbolic entities belonging to the transpersonal realm. *Nirvikalpa samadhi* goes beyond this into the realm of the spirit, where there are no symbols. It is a direct experience of Universal Mind. All dualities and images are totally and cleanly removed, and one no longer contemplates or contacts reality – one becomes reality. This important distinction can be made in terms of psychosynthesis, but not in terms of the Jungian theory. We shall see later just how important this is.

STANISLAV GROF

One of the most important writers about the transpersonal as it comes up in psychotherapy is Stanislav Grof. He came across it through using the drug LSD in Czechoslovakia in the 1950s. He was a psychoanalyst and psychiatrist who got involved in a research project on hallucinogenic drugs in 1956. The original idea was that LSD could give people the same symptoms as schizophrenia, and that therefore LSD could be used to study schizophrenia from the inside, as it were. But what the researchers found was that the LSD experience was nothing like the schizophrenic experience – indeed, if anything, it was just the opposite.

The clearest demonstration of this was given not by the Grof research but by some work of Bernard Aaronson. He put volunteer subjects into a deep hypnotic trance, and then told half of them that there was no depth of vision in their world; the dimension of depth would be gone. The other half were told that the dimension of depth would be expanded. As people talked about their experience (and as their bodies expressed various postures) in each of these conditions, psychiatric observers categorized them as schizophrenic or as healthy. Those in the 'no depth' condition reproduced many of the characteristics of schizophrenia; those in the 'expanded depth' condition seemed not only to be healthy, but to be having experiences which went beyond the ordinary. 'All six subjects responded to this condition with an expanded awareness of the world similar to the experiences described by Huxley in *The Doors of Perception*' (Aaronson 1970, p. 286). In other words, schizophrenia brings with it experiences of the world closing in, while psychedelic states, like the peak experiences we looked at earlier, bring with them experiences of the world opening out.

What Grof began to notice, as the experiments went on, was that many of the visions which people had with the psychedelic drugs seemed to have to do with their inner problems and conflicts. Not only that, but these inner phenomena seemed to come out more vividly and more explicitly with these drugs than they did in the normal analytic session:

> LSD appeared to be a powerful catalyst of the mental processes activating unconscious material from various deep levels of the personality. Many of the phenomena in these sessions could be understood in psychological and psychodynamic terms; they had a structure not dissimilar to that of dreams.
>
> (Grof 1979, p. 19)

This was an exciting time, and many discoveries were made. One of the most interesting things that happened was that much of the thinking in psychoanalysis (particularly the early phantasy postulated by Melanie Klein and her followers) was verified by spontaneous re-experiencing of events under LSD. Grof and his co-workers began to add other elements: listening to music through headphones, the use of physical contact, various experiential techniques, representing a considerable departure from the original psychoanalytic model. Grof began to speak of 'the full appreciation of the therapeutic potential of the mystical and religious dimension of the LSD experience' (Grof 1979, p. 22).

One of Grof's greatest discoveries was of course the Basic Perinatal Matrices – the way in which the birth experience was so important in so many precise and detailed ways. His research gives us an unrivalled view of the stages of the birth process, the psychopathology typically associated with traumas at each of the stages, and the imagery associated with each stage and its specific traumas. But that is not what we are particularly concerned with here.

What he also discovered was a whole range of transpersonal experiences, and in his most practical book he gives a list of them:

Transpersonal Experiences

EXPERIENTIAL EXTENSION WITHIN CONSENSUS
REALITY AND SPACE-TIME

1   Transcendence of Spatial Boundaries
    a. Experience of Dual Unity
    b. Identification with Other Persons
    c. Group Identification and Group Consciousness
    d. Identification with Animals
    e. Identification with Plants and Botanical Processes

  f. Oneness with Life and All Creation
  g. Experience of Inanimate Matter and Inorganic Processes
  h. Planetary Consciousness
  i. Extraterrestrial Experiences
  j. Identification with the Entire Physical Universe
  k. Psychic Phenomena Involving Transcendence of Space
2 Transcendence of the Boundaries of Linear Time
  a. Embryonal and Fetal Experiences
  b. Ancestral Experiences
  c. Racial and Collective Experiences
  d. Past Incarnation Experiences
  e. Phylogenetic Experiences
  f. Experiences of Planetary Evolution
  g. Cosmogenetic Experiences
  h. Psychic Phenomena Involving Transcendence of Time
3 Physical Introversion and Narrowing of Consciousness

EXPERIENTIAL EXTENSION BEYOND CONSENSUS REALITY AND SPACE-TIME

4
  a. Spiritistic and Mediumistic Experiences
  b. Energetic Phenomena of the Subtle Body (Chakras)
  c. Experiences of Animal Spirits
  d. Encounters with Spirit Guides and Suprahuman Beings
  e. Visits to Other Universes and Meetings with Their Inhabitants
  f. Experiences of Mythological and Fairy-Tale Sequences
  g. Experiences of Specific Blissful and Wrathful Deities
  h. Experiences of Universal Archetypes
  i. Intuitive Understanding of Universal Symbols
  j. Creative Inspiration and the Promethean Impulse
  k. Experience of the Demiurge and Insights into Cosmic Creation
  l. Experience of Cosmic Consciousness
  m. The Supracosmic and Metacosmic Void

TRANSPERSONAL EXPERIENCES OF PSYCHOID NATURE

5 Synchronistic Links between Consciousness and Matter
6 Spontaneous Psychoid Events
  a. Supernormal Physical Feats
  b. Spiritistic Phenomena and Physical Mediumship
  c. Recurrent Spontaneous Psychokinesis (Poltergeist)
  d. Unidentified Flying Objects (UFO Phenomena)

7   Intentional Psychokinesis
    a. Ceremonial Magic
    b. Healing and Hexing
    c. Siddhis
    d. Laboratory Psychokinesis

(Grof 1988, pp. 42–4)

With our present understanding, based on the arguments in the Introduction, we can now sort these out somewhat. Almost all the phenomena under 1 and 2 above (except 2a) are what we are calling transpersonal, and we have specifically commented on 1a and 1b. So are 3 (the so-called bad trip) and 4a–j. Items 4k–m have more to do with the different stage of spirit or monotheism. Points 5, 6 and 7 are what we have called extrapersonal rather than transpersonal, though ceremonial magic is a wide-ranging and ill-defined category which may include some transpersonal elements. Healing, too, is a vague category, some forms of which may be included under the transpersonal rubric.

In his latest book (Grof 1992) there are many case histories giving full particulars of how these transpersonal states come across in experience. There is a remarkable realm here, which is very little explored, and it is good to have this further information in such detail.

So Grof has a clearer story than most, and nearly all of it is derived from his actual research and experience with clients, who have come up with these things quite spontaneously. Frances Vaughan, writing under her earlier name of Clark, made a very interesting point about this:

> In his research with LSD psychotherapy, Stanislav Grof (1979) observed that *all* of his subjects transcended the psychodynamic framework and moved into transpersonal realms. This observation implies that a therapist operating in a theoretical context which does not include the transpersonal is necessarily limiting the potential growth of the client.
>
> (Clark 1977, p. 71)

This is an extremely important point, which should never be underestimated. To the extent that we do not cover the transpersonal in our work with clients, we are actually cheating them of their birthright, not allowing them to develop into their full humanity.

And speaking of full humanity, it is worth pointing out that some of these transpersonal phenomena make it easier for people to develop an ecological consciousness. For example, items 1d, 1e, 1f, 1g, 1h, 2e, 2f and 4c enable the person to actually enter into the life of nature and to experience what it is like to go beyond the restrictions of being human in that particular direction. Some of the other spiritual states also make it much more possible to see sympathy with other humans (to the exclusion of animals, plants and nature generally) as just as restricted a position as sympathy with other members of one's family, to the exclusion of other people.

In a later chapter we shall have occasion to look more deeply at some of these phenomena, but here it is sufficient to point out how useful a contribution Grof has extracted from his work first of all with drugs, and more recently with breathing and music.

ABRAHAM MASLOW

Although Abraham Maslow did not make any contribution to the practical aspects of transpersonal psychology, his influence has been very important in it. It was he who insisted, more than anyone else, that peak experiences were a key to the spiritual realms.

His study of peak experiences began in 1946, when he noted that self-actualizing people often had experiences very much like those that mystics had reported in the past. As a confirmed atheist, he found this puzzling, but persevered in his study of the facts.

In fact, the whole idea of self-actualization, which Maslow pursued so intensively, always had mystical overtones. Let us look at this question in detail, because Maslow is such a pioneer in the study of this whole area. Here is what he says:

> Self-actualization is defined in various ways but a solid core of agree-
> ment is perceptible. All definitions accept or imply (a) acceptance and
> expression of the inner core or self, i.e. actualization of these latent
> capacities, and potentialities, 'full functioning', availability of the human
> and personal essence. (b) They all imply minimal presence of ill health,
> neurosis, psychosis, of loss or diminution of the basic human and
> personal capacities.
>
> (Maslow 1962, p. 184)

This clearly suggests that there is just one inner core, which just has to be accepted and expressed. But what exactly is this inner core or self? Maslow became more and convinced that the concept of Being would help to elucidate this: 'This state of Being, rather than of striving, is suspected to be synonymous with selfhood, with being "authenticated", with being a person, with being fully human' (Maslow 1962, p. 188). And he went on to show that it was in peak experiences that people most readily entered into the realm of Being, and therefore obtained a sense of real selfhood in this way:

> Of course, being in a state of Being needs no future, because it is already *there*. Then Becoming ceases for the moment and its promissory notes are cashed in the form of the ultimate rewards, i.e. the peak experiences, in which time disappears and hopes are fulfilled.
>
> (Maslow 1962, p. 200)

This then starts to sound like a fully fledged mystical experience, an experience of enlightenment. And indeed as early as Maslow's first book, he was explicitly making this connection:

> Those subjective expressions that have been called the mystic experience and described so well by William James are a fairly common experience for our subjects... It is quite important to dissociate this experience from any theological or supernatural reference, even though for thousands of years they have been linked... Because this experience is a natural experience, well within the jurisdiction of science, it is probably better to use Freud's term for it, e.g. the oceanic feeling.
>
> (Maslow 1954, p. 216)

In his later books, he makes it very plain that peak experiences are both examples of mystical experience and exemplars of what the self is or could be. And this is of course very different from the oceanic feeling of Freud, which never lost its overtones of the primitive and the unconscious. And it is equally clear that he thinks that there is just one mystical experience, which is the same the world over:

> It has begun to appear strongly that this phenomenon [the peak experience] is a diluted, more secular, more frequent version of the mystical experience that has been described so often as to have become what Huxley called *The Perennial Philosophy*. In various cultures and in various eras it takes on somewhat different coloration – and yet its essence is always recognizable – it is the same.
>
> (Maslow 1973, p. 64)

The sequence now seems clear. If we want to know what self-actualization is, go to the peak experience, go to the experience of Being. When we do this we discover the same kind of unity as that of the mystics down the ages. And this, Maslow tells us, is transcendence:

> Transcendence can mean to live in the realm of Being, speaking the language of Being, B-cognizing, plateau living. It can mean the serene

> B-cognition as well as the climactic peak-experience kind of B-cogni-
> tion. After the insight or the great conversion, or the great mystic
> experience or the great illumination, or the great full awakening, one
> can calm down as the novelty disappears, and as one gets used to good
> things or even great things, live casually in heaven and be on easy terms
> with the eternal and infinite.
>
> (Maslow 1973, p. 287)

The map now appears to be complete. In the process of self-actualization,
which Maslow says is a natural process inherent in the very meaning of
what it is to be a human being, we occasionally have a peak experience.
If we can rise to that occasion and live it and own it, we can get the
experience of Being, and let it change our lives. And that experience of
transcendence can become a plateau experience, which can, with practice,
stay with us. The self we are then talking about is the mystical self, the
actualized self.

In a chapter called 'Theory Z' (Maslow 1973, pp. 293–311), Maslow
distinguishes between nonpeaking self-actualization and peaking self-
actualization, suggesting that the former is a lower state than the latter. This
would mean a two-stage process, whereby contact with the 'real self' comes
first, through a process of integration, rather in the manner that Mahrer
(1989a) has outlined, and then the further state of transcendence comes
later.

At first, then, Maslow thought that self-actualization and transcendence
were one and the same, and then later he thought that the latter succeeded
the former. But either way, the process ends with a mystical unity with
the All. And since Maslow (and Bucke and Huxley) there have been many
humanistic and transpersonal writers all taking it for granted that this is the
whole story. Ronald Havens (1982) says:

> The cosmic consciousness state has been experienced by people
> throughout the world over many centuries and under a variety of
> different labels, including samadhi, satori, moksha, atma-bodhi, enlight-
> enment, revelation, rapture, rebirth, peak experiences and transcen-
> dental consciousness, to name but a few.
>
> (Havens 1982, p. 105)

Carolin Keutzer, another American academic, follows the same line when
she has this to say in the following issue of the same journal:

> Though the terms listed above are obviously not precisely synonymous
> with one another, all are agreed in calling it [cosmic consciousness] (1)
> the highest state of consciousness; (2) a self-transforming perception of

one's total union with the infinite; and (3) an experience beyond time and space – an experience of the timelessness which is eternity, or unlimited unity, with all creation.

(Keutzer 1982, p. 76)

This idea that there is just one thing called 'the unitive consciousness of the mystic' or 'cosmic consciousness' or 'transcendence' seems to me a fundamental error and a classic mistake: it is precisely the one-two-three-infinity view of spirituality which was criticized in the Introduction.

But in his later work, Maslow did recognize that transpersonal psychology could be distinguished from humanistic psychology, and helped, with Anthony Sutich and others, to found the *Journal of Transpersonal Psychology*. It has been said that this is actually the origin of the term 'transpersonal psychology' as it is used today:

It was coined in 1968 by a group of psychologists and psychiatrists consisting of Abraham Maslow, Viktor Frankl, Stanislav Grof and James Fadiman who planned a new journal and had to decide what to call it.

(Guest 1989, p. 62)

Assagioli adopted it at once, thinking that it was more precise than the term 'spiritual' (Assagioli 1991, p. 16). It was perhaps Assagioli and the psychosynthesis school who did most to popularize the word and spread it far and wide.

Be that as it may, Maslow certainly carried the ball for transpersonal psychology and sometimes referred to it as the 'fourth force' in psychology. In the last conference he attended on transpersonal psychology, in 1970, he spoke movingly of his own transcendent experiences, and of how it was these experiences which gave meaning to his writing and his life. The excellent review of his life and work in the third edition of his book *Motivation and personality* ends up by saying:

The harvest of Abraham Maslow's psychology continues to raise unique questions and guide us forward. He opened up a new way of seeing the human universe and in so doing, lifted us up, highlighted the nature of our human potential, encouraged us to reach farther, and reminded us that *greatness is in each and every one of us*. Ultimately, the truth of Maslow's impact lives within each one of us, in the expression of our own search to become more fully human.

(Cox 1987, p. 264)

It is important not to underestimate Maslow, because he has had such a powerful influence worldwide.

Let us now take a break from this historical survey and come back to it in a later chapter, when we see how the whole field was revolutionized by a new map of the territory.

Let us instead go on now to examine in more depth some of the things which are done in the field of transpersonal psychotherapy and counselling, and become more familiar with the techniques which are used.

In the next three chapters we shall go over most of the activities which make up the transpersonal approach and distinguish it from other approaches.

Chapter 2

The practice: 1

In this chapter we shall examine some of the areas covered in the practice of transpersonal therapy. This will also be the subject of the next two chapters.

ACTIVE IMAGINATION

This is an approach which comes out of the Jungian school. It was in 1935 (*Collected Works*, Vol. 6) that Jung first used the concept of 'active imagination'. In active imagination we fix upon a particular point, mood, picture or event, and then allow a fantasy to develop in which certain images become concrete or even personified. Thereafter the images have a life of their own and develop according to their own logic.

A classic in this area was written by Barbara Hannah, who worked with Jung, and then taught at the C.G. Jung Institute in Zurich. She says that this method enables conversations to take place with contents of the unconscious. It does not matter how the image may come; the essential thing is to hold on to it and not let it go until it has revealed its message through dialogue. She emphasizes the distinction between passive imagination, where we merely experience a scene as if looking at it on a screen, and active imagination, where we enter into an interactive discourse which goes back and forth between the personified image and ourselves. Hannah says that she could never do active imagination with someone else in the room – she would have to be quite private to do it. This idea is also put forward by Marie-Louise von Franz, in her introduction to the book:

> In contrast to the numerous existing techniques of passive imagination, active imagination is done *alone*, to which most people must overcome considerable resistance. It is a form of play, but a bloody serious one.
>
> (von Franz in Hannah 1981, p. 2)

This is, as it were, the original and traditional way of using active imagination, but because of its solitary nature, it does seem to be very hard and quite rare.

In recent years the technique of active imagination has been developed by people like Robert Johnson. He goes a considerable way beyond the older tradition represented by Hannah, but is true to it when he says:

> I am convinced that it is nearly impossible to produce anything in the imagination that is not an authentic representation of something in the unconscious. The whole function of the imagination is to draw up the material from the unconscious, clothe it in images, and transmit it to the conscious mind.
>
> (Johnson 1986, p. 150)

So what one has to do is to carry on a dialogue with the image which has been produced spontaneously. Of course there is no one but oneself to play the other role, so it becomes a question of going back and forth between the two or more roles. One can usually tell whether a person is doing real Active Imagination by the feeling responses that come out. If the normal human reaction to the situation in the imagination would be anger, fear or joy, but the client does not express any of these, then the person is detached from the proceedings, just watching from a distance, not really participating, not taking it seriously. Of course the client is perfectly entitled to do this, but let us be clear about what is going on.

Johnson says that it does not have to be a private matter. It can be done in the presence of the therapist. When this is done, the therapist can watch to see that the client does not stray from the zone of participation into the zone of *control*. In Active Imagination we cannot exert control over the inner persons or over what is happening. We have to let the imagination flow where it will, let the experience develop, without trying to determine in advance what is going to happen, what is going to be said, what is going to be done. We must be willing to engage in real dialogue.

This is sometimes not easy: if the client has something which he or she sees as a weakness, a defect, a terrible obstruction to a productive life, it is hard not to approach that part as the enemy. But in Active Imagination it is important to listen to that 'inferior' being as though he or she were the voice of wisdom. Sometimes these figures from the unconscious may be very powerful, especially if they come as archetypal images from the collective unconscious. We may feel we are dealing with something which is more than human. But it will still make sense to treat it as if it were human, because this is really the only way in which we can begin to discover its meaning for us. We have to filter whatever comes through our own experience: there is no other way. In this kind of consciousness work, the energy pattern that we disown turns against us.

This entails a certain humility in working with Active Imagination. As Robert Johnson says:

> One must be willing to say: 'Who are you? What do you have to say? I will listen to you. You may have the floor for this entire hour if you want; you may use any language you want. I am here to listen.' This requires a formidable realignment of attitude for most of us... If our depressions or weaknesses come to us in personified form, we need to honour those characteristics as part of the total self.
>
> (Johnson 1986, p. 183)

But what kind of reality are we talking about here? Is all this something which is way outside anything practical or real? Someone who has written very well about this is another Jungian, Mary Watkins. She says this:

> I shall place before you the view that imaginal dialogues do not merely reflect or distort reality, but *create* reality; that the real is not necessarily antithetical to the imaginal, but can be conceived of more broadly to include the imaginal; and that personifying is not an activity symptomatic of the primitivity of mind, but is expressive of its dramatic and poetic nature.
>
> (Watkins 1986, p. 58)

She goes along with the view of Franklin (1981), when he says that symbolizing does not merely reflect or communicate what is already known, but is formulative, and creates meaning. So the activity we are engaging in when we have a dialogue with our internal subpersonalities is a healthy and constructive one. Hillman (1975) defines personifying rather formally as 'the spontaneous experiencing, envisioning and speaking of the configurations of existence as psychic presences'. This seems a good way of putting the matter.

THE IMAGINAL WORLD

Where does this work of the active imagination take place? We come now to the idea of the *mundus imaginalis*, which we need to discuss in some detail. In plain English this is the imaginal world, the world we enter into when we make up stories or see visions, or hear internal music, and so on.

Now not everything to do with the imagination is part of the transpersonal. To say that would be both imperialistic and confusing. Imagination, like imagery, ranges up and down the whole set of levels or positions which we noticed when we dealt with intuition. Children who have no words yet can still have images, and in that sense imagery is a primitive faculty. Some of us think that even dogs have dreams.

But beginning at the autonomous level and even more at the transpersonal level, we find that images and symbols are better than language in conveying certain things or in allowing ourselves to have certain experiences. At this level we can use images and symbols deliberately, not waiting for them to arrive by chance.

In fact, I sometimes like to say that this conscious use of images and symbols is actually what is meant by the phrase 'opening the third eye'. It is as if we had a faculty which earlier was blocked off, in such a way that things could get through, but only in a patchy and unpredictable way, much as an injured or diseased eye can let through the odd perception here and there. But if we can restore the eye to health, it can be used on a regular basis as a valid source of information.

Henri Ellenberger talks about a 'mythopoetic faculty' which has been inadequately studied in psychotherapy. The word 'mythopoetic' means 'myth-making', and suggests a faculty of consciously entering into a world of myth, story, vision and the like. Frederic Myers, an early researcher of hypnosis and the unconscious, described the mythopoetic function as the unconscious tendency to weave fantasies. It is a 'middle region of the subliminal self where a strange fabrication of inner romances perpetually goes on' (Ellenberger 1970, p. 318).

Henry Corbin on the other hand, in a letter written to the Jungian David Miller, speaks very clearly of:

> a mediating and intermediary world which I call *mundus imaginalis* (Arabic *'âlam al-mithâl*). This is an *imaginal* world not to be confused with the *imaginary*.
>
> (Miller 1981, p. 4)

The difference is that the imaginal world is a world where real things happen; and one of the things which happens is 'the self open to others'. If we pay attention to the imaginal world, and open ourselves up to it, it becomes possible to share in another person's imaginal world, and in fact to see that we have here only one world.

This is connected with the whole business of questioning barriers and boundaries around the self which we said earlier was so important in understanding what the transpersonal was all about. It is important to emphasize, however, that this is not the neurotic confluence which Perls defined and talked about. 'Confluence is a phantom pursued by people

who want to reduce difference so as to moderate the upsetting experience
of novelty and otherness' (Polster and Polster 1974, p. 92).

Confluence has been particularly identified as a potential problem
between therapist and client.

> The therapist's greatest enemy is that state in which he finds himself
> deeply identified with his client, embedded in the other's psychological
> skin... This state is called confluence: the loss of differentiation between
> two people... Creative conflict, or simply good contact, is sacrificed for
> routine interactions which are flat, static and safe.
>
> (Zinker 1978, p. 46)

It is true that more recent texts have a good word to say for some forms
of confluence, as a kind of peak experience:

> Some confluence in relationships can be beneficial – for example,
> empathic understanding of a partner's bereavement. Some confluence
> with the environment can be life-enriching and enhancing. For
> example, in a meditational peak experience, or in certain forms of
> expressive art such as painting, the loss of self boundaries can be crucial
> to the full richness of the experience.
>
> (Clarkson 1989, p. 56)

In intimate lovemaking, for example, a kind of confluence may be an
intensely rich, ego-transcending, self-forgetful, egoless experience, and 'An
I-Thou experience in therapy may have these qualities' (Korb et al. 1989,
p. 61). But this is seen as a momentary event which is unpredictable and
does not last.

So what we are talking about here, as the self open to others, is not
confluence at all. It is something conscious and chosen. How does it work?
Let us look at some different examples. John Watkins, an ego–state therapist
who makes a good deal of use of hypnosis (Watkins 1978), describes this
as resonance, and likens it to the phenomenon where two pianos are put
side by side, and the note A is hit on one of them. The A string in the
other piano resonates in sympathy. In the kind of therapy, he says, where
this approach is used, what actually happens is that the therapist sets up an
ego state corresponding to the client and puts energy into that. In that way
the therapist can be with the client from the inside, and share the client's
subjectivity. So resonance is that inner experience within the therapist
during which he or she co-feels, co-enjoys, co-suffers and co-understands
with the client.

At the same time Alvin Mahrer, who is a therapist in the humanistic-
existential tradition (Mahrer 1983), was describing this new approach as

experiential listening, and saying that this kind of listening involves a complete sharing of the client's phenomenal world. The therapist becomes part of the personality of the client. The therapist and client can integrate with one another. The personhood and identity of one can assimilate or fuse with that of the other, and then the therapist will have experiencings which are also occurring in the client. Recently Mahrer has been giving workshops on exactly how to do this, and has produced a short manual (Mahrer 1989b) on how to do it.

One of the main things which has to be done, in this understanding of the matter, is to reproduce in one's own body (as a therapist) whatever the client is describing as going on in his or her own body. One gets into the same position as the client, and if the client says there is a pain in the middle of the back, the therapist also sets up a pain in the middle of the back. It is OK for the therapist to exaggerate what the client is saying, in order to get deeper into the experience, and to encourage the client to get deeper into the experience. This is a very active approach which is easy to teach and to use, much to the surprise of those taking part.

At the same time Andrew Samuels, a British Jungian who has written a great deal on Jungian thought, describes this as 'embodied countertransference', and gives examples of it where he seems to become part of the client's inner world.

> After the memories came, she was very angry with me indeed. One session, she got up and sat in the desk chair which is located behind my usual chair... She told me what she would like to do to my head with an instrument, and this became an expressed fantasy of what she *was* doing... But I was not frightened. In fact I had the most pleasant, warm sensation in my lower legs and feet, as if seated before a fire. I went on to have a vision of a small and comfortable living-room in which we were both sitting. In my mind's ear I could hear the rustle of 'my' newspaper. I was smoking my pipe anyway. I said 'You're watching daddy read his paper. It's pleasant. Part of you wants it to go on for ever. Part of you wants him to look up and acknowledge you. The tension is what is making you angry. You're smashing my brains up because that settles the question of whether I'll notice you of my own accord.' For the first time, she and I could grasp the *telos* of her exceedingly dramatic and demanding behaviour... I had experienced an embodied countertransference.
>
> (Samuels 1989, p. 81)

He says that using the word 'embodied' emphasizes that we are talking here of a physical, actual, material, sensual expression in the therapist of something in the client's inner world. Again we may find the words hard to understand or to take, if we have never had this sort of experience.

It is common in psychoanalysis today to recognize that some counter-transference reactions in the analyst stem from, and may be regarded as communications from the patient, and that the analyst's inner world, as it appears to him or her, is the *via regia* into the inner world of the patient; but this goes further in stressing the idea of the *mundus imaginalis* as shared territory.

Similarly, Benjamin Wolman, a psychoanalyst who uses hypnosis (Wolman 1986), speaks of those times when we become aware of another person's feelings without sensory perceptions and without any possibility of proving or disproving them. He says that such experiences belong in the region of the 'protoconscious'. The protoconscious is not the conscious or preconscious mind, because there things are under control and are available to logic and language. Nor is it the unconscious, because the unconscious is what we are unaware of and cannot simply get in touch with at will.

Wolman says that meditation is the best-known method of contacting the protoconscious mind. My own view is that actually the use of imagery is the most common method, and as Jerome Singer (1974) has made clear, imagery is used by many different kinds of therapists. However, as we saw earlier, the use of imagery in behaviour therapy is not transpersonal in any way – it is simply using a technique in a quite mechanical way to achieve a preordained result.

The best general discussion of imagery in psychotherapy that I know of is to be found in the work of Mary Watkins. The term she uses is 'waking dream' to cover the phenomena of a spiritual nature in which we are interested.

> By waking dream we mean not just an experience of dreamlike character received while awake, but an experience of the imagination undertaken with a certain quality or attitude of awareness. This conscious awareness differentiates the experience of imagination... from daydreams and hallucinations.
>
> (Watkins 1976, p. 31)

She discusses many aspects of this, and finds in Jung a real respect for and understanding of this area of human experience. His concept of active imagination is very much in line with what she herself is saying. Another concept of his is also very relevant: the transcendent function. If we are looking for an attitude through which the conscious and the unconscious can work together, we can find it in this function:

I have called this process the *transcendent function*, 'function' being here understood not as a basic function but as a complex function made up of other functions, and '*transcendent*' not as denoting a metaphysical quality but merely the fact that this function facilitates a transition from one attitude to another. The raw material shaped by thesis and antithesis, and in the shaping of which the opposites are united, is the living symbol; its profundity of meaning is inherent in the raw material itself, the very stuff of the psyche, transcending time and dissolution, and its configuration by the opposites ensures its sovereign power over all the psychic functions.

(Jung 1971, par. 828)

Through his own experiences, says Mary Watkins, Jung found that he was able to withdraw his awareness from distractions and enter into the world of the mythopoetic at will. These experiences provided a way of establishing contact with the imaginal.

I think the best account of where all this is taking place is given by Samuels (1989), where he says that it takes place in the imaginal world. This imaginal world is an in-between state, where images take the place of language. It is between the conscious and the unconscious, and also between the therapist and the client. Both persons have access to it and can share it. It is the therapist's body, the therapist's imagery, the therapist's feelings or fantasies; but these things also belong to the client, and have been squeezed into being and given substance by the therapeutic relationship. And Samuels emphasizes that these are visionary states, concluding that such experiences may usefully be regarded as religious or mystical.

I have certainly found this approach very useful in my own work in primal integration. I have also found that it is possible to give people a taste of what it is like in quite ordinary workshops of an educational kind, by simply asking people to follow Mahrer's instructions.

One of the best writers on the imaginal world is James Hillman, who links it with the idea of soul. His distinction between soul and spirit parallels the distinction we shall be making later between the transpersonal and the causal. So what he says about the soul will feed into our definition of the transpersonal and the imaginal very directly and naturally.

Soul sticks to the realm of experience and to reflections within experience. It moves indirectly in circular reasonings where retreats are as important as advances, preferring labyrinths and corners, giving a metaphorical sense to life through such words as *close*, *near*, *slow* and *deep*. Soul involves us in the pack and welter of phenomena and the flow of impressions. It is the 'patient' part of us. Soul is vulnerable and suffers;

it is passive and remembers... *Soul is imagination*, a cavernous treasury... a confusion and richness, both... The cooking vessel of the soul takes in everything, everything can become soul; and by taking into its imagination any and all events, psychic space grows.

(Hillman 1990, pp. 122–3)

For Hillman, psychotherapy is all about soul-making. And he says that symptoms are the gateway to soul. Dreams are about the world and realm of soul, and belong to soul. Hillman goes on to push further, and to say that our lives are full of images and myths – we constantly make up stories about our lives and what they mean – and as soon as we take them too literally as being the truth, we are liable to go astray. It is much better to take them as fictions, and to ask how these fictions are constructed, what their function is, how they work in our lives. 'We don't know we are telling stories. And that's part of the trouble in the training of psychotherapy, that psychotherapists don't learn enough literature, enough drama, or enough biography' (Hillman and Ventura 1992, p. 28). It is strange that people whose work will largely consist of listening to stories are taught so little about how people tell stories. Mary Watkins says:

The imaginal resists being known except in its own terms. Image requires image. Image evokes image. Systems of understanding arise, themselves symbolic. It is as if one can say what the imaginal *is like*, but cannot utter what it *is*.

(Watkins 1976, p. 99)

So there are two elements to this imaginal world. One is that it must be entered consciously and by an act of will, and the second is that control must be abandoned as soon as one enters this world. Exploration, yes; action, yes; control, no. This was well expressed once by Jung:

The art of letting things happen, action through non-action, letting go of oneself, as taught by Meister Eckhart, became for me the key opening the door to the way. We must be able to let things happen in the psyche. For us, this actually is an art of which few people know anything. Consciousness is forever interfering, helping, correcting and negating, and never leaving the simple growth of the psychic processes in peace.

(Jung 1968, p. 93)

This is particularly important when we are dealing with the archetype. One of the most important archetypes is the Anima, who is a goddess and also stands for the soul. Jung says:

> start some dialogue with your anima... put a question or two to her: why she appears as Beatrice? why is she so big? why she nurses your wife and not yourself?... Treat her as a person, if you like as a patient or as a goddess, but above all treat her as something that does exist.
>
> (Jung, 7 May 1947, letter to Mr O)

Even so, however, we have to be careful. It is important not to turn the Anima (or to try to turn her) into something neat and delimited and hard-edged, as if she were something less than a complete human being. The whole point about archetypes is that they are more than a human being: they go back further, they carry more of what Jung calls the *numinosum* – the quality of divinity which as we have seen so many times is the hallmark of the truly transpersonal.

James Hillman warns against literalization and externalization, even to the point of questioning the value of dialogue with the Anima at all. He wants to see in the Anima the very essence of the imaginal, of the world of soul:

> Anima consciousness not only relativizes ego consciousness but also relativizes the very idea of consciousness itself. It then is no longer clear when we are psychologically conscious and when unconscious. Even this fundamental discrimination, so important to the ego–complex, becomes ambiguous. Ego therefore tends to regard anima consciousness as elusive, capricious, vacillating. But these words describe a consciousness that is mediated to the unknown, conscious of its unconsciousness and, so, truly reflecting psychic reality.
>
> (Hillman 1985, p. 141)

It seems clear that the key idea here is surrender. As we have seen so many times in our pursuit of the transpersonal, surrender and opening are much more important than control and order. We really have to give up the kind of control which the ego demands, and even the kind of control which the real self demands, if we are to do justice to the transpersonal realm.

One of Jung's patients complained that he was worried because he could not understand what was required of him in active imagination. At the railway station one day he decided to look at a poster and pretend he was in it, in order to try to find out more of what active imagination might mean to him personally. He found himself walking through the country and down a path to a chapel. When he entered the chapel he saw something with pointed ears behind the altar. He thought, 'Well, that's all nonsense', and instantly the whole fantasy was gone.

But he decided to test the method a little further. He went into the poster as before, walking through the country toward the chapel. Everything was the same, up to and including the pointed ears. 'Then he was able to trust that in fact his imagination was intent on making this scene and that he could learn further' (Jung 1968, p. 190).

There was something uncanny about this scene, and in fact the uncanny is one of the marks of the transpersonal. If something in a dream or vision seems to be uncanny, it very often turns out to be something numinous or spiritual or holy.

Mary Watkins has a useful list of some of the possible different imaginal involvements which are possible:

1   You are watching the images but are not yourself among the images. You, as you know yourself, are the one watching.
2   You see yourself watching the images from within the imaginal scene. For example, you see yourself looking down from a tree.
3   You see yourself interacting with images within the landscape of the imagination.
4   You are within the scene watching the images (you yourself are in the tree).
5   You are interacting with images within the landscape of the imagination as yourself.
6   You are interacting with other images in an imaginal body not your own. You are still willing your actions.
7   You are interacting within the imaginal landscape, but not as you usually would. Your actions are not initiated from your conscious ego. *You* are moved, as well as the rest of the images.
8   You are interacting within the imaginal landscape not as yourself but as a peripheral image to the scene. For example, you are a tree and being the tree are in touch with the other images around the tree. Here also you do not think what the tree is going to do. You are whatever the tree does.
9   You are an image. You are not in your imaginary ego or body. You feel and move and are the ground or the bird. You are not your normal ego in the bird's body. You are the bird.
10 You are watching the images from within the imaginal scene but the you that is watching them is a different kind of ego with different ways of perceiving and movement than we would notice at first.

(Watkins 1976, p. 114)

Looking back now at the example of the man walking down the path into the chapel, this is an example of headings 3, 4 or 5 on this list. The later items on the list tend to be more in the area of the transpersonal, though they all can be. The key thing about the transpersonal is this working with symbols for their own sake and in their own terms, moving about in the language of symbols and not being too eager to translate them into other terms.

For those who are interested in working with subpersonalities, suffice it to say that work with subpersonalities comes under headings 5 and 6 on this list.

Mary Watkins has some interesting things to say about the seventh form of entering into the imaginal world mentioned above:

> These imaginal egos are a great source of insight. By moving in them we see the imagination from different standpoints than we ever have before – for now we are part of it. We are not only moving within the imaginal, we are being moved *by* it. We are not limited by the ways of our heroic ego which are often quite clumsy and insensitive when it is not in its own realm... [We may] begin to move in an ego that is more attuned to the imaginal.
>
> (Watkins 1976, p. 117)

She points out that the ego psychologist – that is, the psychologist who is wary of the unconscious and what it contains – would never encourage a client to have anything to do with the later forms of imagination detailed above, from 7 onwards. I would add that even people working at the autonomous level would be uneasy about these forms, because of the seeming denial of responsibility involved.

This is so important and challenging that I want to underline it even more. To move out of our usual ego, to experience things in a different way, is a frightening prospect for many people, yet we have seen that it is possible and that we always have the power to come back into our usual frame of thought if and when we want to.

To deal with imaginal symbols in an imaginal way – what would that be like? Mary Watkins warns against being too afraid of losing the ego. She is not talking about losing, dissolving or dropping the ego: she is talking about relativizing the ego. This is what we have been saying all along – that as we move from position to position, from level to level, we change our whole idea of the ego, as we shall see in more detail when we come to discuss the work of Ken Wilber. Here we are talking about it as soul, and saying that if we want to do justice to the soul, we must not try to translate it all the time into terms of the mental ego or even the real self.

While engaging in the latter types of imagining described here (types seven through ten) one does create for oneself a home (as Dionysus had) in the imaginal. This home, the various imaginal egos, is created from the very material of the imaginal – images. With its creation the non-material side of metaphor becomes more apparent, more inhabited, more clearly a part of our wanderings. We are not only living with the image but aware that we are doing so. One is not just involved in fantasy (daydream) and identified with it, but is aware of the fantasy as fantasy, of the image as image.

(Watkins 1976, p. 124)

As we shall see later in our discussion of guided fantasy, we do not get caught up, deceived, in our fantasy: it is our choice to surrender to it, and all the time we realize that we could withdraw from it at any instant. We could open our eyes and be right back in the room.

Watkins speaks of the 'imaginal real', and it is crucial to understand that the imaginal world has a reality of its own, within the four walls of its own realm. It is not something to be treated as merely offering clues about our ordinary everyday world – rather it has to be treated as something different and valuable in its own right. This is hard for most of us to do, because we are persistently told that the everyday world is the real world, and that the imaginal world is 'just fantasy'. But this is just the same lie as we are told when we are led to believe that the mental ego is all there is, and that the real self, the transpersonal self, and so on do none of them exist.

We often do not realize that images are safer than words in human relations and human interactions. In one of her books, Eileen Walkenstein (1975) diagnoses a psychiatric patient as a 'Zombie'. Another one she diagnoses as 'Peanut Brittle', and another as a 'Marshmallow'. These are expressive labels, which are clearly temporary and provisional. They carry no weight of authority, they are not in the medical dictionary or the diagnostic manual. They stimulate rather than anaesthetize. They arouse rather than depress. They communicated to the particular people they were directed towards, at the particular time when this happened. This is the thing about images – they are many, they emerge from the moment, they are caught on the wing or not at all.

And this is what metaphysics is all about. John Wisdom once gave a wonderful example of metaphysics in his story of two women in a boutique trying on hats. One woman puts on a hat and looks questioningly at the other. The other woman says – 'Taj Mahal'. The first woman laughs and puts the hat away. There is no argument here, no question of right and wrong, true or false. It is nothing more or less than a metaphorical image.

If we are to move about in the transpersonal world, the imaginal world, the world of soul, we have to acknowledge without reservation that we may have to abandon our usual standpoint. We may have to enter into the consciousness of another person (as we saw earlier in this chapter); we may have to enter into the character of a licence-plate (as we shall see in our discussion of dreams), we may have to enter into the character of an eagle, or an electron (as we saw earlier). And when we do this we are entering the land of symbols, the realm of soul.

PERSONAL MYTHOLOGY

This idea has been taken further by David Feinstein, a clinical psychologist who lives in Oregon. Back in 1982 Stanley Krippner (then professor of psychology at Saybrook Institute) edited a special edition of the *AHP Newsletter* (San Francisco) entitled 'Into the mythic underground', featuring articles by Feinstein, Jean Houston, Anne Dosher, Cecil Burney (on sandplay), Stephen Larsen, Robin Larsen and Trisha Colt. This was very stimulating but really quite brief.

In October 1988 was published at last the book, co-authored by David Feinstein and Stan Krippner. In it they say that their approach is organized on three basic premises:

1   Myth-making, at both the individual and the collective levels, is the primary though often unperceived psychological mechanism by which human beings navigate their way through life.
2   More than in any previous period of history, people are capable of carving out distinctively personal mythologies and reflecting upon those mythologies – and the need to become conscious of our mythologies is more urgent than ever before.
3   By understanding the principles that govern their underlying myths, people become less bound by the mythologies of their childhood and of their culture, and they may begin to influence patterns in their lives that once seemed predetermined and went unquestioned.

(Feinstein and Krippner 1988, p. 4)

A well-articulated, carefully examined mythology, say Krippner and Feinstein, is one of the most effective devices available for countering the disorienting grip of a world in mythic turmoil. It also points the way back to the deeper world of the psyche, as we saw in the previous section.

To live mythically, they say, is to seek guidance from your dreams, imagination and other reflections of your inner being, as well as from the most inspiring people, practices and institutions of your society. To live mythically is also to cultivate an ever-deepening relationship with the cosmos and its great mysteries.

They quote Jean Houston (1987) as saying that in the ancient mystery schools, one is required to die to one story, one myth, in order to be reborn to a larger one. This idea, that development involves giving up a smaller story in order to wake up to a larger story, ties in very well with the ideas of Ken Wilber which we shall be looking at later. But by putting it in this mythic form it is easier to see the pain which may be involved. Giving up one's myth may be difficult.

They also quote Jerome Bruner as saying:

> when the myths no longer fit the internal plights of those who require them, the transition to newly created myths may take the form of a chaotic voyage into the interior, the certitudes of externalization replaced by the anguish of the internal voyage.
>
> (Bruner 1960, p. 286)

This is well said.

But because all this is at a mythic level, there is something sacred about it. It is not just something personal, although it certainly is personal, but also involves the gods, the archetypes. This is why it can hit with such force sometimes as to overthrow the person completely. This is something we shall look at in detail in Chapter 9, but here it is more a question of what comes up in a more amenable manner in the course of therapy.

One helpful move is to introduce the client to his or her inner shaman. There has been much written in recent years about the shaman, and this is an acceptable idea to many people. One can explain that 'the inner shaman has three essential responsibilities: to guide the evolution of your existing myth, making sure that the new myth is not a mere addition to what is there already, but has a convincing negative relationship with it; to creatively and effectively bring into being new circumstances in line with your new myth, so that it is consolidated and made more firm; and to maintain a channel between your waking consciousness and the imaginal world, by being ready to go back and forth between them.' This latter is of course very close to the idea of Hermes, the god who goes back and forth between the upper world and the underworld, bringing messages from one to the other.

Because the shaman is always close to nature and to the plant and animal worlds, a guided fantasy to meet the inner shaman will involve coming to a gateway consisting of two trees, and passing through this gateway.

The strength of this approach, in my opinion, is in its dialectical view of the process – taking the existing myth as the thesis, the countermyth as the antithesis, and the new myth as the synthesis. The existing myth is our story, the story we tell about ourselves to account for why we are the way we are. It is the story we tell to our therapist and anyone else we trust enough to tell it.

To say more would be to paraphrase the book, and all we need to do here is to point out how relevant this book is to the whole case being made in the present work.

Chapter 3

The practice: 2

Still in the realm of the imaginal world, we have now to look at two of the most important ways of working: guided fantasy and dreams. But before we come to guided fantasy, it may be worthwhile to say a few words about visualization. It is obvious that guided fantasy relies a great deal upon the ability to visualize, and this cannot be taken for granted.

VISUALIZATION

Let us start with the question of the sequencing of visualization exercises. The best answer to how to begin that I know is to be found in the book by Hanscarl Leuner, where he suggests that the easiest thing to begin with is a flower. He uses the words – 'Can you imagine a flower?' And he adds that in all his exercises he never uses the word 'see', but always uses the word 'imagine'.

> Some patients believe they have to 'see' something and are consequently disappointed if, as a phenomenon, what is imagined does not compare with seeing but perhaps is pale, without good contours, and also varies in clarity at first.
>
> (Leuner 1984, p. 102)

This I think is a very helpful hint, from a long experienced master of this kind of technique, and he has many other helpful things to say.

Janette Rainwater (1981) asks the person to 'visualise a large blank white movie screen' and to 'visualise a flower on the screen'. This is very similar, but lays much more stress on seeing rather than imagining. Again, I think she is a reliable guide.

Jean Houston gets the person to start by looking for a few seconds at a candle flame, then closing the eyes and looking at the after-image.

> Now see this ball of light you are looking at behind your closed eyes
> turn into a sunflower with bright yellow petals, a brown seeded centre
> and a long green stalk.
>
> (Houston 1982, p. 144)

So here again a flower is the starting point. This whole chapter (7) is very
interesting and provocative.

My own experience is that people do well if they are given something
dramatic to visualize. My favourite first exercise, which I have done many
times with totally unprepared groups, is this:

> Relax, close your eyes... Now you are an animal in a cage... What is
> your experience, as the animal?... What do you say, as the animal?...
> Now you are the cage. What is your experience, as the cage?... What
> do you say, as the cage?... Carry on this dialogue for a while... Now
> you notice that the door of the cage is open. What happens now?...

Of course, appropriate pauses are inserted, and the whole thing normally
takes 5 minutes from beginning to end. I've not found a single person so
far who has failed to complete this exercise, and the answers are always
interesting. I ask – 'What animal were you? What kind of cage were you?
Did you feel stronger as the animal, or as the cage? What happened when
the door opened? Does any of this have relevance to your life?' Then
having done an exercise like this, people are more willing to do other and
more difficult things.

Someone else who prefers to start with dramatic situations is Joseph
Shorr. He plunges in straight away with things like – 'Imagine yourself
taking a shower with your father. How do you feel? What do you say to
him? What does he say to you?' (Shorr 1983, p. 17).

So there seem to be two basic approaches here. One says that the way
to start is through something non-threatening and simple: the other says
that the way to start is through something which has a lot of dramatic
meaning for the person. From a *safety* point of view, which could be
important in a child abuse context, I think I would go for the former. But
in other situations, where there are no contra-indications, I would go for
the latter.

GUIDED FANTASY

This is one of the prime areas where the transpersonal approach has
dominated and led the field. So much so, that a few years ago I came across
a whole body of writing by one man who was convinced that guided

fantasy and psychosynthesis were one and the same thing. Of course they are not: psychosynthesis is much broader and wider than that, as we have seen many times in this book already, and shall do again.

So where did guided fantasy come from? Fortunately the story here is quite clear. After a number of pioneers had concentrated on imagery as very important for exploring certain psychological areas, an engineer named Desoille developed quite a sophisticated way of working, using scenes for people to imagine, which were calculated to take them up or down into relevant areas of the psyche for self-development. He called this the 'waking dream' method.

He suggested to people, without putting them into a hypnotic trance, that they imagine a scene. These scenes were carefully planned beforehand, but mostly involved ascents and descents. The ascent put the person in touch with their spiritual nature, and the descent put them in touch with the personal unconscious. In both cases archetypes (as defined by Jung) could be evoked, and were regarded by Desoille as most important. This work was developed during the 1930s.

Of course the basic approach can be used more spontaneously, taking off from a dream or fantasy which emerges from the client. Assagioli gives the example, from the practice of an American doctor, where the client had the image of an octopus in the depth of the sea which threatened to engulf him. Many people might work with this as a subpersonality (Rowan 1990), but the therapist here asked the client to rise up to the surface of the water, taking the octopus with him. On reaching the surface, 'to the surprise of the subject', the octopus changed itself into the face of his mother. Again this could have been worked with in various other ways, but the therapist here guided the client into climbing a mountain in company with his mother.

As he climbed higher and higher with her, he began to see her in a different light, as a human being in her own right, a person with both qualities and limitations, who had struggled under difficult circumstances. She was no longer threatening to him. This experience contributed toward a marked improvement in his affective life.

(Assagioli 1975, p. 213)

This is very much along the original Desoille lines, with the Desoille emphasis on ascent and descent, and also on the meeting with the archetypes. Desoille believed that this entry into the world of the collective unconscious was one of the most powerful change agencies in psychotherapy. The client experiences his personal conflicts as having an impersonal and collective background. 'The motivational (libidinal) conflict is not resolved by being transferred upon the therapist, as in psychoanalysis, rather, the patient uncovers, in himself, the basic roots of the conflict' (Assagioli 1965, p. 310).

Quite independently, in the 1940s and 1950s, Hanscarl Leuner was developing a system which he called Guided Affective Imagery, based on some of the same sources which had inspired Desoille. In the 1960s many people took this up and Leuner renamed it 'symboldrama'. He remarks:

> Symboldrama with its imaginings conveyed by fantasy can also be considered a form of projective self-representation. It has the advantage over all of the familiar test procedures in that no limits are placed on it by the type of presentation and technique and that even the slightest change of inner emotion is immediately reflected in changes of the image. I have called this active course of projections *mobile projection.*
>
> (Leuner 1984, p. 20)

Symboldrama uses a series of well-worked-out scenes, and invites the client to enter the scene. There is no need to induce a hypnotic state nor even a particularly deep state of relaxation. Leuner says that simply asking the client to sit back and imagine a flower is sufficient as a check to see whether the person is capable of symboldrama. The type of flower reported can then be a good indication of whether it is wise to proceed with this approach: a black rose, a flower that quickly wilts, a flower made of steel, a flower that develops menacing teeth, might all be indications not to use this technique for a while.

There is a sequence of scenes, and the first one is the meadow. The instructions are given like this:

> Now please try to imagine a meadow. Imagining is not difficult. Simply any meadow. If something else appears before your eyes, that's all right, too. Everything that comes along is fine. (Pause) Wait calmly and patiently until something appears before your eyes, perhaps a meadow or something else too. (Pause) And when an image appears, please talk about it. (Pause) But even if this should cause difficulties, tell me that, too, so that I can perhaps help. (Pause) You can also nod your head as a first sign that you have something in view.
>
> (Leuner 1984, p. 31)

Then the person is asked to explore the meadow and tell about anything that appears. This running commentary can be interrupted by the therapist if the client gets into difficulties of any kind. In one session the client was climbing a mountain, and met a huge boulder blocking the path. The therapist proposed that a bulldozer was now removing the boulder, enabling the journey to continue. This would not always be done, but it does show the range of interventions which are possible.

Mary Watkins enters an important caution at this point, by pointing out some of the possible drawbacks of the therapist introducing helpful symbols in this way:

> Desoille felt that the introduction of new symbols to the person's unconscious liberated him from 'vicious circles'. These 'vicious circles' may, however, be that person's means of getting in touch with his psyche. It is true that they may stand in the way of certain lines of growth, but are these preferred lines the choice of the therapist or of the patient? In my opinion, directivity should not seek certain ends which are not the patient's.
>
> (Watkins 1976, p. 63)

What the therapist can always do, however, is to act as if the situation were real, and ask appropriate questions, as for example – what colour is it? what does it do next? what else can you see? So in a sense the therapist is right there in the scene with the client, 'in the picture' at the same time, not leading but facilitating.

Besides the meadow, other scenes include: climbing up a mountain; following the course of a stream (either from the source to the sea, or from the estuary to the source); visiting a house; the edge of the woods (these first five form the basic level for Leuner, and can be carried out with most people); an ideal person of the same sex; a cow; an elephant or bull; a lion; (for men) a rose bush; (for women) being offered a lift in a car (these form the intermediate level, and should only be used by an experienced therapist, according to Leuner); a pool of water in a swamp; waiting for a figure to emerge from a cave; eruption of a volcano; and an old picture book (these last items are described as advanced, and are not so often used).

Assagioli did not discover these methods until the 1960s, but they immediately became a part of psychosynthesis, so much so that when they were introduced into encounter groups and other types of growth groups in the 1960s and early 1970s they were almost always introduced as something out of psychosynthesis. It is clear in the book by Ferrucci (1982) that guided fantasy (as psychosynthesis preferred to call it) can be used in a masterly and very flexible way in this discipline.

Ira Progoff has also worked in this area, and has suggested a guided fantasy of 'the road of life' (Progoff 1975). This too has been taken up in psychosynthesis, and the client encouraged to come to a crossroads and explore travelling in each direction to discover its implications.

Recently a fantasy has been used of a sphere with many concentric layers, each representing a different level of the client's personality, until the central Self is reached (Whitmore 1991, p. 124).

Let us look now at a well-worked-out list of what can be done in this area, adapted from the work of Robert Gerard and Mary Watkins.

FORMS AND TYPES

A. Controlled symbolic visualization
    Although some of the details may be spontaneous, the basic pictorial content is specified in advance. A preparatory state consists of sitting in a comfortable chair, closing the eyes and achieving as relaxed a state as possible.

    1   Controlled visualization of symbols.
        a. Focusing on a single symbol.
            i)   Symbols of synthesis, such as a flower, a mandala, a yantra, the sun (F117–18), a diamond (F123–4), the sky (F124), a work of art (F236–7).
            ii) Symbols of harmonious human relations, such as clasped hands, people joined in a circle, people embracing.
            iii) Symbols of masculinity, such as a sword, a phallus, a tower, a wolf.
            iv) Symbols of femininity, such as a chalice, a womb with tubes extending from it, a downward-pointing triangle, a cat.
            v)   Symbols of affective states. Colours, water (F123), fire (F123), earth, a skeleton, a decaying corpse, a bell (F125), meditation on love (F237–8).
        b. Controlled change of symbols.
            i)   Symbols of transformation, such as caterpillar to chrysalis to butterfly (F121–2), or synthesis of opposite attitudes (F206–7), or through drawings (F211).
            ii) Symbols of renewal, such as a snake sloughing its old skin and revealing itself in its colourful new skin, seeing one's own life crises as forms of renewal (F236).
            iii) Symbols of growth, such as a rose opening (F132–3), a seed growing into a tree.

    2   Controlled visualization of symbolic scenes.
        a. Controlled visualization of desirable personality characteristics.
            i)   Imagine someone of the same sex with another name. Describe that person in detail.

    ii) Imagine discovering a statue of someone of the same sex.
    Read the inscription.
  b. Symbolic representations of personality reconstruction, such as
    rebuilding a house and garden (F126–7), landscaping a park.
  c. Symbolic discovery of a centre, such as reaching safety after a
    dangerous experience, reaching a high vantage point, getting to
    the centre of a labyrinth, discovering a lighthouse (F119), suc-
    cessfully completing a voyage (F124–5).
  d. Symbolic discovery of relationship, such as two people helping
    each other over difficult terrain, people passing buckets of water
    down a human chain to put out a fire, rescuing children from
    danger, work with pencil and paper (F178–9).

B. Spontaneous symbolic visualization
   No attempt is made to predetermine the form or sequence of symbolic
   representations, although a starting image may be given to induce the
   process. Again relaxation is a helpful preliminary.

1 Symbolic visualization of somatic states.
  a. Visualize any pain or tension you experience.
  b. Visualize aggressive energy and transform it.

2 Symbolic visualization of emotional states.
  a. Notice how you are feeling, and find a metaphor for that.
    Visualize it in detail.
  b. Imagine a door marked with the emotion you want to explore.
    Walk through it and notice what you find (F176–7).
  c. Let an image emerge of how you would like to feel, and focus
    on that (F183), contrast beauty and ugliness (F196).

3 Symbolic visualizations based on projective techniques.
  a. Visualize a TAT scene which is meaningful to you.
  b. Visualize a Rorschach image and notice what happens to it.

4 Symbolic visualizations based on dreams, daydreams, hypnagogic
  images.
  a. Visualize a specific image.
  b. Visualize a whole scene.

5 Symbolic visualizations of thought content.
  a. Translate your thoughts into metaphors, and visualize them.

C. Symbolic visualization for psychospiritual development
   These may simply take off from one of the previous ideas and take it

further, or they may particularly focus on inner wisdom and inspiration or ethical humanitarian and altruistic values.

1   Guided fantasy technique.
   a. The wise being (F144–6), the inner teacher, the goddess within.
   b. The creative place inside.
   c. Taking a wider view (F215–16).
   d. Exploring silence (F219–20), in a busy town (F239–40).
   e. Potential of humanity (F227–8).
   f. Inevitable grace (F238–9).

2   Fostering of desirable qualities.
   a. Directly (F104–5), through ideal forms (F165), through the ideal person (F167), through inner beauty (F193–4).
   b. Indirectly (F125–6)

3   Technique of inner dialogue.
   a. Working with one subpersonality, writing a letter to the self (F148–9).
   b. Developing a subpersonality positively (F235–6).
   c. Meetings of subpersonalities.

(N.B. I have added to these general divisions specific exercises, marked with the letter F and a page number, taken from Ferrucci's book *What we may be.*)

DREAMS

Dreams are one of the most important areas where transpersonal material can appear. It is sometimes said that people will only have transpersonal dreams if they are working with a transpersonal therapist, but this is not true. Many dreams have transpersonal elements or overtones, and a good therapist will pick these up. For example, in a therapy group which was by no means dominated by transpersonal ideas, a woman had a dream of a frightening house. As she was feeling this fear, there appeared an androgynous figure from Mars, supple and radiant in white and silver. The group leader encouraged her to get into and be the person from Mars:

> Diana speaks as the androgynous person from Mars: 'I'm supple and silver and beautiful...' but after a few sentences she dries up. The group notice a funny expression on her face and ask her what is stopping her.
> 'It doesn't feel like me at all. This person is so radiant and alive, I feel such a mess...' Diana starts to sob.

'Diana, it's your dream, it *is* you. See if you can carry on.'
Through her tears, Diana carries on describing herself as the space-person and gradually manages to own that radiance.

(Ernst and Goodison 1981, p. 154)

Later Diana identified the spaceperson as her spirituality, a part of her personality she had repressed and been scared of.

In a group of my own, a woman visualized a flower, a rose, which again turned out to represent her own spirituality. This happened quite sponta-neously, but later I found out that Ferrucci (1982) had an exercise which was based on the same idea. He makes the point that these experiences are intensely real to the person having them. He insists that when a person has such an experience:

It is not an intellectual concept.
It is not a byproduct of the superego.
It is not the result of suggestion.
It is not a parapsychological phenomenon.
It is not a state of lowered awareness.

(Ferrucci 1982, p. 133)

What it actually is we have described as an aspect of the imaginal world, which is crucial to all work at the transpersonal level.

Another example is to be found in the work of Fritz Perls, which was actually filmed, where he is helping a woman named Madeline work with a dream about a circular lake. In the middle of the lake is a statue. It's a little boy, and he's pouring water from a vase that has a large bottom and a small neck. This water is extremely pure and good to drink. Perls asks her to get into and become the water, speak on behalf of the water.

Madeline: I don't know much about myself. (Pause, begins to cry.) I come. I don't know how I come but I know I'm good, that's all I know... I'm there and I'm white and pure, and if you ask me where I come from I can't tell you. But it's a miracle, I always come out, just for you to drink me... and you have to drink me, every little bit of it.

(Perls 1976, pp. 193–4)

It is clear from the context and from what she says later that the water represents Madeline's spirituality. It was a very moving scene, where Madeline was crying much of the time, and other people in the group were crying too. She had had the dream before, but had woken up before being able to drink the water, feeling somehow not worthy to drink the water.

The realization that perhaps she in some sense *was* the water was a revelation.

This leads to the realization that working in a genuinely Gestalt way with dreams may itself be a transpersonal activity. I did not realize this in my earlier writings, thinking, as I suppose one naturally would, that work in Gestalt therapy was always work at a more ordinary everyday level. Gestalt therapy is so full of the existential spirit, so characteristically down-to-earth in so many of the pronouncements of Fritz Perls, that we are misled into thinking that Gestalt work with dreams is necessarily work at this everyday kind of level.

Yet if we look at what actually happens, instead of at the pronounce-ments and the theory, what do we find? We find that there is a consistent emphasis on staying with the image, on respecting the image, on not interpreting or reducing the image, on loving the image for its own sake. And these are characteristic themes of the transpersonal approach.

Every time we let the image speak for itself, every time we encourage the client to simply *be* the image instead of thinking about it, reasoning about it, intellectually taking it apart, we are taking up the transpersonal approach, we are entering into the reality of what Watkins (1976) calls the imaginal and what Hillman (1975) calls the soul.

Sometimes the therapist can play an important part in helping the client to see something which was not obvious to them about the dream, and which has to do with the symbols of the transpersonal. Norman Don tells us of a client of his where this happened. In the course of a long case history he says:

> At this time Wendy had a dream. She was on a ship crossing a storm-tossed ocean. The captain of the ship – an old 'caretaker' who walked around carrying a staff – warned her not to go too close to the railing, lest she fall in. Just after this she did fall overboard and as she was falling she realized that rescue was impossible under these violent conditions. She did not actually fall into the water, but next found herself back on the ship. The caretaker came to her, lent her his staff, and told her that this would keep her from falling into the water again.
>
> The 'caretaker' is of course a representation of the archetype of the Wise Old Man, while the ocean is the unconscious. The staff is particularly important to us here, for it is the *caduceus*, representing the healing process through unification and the rising of energy. The energy is the *kundalini* and the staff is the central channel for its ascent, the *sushumna*.
>
> (Don 1980, p. 290)

In the context of the case study as a whole, this made a lot of sense, and was accepted and used very readily.

However, the person may or may not be ready to deal with this material at a given time in their life. Here is an example of where this happened, in the case of a patient of Crittenden Brookes:

> One of the dreams presented by this woman was recurring: she walks alone through a kind of enchanted wood to an open clearing on top of a hill. As she walks into the clearing, a figure, at once human and not human, unusually tall and wearing a hooded white robe, advances towards her from the other side of the clearing. There is a vaguely feminine 'feel' to the figure. The dreamer is terrified but unable to prevent herself from advancing to meet the figure. In the midst of her terror she is fascinated that in the figure's hands is a white flower, so perfectly beautiful and radiant as to inspire feelings of the deepest awe and wonder, even in the midst of her terror. In each of the recurring dreams, the figure holds the flower out to her as if inviting her to take it for herself. And in each dream the dreamer, filled with terror, forces herself to awaken.
>
> (Brookes 1980, pp. 63–4)

It was unfortunately true in this case that the person never did get up the strength to deal with this dream, and left therapy before there was any chance to do so.

I used to believe that it was wrong for therapists to offer interpretations of dreams. I held the view, very strongly, that the client should be the sole and sovereign authority as to the meaning of their dreams. But more recently I have had one or two experiences which suggest that this is too rigid a shibboleth, and that it is sometimes all right for the therapist to offer something.

I had always held the opinion that there is never just one meaning to a dream, and two, three or four or more interpretations may all be valid and useful. But I had always wanted these to come from the client.

The event which changed my mind was when a woman client had a dream involving a vulture. The vulture played a major role, and seemed to be one of the most significant features of the dream. All the client's associations with the vulture were negative, and for her it was quite a frightening dream for this reason.

It just so happened that the previous day I had been reading about Nekhbet, the vulture goddess of ancient Egypt. She was regarded as the origin of all things, and the greatest oracle in Egypt was located at her shrine in Nekhen (modern Al-Kab). She was the pre-dynastic matriarch, and the hieroglyph for 'grandmother' was the symbol of the vulture goddess with the flail of authority. The hieroglyph for 'mother' was the vulture on its own. So in ancient Egypt, and in other places too, the vulture was sacred and highly valued, a major goddess and a powerful cult figure.

This made the dream quite different in meaning, and the client was greatly reassured and relieved. In this particular case, I am sure that the new interpretation was much closer to the truth for this client. It would not necessarily be so for another client at another time.

Another time a client had a dream about a powerful woman, who was dominant and aggressive, both defeating people with words and also cutting off their heads with a sword. My client was inclined to see in this her *animus*, or inner male archetype, and to deplore the masculine qualities being exhibited by this woman, who seemed to her more masculine than feminine.

But this character seemed to me more like the goddess Athena, who was both powerful in reason and logic, and also warlike, inspiring heroes and going with them into battle. She was the only goddess on Olympus who wore armour. Jean Bolen tells us that: 'Strategy, practicality and tangible results are hallmarks of her particular wisdom. Athena values rational thinking and stands for the domination of will and intellect over instinct and nature' (Bolen 1984, p. 76). Yet Athena is a goddess, completely female, nothing masculine about her at all. She proves, like many other goddesses, that many so-called 'masculine qualities' can be true of the feminine too. There is nothing about being female which precludes women from getting in touch with these forceful qualities and using them to the full. This idea appealed very much to my client, and meant a lot to her at this particular point in her life.

It is important not to let ourselves be talked out of these truths. In the case of Athena, people have said to me very seriously – 'Of course, you must realize that Athena is a patriarchal fiction herself, supposedly born from the forehead of Zeus, a male creation.' But Barbara Walker reminds us that:

> Athena was the virgin form of the same goddess [Metis], born not from Zeus's head but from the triple Gorgon in the land of Libyan Amazons, who worshipped Medusa-Metis as the Mother of Fate. A later, Gnostic-Christian version of the same Goddess was Sophia, whose name also meant 'Wisdom'.
>
> (Walker 1983, p. 653)

So I now believe that a knowledge of mythology can be very useful when dealing with dreams, because they can enable a different light to be thrown on something, and another meaning to be extracted, which may be highly relevant and very useful to the client.

Let us also remember, however, that to work in a transpersonal way is not always to be looking for myths and spirituality, but more importantly to be working at the level of soul, to be working in the imaginal space in such a way as not to falsify it or make it into something it is not.

Chapter 4

The practice: 3

One of the tricky things to deal with is meditation, because in a way it is part of therapy, and in a way it is not. Let us examine it now.

MEDITATION

Meditation is one of the main things which people think of when they think about the transpersonal, and indeed it is quite a key activity in this area of work. It can be a preparation for therapy, or an adjunct to therapy, or a follow-up to therapy. But let us first ask the question – what is meditation?

The triangle model of meditation presented in Naranjo and Ornstein's book (1976) is well known, and I have used it for years. It says that there are three types of meditation – the Way of Forms, the Expressive Way and the Negative way.

Through working with the developmental model of Ken Wilber (1983b) however, I have come to see not only that there is a very important fourth type, but that the actual relationships between all four are very much clarified when we use this model. The work of John Southgate (1983) is also very relevant to this.

Wilber says that in understanding the process of psychospiritual development, we have to use two dimensions, both of which, in quite different ways, could be called *eros* versus *thanatos* (love versus death). The horizontal dimension we could call preserve (eros) against release (thanatos). When we preserve something or somebody, we hang on to them, we want to keep them, we want to be near them, we want to be involved with them, we want to know what they are doing – all of these involve some kind of *desire*, as Southgate has underlined.

Conversely, at the other pole of this dimension, we are willing to let go, willing to be separate, willing to be independent or autonomous, willing to be alone, willing to be free, willing to finish with something or somebody. These again are in the realm of desire.

The vertical dimensions we could label ascend (eros) versus descend (thanatos). When we ascend we push towards creativity, we go towards love, we move towards orgasm, we thrust towards satisfaction – all these, as Southgate has remarked, have the nature of *drives*. And again if we look at the opposite pole, we push towards destruction, we go towards hate, we move towards violence, we thrust towards depression. This again is seen as an active drive: as Wilber puts it – 'Not a fear of death, but a drive towards it'.

Now we can come back to the types of meditation outlined by Naranjo and Ornstein, and see where they fit in on Figure 4.1.

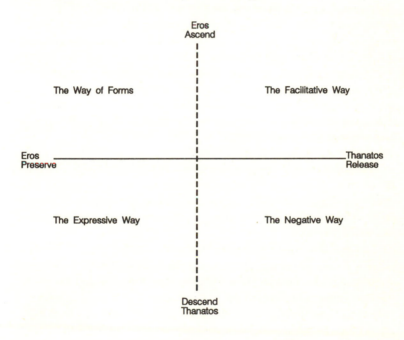

Figure 4.1   Four quadrants of meditation.

The Way of Forms, otherwise known as concentrative or absorptive meditation, is any way of working which involves a definite object which is held to. This object may be a mantra (word or phrase), a yantra (symbolic design), a mudra (movement of the hands), a bija (seed affirmation), a kasina (plain surface or colour), a symbol (such as serpent, cross, lotus, heart, sun, etc.) or something else. In the meditation we focus on this object, and if we find ourselves drifting away from it, we bring ourselves back to it. This is an Apollonian, outer-directed form of meditation, which fits very well into the 'ascend–preserve' quadrant of our model. Very often the symbols chosen represent some form of aspiration, as in Bhakti yoga.

The Expressive Way is more Dionysian, and may include possession by gods, spirits or energies. A familiar version of it is the Rajneesh dynamic meditation, which involves heavy breathing, fast movement, loud chanting and so on. In this form we take the things which distract us, and which in other forms of meditation are often the enemy, so to speak, and make them the very centre of the meditation. Some of the shamanic forms, such as the sweat-lodge, use this approach, so do some of the Tantric methods, and Sufi dancing works in this way. 'Speaking in tongues', as in the Charismatic Church, can also be regarded as an example of this way of approaching the divine. But because it also includes the martial arts, we put this way into the 'descend–preserve' quadrant. We actually focus on the opponent, so to speak, as the thing we need to keep in front of our gaze.

The Negative Way is where we try to eliminate all forms, all expression. The yoga meditation of Patanjali is a good example of this. The Zen practice of shikan-taza is another. The phrase neti-neti, loosely translated 'not this, not that', is appropriate too. The work is done by letting go, but in a way which merely empties the mind. One way of looking at this is to say that we can progress by attending more and more intensely to fewer and fewer things, until the zero point is reached. Because this is a kind of deprivation, we place it appropriately in the 'descend–release' quadrant of our model.

This now leaves the Facilitative Way, which simply opens awareness to what is there. These are the forms of meditation which are all about witnessing whatever takes place. Whereas most forms of meditation focus on one thing, this form flows with whatever is being experienced, following it and allowing it. In Vipassana, Mahavipassana and Satipatthana meditation, we are mindful of whatever passes. This mindfulness can be extended in every direction – 'If any further comment, judgement or reflection arises in the meditator's mind, these are themselves made the focus of bare attention' (Goleman 1977). So this fits into the 'ascend–release' quadrant, because it is friendly to everything, and enables fresh movement to take place.

The advantage of putting matters in this way is to see that there are real differences in the various forms of meditation, depending on where they fall in the structure. The Way of Forms and the Expressive Way are both seen to be quite conservative, in the sense that they tend to hold on to what is. This is quite easy to see in the case of the classic, Apollonian, Way of Forms, which so often is attached to an orthodox religious structure of discipline, but it is much harder to accept in the case of the apparently Dionysian and romantic Expressive Way. Certainly the followers of the Expressive Way often see it as radical or challenging. But the proof of the pudding is in the eating. The followers of the Expressive Way seem in practice to be as powerfully attached to a strong structure of firm leadership as any of those following the Way of Forms. They are in fact very orthodox in their adherence to a guru or other head. So in social terms, things stay as they are.

In the case of the Negative Way, social impotence is the result. Because good is no better than bad, because all distinctions ebb away, there is no impulse to do anything in the world.

But in the Facilitative Way – and if we are correct in our location of these forms in our fourfold structure – both Wilber and Southgate say that it is here that real change and development can take place. And we can now see the connection and similarity between this way and the best in therapy. As David Levin puts it:

> Health, radically understood, is simply a question of *staying* with the situated experiential process just as it presents itself, and letting the spontaneous play of energies flow freely, not separated by conflict into subject and object, inner and outer, myself and others, nor myself (here) and the situation (there). The wholesome flow, or creative interplay, of the process is what principally matters.
>
> (Levin 1981, p. 249)

He is talking here about Tibetan Buddhist therapy, which seems very close to what I try to do as a practitioner. And the results of therapy can be very dynamic in changing the lives of people and the people around them. Furthermore, since the Facilitative Way of meditation is so similar to good therapy, it can be used along with such therapy as a valuable preparation and follow-up, taking the person further along the path, and encouraging the same mindfulness to be extended to other people and their interdependence.

Having said this much, there are certain features of meditation which need to be spelled out. It is a method which is almost tailor-made for self-deception if practised alone. It is possible to kid oneself that one has gone much further along the path than one really has. For this reason it is best, if practising meditation, to go to a definite school and to do it in the company of others. One can then practise further on one's own, but continually return to the discipline of the group and teacher.

Meditation was originally part of a unique and individually prescribed pattern of development. It has now been extracted from its original context and offered for consumption, sometimes as if it were a kind of vitamin that was good for everyone, ridiculously cheap, and devoid of side-effects. Those who use it in this way may obtain increased calmness, enjoyment, and improvement of efficiency – but without noticeable gain in wisdom. And it is all too possible for schizoid withdrawal, grandiosity, vanity and dependency to flourish under the disguise of spiritual practice. The end result is that casual experimenters may 'confirm and strengthen their conceptual prison, from which they desperately need to escape' (Deikman 1980, p. 204).

However, Carrington has something interesting to add at this point about the relationship between meditation and psychotherapy:

> I have, for example, seen long-term meditators who have become more emotionally responsive, tranquil, personally insightful, energetic and sensitive to the world around them through meditation. But these same people still carried the burden of unresolved conflicts – sexual adjustments, social maturity, marriage, career. These conflicts remained to be handled by some form of psychotherapeutic intervention. However, I have also seen people who had recently learned to meditate and were benefiting from it considerably, enter psychotherapy (after commencing meditation) to work out specific personality problems. According to them, meditation had reduced their anxiety to a point where they could contemplate exploring their emotional problems in depth for the first time.
>
> (Carrington 1980, p. 253)

This is a comment from someone who has wide and deep experience of both meditation and psychotherapy.

The complementary nature of the two processes, meditation and psychotherapy, particularly impresses me, especially when the Facilitative Way of meditation is used. By far the best and fullest account of the relationship between psychotherapy and meditation is to be found in the book which Ken Wilber wrote about his wife dying of cancer. He examines there the question of what psychotherapy can do, what medicine can do, what healing can do, what meditation can do, in a moving and complete way which can hardly be surpassed (Wilber 1991).

Deikman (1980) has shown that meditation can be used at the beginning of a session to increase the value of the therapy session, and this is a quite legitimate and proper way to engage in meditation. There are also other similar exercises which can be used at the beginning of a session with certain clients, such as the standard relaxation exercises of Jacobson and others. (It is fascinating, by the way, to notice how many of these relaxation exercises completely skip the genital and pelvic area, including the rectum, where a good deal of tension can be held. Don't make this mistake yourself.)

There is a fascinating practice called 'Open Focus', which can also be used instead of meditation at the beginning of a session to put the very anxious or agitated client into a better state to commence the session proper (Fehmi and Selzer 1980).

The Open Focus exercise consists of a series of questions about the ability to imagine certain experiences. For example, when it asks, 'Can you imagine the space between your eyes?' you might naturally experience your eyes and then let your imagination flow to the region between your eyes and imagine the distance between them. Your objective is not to come up with some number or other abstraction, such as 'There are two inches between my eyes.' The objective is very gently to imagine or experience that distance or region between your eyes. You initially may imagine or experience the distance as a very small region or vague feeling and the distance may then expand or change as you continue to maintain your orientation in that region.

These questions are usually put on tape, with approximately 15 seconds between questions; for that period of time the client is asked to maintain attention on the subject of the last question. The usual instructions for meditative exercises are given: don't strain, take it easy, if your attention wanders, gently bring it back, and so on.

While most people find it helpful to close their eyes while practising, after some facility is gained the practice may be done with eyes open or half open. Practising with eyes fully or partially open enhances the transfer of the Open Focus to daily life situations. Again, in order to facilitate transfer of Open Focus effects to daily life situations, a relatively erect body posture is recommended, sitting or standing.

Open Focus exercise

Is it possible for you to imagine the space between your eyes?
Is it possible for you to imagine the space between your ears?
Is it possible for you to imagine the space within your throat?
Is it possible for you to imagine the space between your shoulders?
Is it possible for you to imagine the space between your hips?

Is it possible for you to imagine that the space inside your bladder is filled with space?

Is it possible for you to imagine that the region between your kidneys is filled with space?

Is it possible for you to imagine that the region inside your kidneys is filled with space?

Is it possible for you to imagine that the region between your navel and your backbone is filled with space?

Is it possible for you to imagine the space within your stomach?

Is it possible for you to imagine the space within your rib cage?

Is it possible for you to imagine the space between your ribs?

Is it possible for you to imagine the space between your shoulder blades?

Is it possible for you to imagine the space inside your breasts?

Is it possible for you to imagine the space between your breastbone and your backbone?

Is it possible for you to imagine the space between your shoulders and your ribs?

Is it possible for you to imagine that your neck is filled with space?

Is it possible for you to imagine that the region between your shoulder blades and your chin is filled with space?

Is it possible for you to imagine that your lungs are filled with space?

Is it possible for you to imagine that your bronchial tubes as you inhale and exhale are filled with space?

Is it possible for you to imagine that your whole body, from the chin down, is filled with space, including your hands and fingers, your heart, your genitals, your anus, and your feet and toes?

Is it possible for you to imagine that your throat is filled with space?

Is it possible for you to imagine that your nose as you inhale and exhale is filled with space?

...

At the same time that you are imagining the space inside your whole body, is it possible for you to imagine the space around your body?

Is it possible for you to imagine the space between your fingers and toes?

Is it possible for you to imagine the space behind your neck and back?

Is it possible for you to imagine the space above your head and beneath your chair?

Is it possible for you to imagine the space in front of you and to your sides?

Is it possible for you to imagine that the boundaries between the space inside and the space outside become one continuous and unified space?

Is it possible for you to imagine that this unified space, which is coextensive inside and outside, proceeds in three dimensions front to back, right to left, and up and down?

Is it possible for you to imagine that, at the same time you imagine this unified space, you can simultaneously let yourself attend equally to all the sounds that are available to you, the sound of my voice, the sounds issuing from you, and any other sounds you may be able to hear?

Is it possible for you to imagine that these sounds are issuing from and pervaded by unified space?

Is it possible for you to imagine that at the same time you are attending to the space and the sounds you can also attend simultaneously to any emotions, tensions, feelings, or pains that might also be present?

Is it possible for you to imagine that these sensations and perceptions are permeated by space?

Is it possible for you to imagine that at the same time that you are aware of the space, the sounds, emotions, and other body feelings, you can also be simultaneously aware of any tastes, smells, thoughts, and imagery that might also be present?

Is it possible for you to imagine that you can admit also to awareness any sensation or experience which may have been inadvertently omitted thus far, so that you are now simultaneously aware of your entire being, of all that is you?

Is it possible for you to imagine that all your experience is permeated and pervaded by space?

Is it possible for you to imagine that, as you continue to practise this Open Focus exercise, you will increase your ability to enter into Open Focus more quickly, more completely, and more effortlessly?

Is it possible for you to imagine that, as you continue to practise this Open Focus exercise, your imagery of space will become more vivid and more pervasive?

Is it possible for you to imagine that, as you continue to practise this Open Focus exercise, your ability to imagine space permeating all of your experience will continue to become more vivid and ever present?

The full version of the exercise takes 45 minutes to go through, which makes it impractical for use at the beginning of a therapy session, unless the session is unusually long. But I have used a briefer version with good effect, and the full version can be used by the client at home. It does seem to have many of the same effects as meditation when combined with therapy.

GENERAL PRACTICE

It will be noted that in the whole discussion of practice, there has been no mention of the general conduct of a case. How does the transpersonal practitioner start with a client, how does the relationship continue, what happens along the way, how does it come to an end?

All these questions, which in my view require a book to themselves, are dealt with very well in other publications. Indeed the practice of the transpersonal practitioner is not so very different from the practice of anyone else, very often. All the ordinary questions of transference, counter-transference, resistance and so forth come up. Good texts include the following:

1   Diana Whitmore's *Psychosynthesis counselling in action* gives a very good account of the therapeutic process and some of its ramifications.
2   Jocelyn Chaplin's *Feminist counselling in action* treats the whole journey of therapy as a mythological trip into and out of the labyrinth. This is an excellent account of the whole process, seen from a deeply trans-personal viewpoint.
3   'Transpersonal psychotherapy', the chapter by Ian Gordon-Brown and Barbara Somers in the book *Innovative therapy in Britain* edited by John Rowan and Windy Dryden, is excellent, and answers many of the most crucial questions which may be asked. The two authors are the greatest authorities on the transpersonal in Britain, in my opinion, and have done a great deal over the years to establish a transpersonal theory and practice. Their chapter is essential reading for anyone interested in this area.

It is good that these books on the actual conduct of a case are now available, which was not the case even five years ago. I am sure that in the future even more will come on the scene and be usable.

However, there are one or two points which seem so important that it would be good to mention them here. In 1977 Frances Vaughan brought out an article in the *Journal of Humanistic Psychology* (under her earlier name of Clark) which is well worth attention. In it she makes a comparison between the approach of mainstream humanistic psychotherapy and transpersonal psychotherapy:

> One of the underlying assumptions of transpersonal psychotherapy is that each human being has impulses toward spiritual growth, the capacity for growing and learning throughout life, and that this process can be facilitated and enhanced by psychotherapy. In this respect, it has much in common with growth-oriented humanistic approaches such as client-centred therapy, but goes beyond them in affirming the potentiality for self-transcendence beyond self-actualization.
>
> (Clark 1977, p. 70)

> The change in attitude which occurs when a therapist moves toward a transpersonal orientation has been described as a shift from working *on* yourself to working *with* yourself.
>
> (Clark 1977, p. 72)

These are helpful pointers to what exactly the difference is between working in one way and another. It is not so much a question of doing anything different, but more a question of extending one's horizons. If we ask then how this is to be done, this can be answered too:

> Helping the client to differentiate between the true inner teacher or transpersonal self and the many distracting solicitations of false teachers, both inner and outer, is one of the principal tasks of the therapist. This is a twofold process: First the client learns to tune into him/herself and to listen to his/her own inner truth. This may include learning to quiet the mind, to give honest expression to real feelings, and to be assertive in accordance with felt needs. The second step is one of learning to trust the intuition or inner voice which determines choices and allows one to assume responsibility for oneself. Here the task is a continuing one of being alert to distractions and uncovering self-deceptions, insofar as possible. The concept of the transpersonal self as that center of pure awareness which simultaneously transcends and observes conflicts at the level of ego and personality is useful here in giving a point of reference for the newly awakened sense of self. The continuing search for inner

truth requires a sincere commitment to this transpersonal self and calls
for the deepest level of self-awareness that can be attained.

(Clark 1977, p. 76)

This is well said, and recalls us to the purpose of the whole thing. The
process of therapy may be defined in this frame of reference as one of
expanding consciousness, allowing the client to discover and integrate the
inner wellsprings of transpersonal experience. But as can be seen from the
quote above, this does not exclude the necessary work of exploring feelings
and dealing with the everyday world effectively. As Norman Don tells us:

> It is a serious error to attempt therapy exclusively on a transpersonal
> basis... The energies, feelings, images and thoughts so activated must be
> brought down and grounded in the life of the person. This grounding
> is considered to be essential both in bioenergetic work and in Qabalistic
> philosophy (Fortune 1979). If this grounding does not occur, then one
> has a spiritual person whose life still does not work. Grounding must
> ultimately be in the body and its vitality. This leads, ideally, to
> contactfulness in all areas of life.
>
> (Don 1980, pp. 294–5)

This agrees very much with the analysis to be presented in the next chapter.
Yet there must not be too much emphasis on grounding. We need wings
as well as roots, in this business. If we are too hard on inflation, how are
we ever to take off?

In my own work, developed with Jocelyn Chaplin at the Serpent
Institute, I have found that the concept of Goddess spirituality has a great
deal to offer. What does this mean? It means that we respect the principle
of rhythm as the dance of life energies interweaves in or out of opposites
and polarities throughout nature and human life. Sometimes this is called
the feminine principle, but we also stress the importance of the male
polarity and of male sexuality as an essential part of Goddess spirituality.

One of the things involved here is a reclaiming of very ancient
pre-Christian pagan symbols and rituals that embody more of the 'feminine' principle. The serpent is one of these symbols, representing wisdom,
transformation, connections between the worlds and even the spiralling
shape of the primal earth and human energies themselves.

This rhythmic and fundamentally erotic model of life is contrasted with
patriarchal relationships based on dominance and submission. It celebrates
difference and interconnectedness through dance and sometimes struggle.
It is not rigidly hierarchical and is in a constant state of change. It represents
both male and female inner powerfulness rather than 'power-over'. The

emphasis is on partnership, social equality and justice as well as individual well-being.

The vision that we arrived at was to see therapy and counselling as a kind of initiation process. The kind of initiation we are talking about is a process of symbolic death and rebirth, leading to a new phase of life or a new existence as a different kind of woman or man. Each individual starts at a different point in this process and may need different styles of therapy at different times. Some need to develop a well-functioning ego before they can begin to question it. Some need to work through problems to do with their sexual identity in a patriarchal society. Some have to clean up their karma before they can go on. Some need a counsellor, while others need a guide.

This means that a proper training along these lines has to cover a much broader range than was thought necessary in the past. For example, we have to use non-possessive warmth, but also to understand the world of myths and symbols.

One of the major symbols which we discovered was the labyrinth. As therapists we are privileged witnesses to other people's stories and can help them follow their threads through their own journeys in and out of the labyrinths of self-discovery. Psychotherapy can indeed be thought of as a seven-stage journey into and out of the labyrinth. It starts with an emphasis on mothering, trust and childhood, and goes on to deal with separation from the mother and difference. This may lead to the exploration of life myths and stories, which may in turn enable the client to face the loss of illusion and ambivalence at the centre. Then there is the return to the world with new awareness and assertiveness, learning to dance to our own rhythms. Finally we deal with endings and new beginnings.

> To the ancients, the cosmic serpent – the spirit of earth and water – was everywhere known as the energy source of life: of healing and oracular powers, fertility and maternal blessing.
>
> (Sjöö and Mor 1987, p. 251)

So the serpent became for us a symbol of this journey, of this path through the labyrinth. And it was good for men too, because of its basic ambivalence and dual nature:

> Finally, the snake came to symbolize the phallus, male sexual energy, which was understood to be originally contained within the Goddess – born from her, and returning to her again, when at the end of each world cycle (expansion–contraction) she curls up in dark sleep... But these are not aggressive or misogynistic phallic images; rather, they seem

to represent the phallus *serving* the Goddess, women, and the life processes of all.

(Sjöö and Mor 1987, p. 61)

This then seems a rich source of imagery for the whole process of psychotherapy and counselling.

But there are also one or two things to be said about the therapist in all this. How far does a counsellor or psychotherapist have to go before they can do this work?

> In this context a holistic approach to psychological health means an integration of physical, emotional, mental and spiritual dimensions of the person. The spiritual quest is affirmed as a vital aspect of human potential, and its validity is affirmed in both theory and practice. Thus a transpersonal therapist is necessarily on his/her own spiritual path, though this need not imply formal affiliation with an organized group or particular religious beliefs. On the contrary, it is important that the therapist not be identified with a particular belief system in such a way as to interfere with the right and the responsibility of his/her clients to choose freely their own paths to transpersonal development.
>
> (Clark 1977, p. 72)

This again is well said, and seems to be putting the matter very much in its proper proportion. The therapist does not have to be a superbeing of any kind, but simply has to take seriously their own process and their own development. This is something which the humanistic practitioner has always recognized, and all this does is to take it one step further. But this means that there is no end to the process of development. There is no point at which the transpersonal therapist has got there finally, and has to learn no more:

> Jung (1973), Ram Dass (1974), and others have noted the fact that a psychotherapist cannot take someone beyond where he/she has been. However, it is possible for therapist and client to break new ground together if both are willing to learn from each other as companions on the journey of self-discovery.
>
> (Clark 1977, p. 80)

In other words, the therapist can learn from the client. And in fact my own experience is that we learn most from our most difficult clients. It is the clients who press us beyond our existing limits who force us to learn new things, about them and about ourselves, and about the whole process of psychotherapy. This opinion is I think common to all good therapists of all persuasions, but it is only the best, perhaps, who can actually carry it out in practice.

Part II
The Wilber revolution

Chapter 5

The basic map

In 1977 something happened to the world of the transpersonal. There came on the scene a writer who had the ambitious plan of linking and reconciling the psychological and the spiritual. In a series of books, some about mysticism, some about psychology, some about world-historical developments, some about religion, some about physics, he has applied his ideas over a very wide range, illuminating everything he touches. His name is Ken Wilber, an American living in Colorado, who seldom goes to conferences or meetings, but has a tremendous talent for writing.

If we say that the transpersonal is the shallows of mysticism, what is mysticism? People often use such a term in a derogatory or dismissive way, as if to say that if something is mystical then it can be ignored. But the great contribution of the mystics down the ages, and in many different traditions, has been the discovery that authentic spiritual experience is only to be had for oneself. It cannot be given by someone else – not a person, not a book, not a sermon.

To say that something can be an authentic spiritual experience is to say that it is a form of consciousness. Evelyn Underhill says well of mysticism:

> One of the most abused words in the English language, it has been used in different and often mutually exclusive senses by religion, poetry and philosophy: has been claimed as an excuse for every kind of occultism, for dilute transcendentalism, vapid symbolism, religious or aesthetic sentimentality, and bad metaphysics. On the other hand, it has been freely employed as a term of contempt by those who have criticised these things. It is much to be hoped that it may be restored sooner or later to its old meaning, as the science or art of the spiritual life.
>
> (Underhill 1961, p. xiv)

This is a classic statement, but the most succint discussion of mysticism I have seen is the book by Horne (1978), where he makes two important distinctions: between introvertive and extravertive mysticism, and between casual and serious mysticism. (In all these cases we are speaking of authentic spiritual experiences.) In introvertive mysticism the person has an experience of transformation of the self; in extravertive mysticism the person has an experience of transformation of the world. In casual mysticism the experience comes unexpectedly and with little or no preparation; in serious mysticism the experience comes as a result of intention and commitment.

With the help of this terminology we can see that the typical peak experience, which we saw described in the Introduction to this book, is an experience of casual extraverted mysticism. The practice of psychotherapy, on the other hand, is an intentional and committed process of self-development, and as such is more likely to lead to serious introverted mystical experiences, such as the experience of contacting the Real Self (as described by Jung, Adler, Federn, Perls, Assagioli, Winnicott, Guntrip, Laing, Janov, Love, Johnson, Koestenbaum, Heron, Sullivan, Loevinger, Maslow, Fromm, Riesman, Kohlberg, Alderfer, Mahrer, Broughton, Wilber, Rogers, Buber, Jaspers and others), or the experience of contacting the Transpersonal Self, as described by Assagioli, Grof, Jung, Heron and others.

What we are saying, then, is that mystical experiences are states of consciousness which can come suddenly and with no preparation, or as the result of a long period of preparation and work. They can have to do with the world outside us, or with the inner world. So to understand them better, one way to go is to work up to them by a full discussion of states of consciousness with which we are much more familiar. We can then see how they fit in naturally, rather than being something quite special and isolated.

The symbiotic consciousness of early babyhood is something we have all experienced; the body consciousness of the small child is something familiar; the membership consciousness we had in our early family life is common to us all; the ego consciousness of our adolescence and the years immediately following is well known to all of us; the existential and authentic consciousness which we get from working on ourselves is known to some of us; and transpersonal consciousness is a mystical experience, but something which most of us have had in glimpses, here and there.

LEVELS OF CONSCIOUSNESS

One of the most productive ways of looking at consciousness has been the idea of levels. Some people prefer to use the term 'positions', because it is nonhierarchical, and I have followed this usage myself in the Introduction to this book, but I think it is equally legitimate to outline positive uses of the term 'hierarchical', and we shall be looking at this in due course.

The most common idea of levels is to distinguish between body and mind. This goes back so far, and has been taken up so vigorously by Christianism (I believe Hillman is right when he chooses to use this term in preference to Christianity, because it puts it more on a level with Taoism, Buddhism, Sikhism and so forth) that we hardly need to establish its credentials and origins. In this view the body is seen as a rather unruly animal ('brother ass') which has to be disciplined by the mind, which is rational and in charge and in control, or ought to be.

Almost equally common is the idea of the body, the mind and the soul or spirit. This is so popular that it has become the title of a yearly exhibition which brings in thousands of people each time. The reason why this has become more understandable is that the idea has been developed that spirituality is different from religion. This has to do with the distinction which is often made between the authentic and the normative in religious practice. Authentic experience is experience one has for oneself, and does not necessarily get from someone else. The normative, on the other hand, has to do with observances, rules, rituals, dogmas and so forth, which are laid down by a religious group and policed in some way. Spirituality has to do with the authentic rather than the normative, and many people these days are paying more attention to their own experience and valuing that.

Going on from there, we can easily move to a four-level model, and talk about body, mind, soul and spirit. Huston Smith (1976) suggests that this is a better model, because it enables us to distinguish between the soul level, where the multiple and the symbolic are important, and the spirit level, where the emphasis is on unity and leaving the symbolic behind. It is important to understand this properly, because it will come in again and again as one of the most important distinctions. The soul level is the level we discover when we fully go into and accept our own imaginative qualities. So many people put down their own imagination as distracting or fantastic, perhaps even dangerous. And yet we all have dreams and daydreams. I remember once asking a group of housewives whether they ever had fantasies, and one of them said: 'What do you think we do when we are standing at the sink with a pile of dishes?' And it turned out that many of them had fantasies while taking a bath. So this is not something recondite or unusual. But we need to recognize that if we can feed our imagination, enrich it, take it seriously (by remembering our dreams, for example), we can cultivate our soul in a very effective way.

It is then quite easy to accept a five-level model, where we refer to body, emotions, intellect, soul and spirit. This divides the mind into emotions and intellect, which seems quite reasonable and in tune with experience and a good deal of philosophy and common sense. All the time we are saying that any human being has potential access to these levels of consciousness – they are within us all, so to speak – though we may not be in touch with them all at a given time.

From there it is not far to the *chakra* system in Yoga. This holds (and I am deliberately changing some of the traditional naming of parts in order to fit in better with the model we have developed so far) that there are seven levels involved here: the base level (part of what we have called the body earlier); the sexual level (another part of the body); the active energy level (a third part of the body); the heart level (what we have called the emotions); the throat level, which has to do with communication (what we have called the intellect); the level of the third eye (what we have called the soul level); and the level of the thousand-petalled lotus at the crown of the head (what we have called the level of spirit). So here we have expanded the notion of the body to allow the separation of various aspects of it, just as before we expanded the notion of the spirit, seeing in it two levels rather than one.

Von Eckartsberg (1981) takes this further, and gives us a pyramid, where at the bottom we have death, and then going upwards from there, coma and sleep. Going up further, awakeness, and then further up still, everyday thinking. Still going up the pyramid, we get cognitive mapping and systematic thinking, the highest reaches of the intellect. Going on again upwards, we get aesthetic experience and intuition, and then moral experience and sacred experience. Above this like a rainbow above the pyramid we get the infinite divine psychic energy field radiating outwards. This puts together many of the themes we have been noticing up to now.

KEN WILBER'S MAP

But as we saw at the beginning of this chapter, a writer has come along who takes this idea of levels and pushes it much further. He has actually gone through all the established systems of levels and reconciled them, showing that they are really all talking about the same thing – it is just that different systems leave out different things. When we include everything, we get a consistent and very convincing plan, with no less than seventeen distinguishable levels, not all of which he deals with in detail.

What he says is that there is a process of psychospiritual development which we are all going through, both as individuals and as members of a historically located culture. In a series of books he has outlined this process, and shows that we are very familiar with its early stages. The later stages are much more controversial, but follow exactly the same form.

The easiest way to describe this model seems to be by going through Figure 5.1. It can be seen from this that there are three broad sections, labelled as prepersonal, personal and transpersonal. We are already familiar with these terms and these distinctions from our earlier discussions. One of Wilber's most insistent themes is that we tend to suffer from the pre/trans fallacy – that is, we confuse what is prepersonal with what is transpersonal. Some do it (like Freud) by saying that the transpersonal does not really exist – it is just a projection from the prepersonal; others do it (like Jung) by saying that the prepersonal does not really exist – anything beyond the personal must be transpersonal.

What is so reassuring about Wilber is that he says that the move from the personal to the transpersonal is no great leap into the deep waters of spirituality (or religion, or occultism), but a change no greater than that which we have experienced several times before, in the course of our development so far. We have already gone from symbiosis with the mother to separation, and from body-self to membership-self, and from there to the mental ego. At each of these transitions we had to revise our whole notion of who we were, and even what kind of self we were. So we know what it is like to revise our self-definition. The move from mental ego to the centaur stage is just another such change, and peak experiences are a very common harbinger of this particular transition.

Let us now look at each of the positions which Wilber (1980) marks out separately.

Pleroma

This is the first state of consciousness, but perhaps it should not be counted as a state of consciousness at all. It is completely empty. This is not the full and complete emptiness we shall meet at the end of the road, but an ignorant emptiness which has not had to make any distinctions yet. It is objectless and spaceless. Wilber says it is 'Desireless, choiceless, timeless'. Yet it is the starting point for all our development. Perhaps it is a myth, in the sense of not being verifiable or pinned-down in time, but it seems to be a necessary myth, in that it helps to make sense of the whole process which is to follow.

Dual unity

This is used to represent an unfamiliar state, which most of us have not

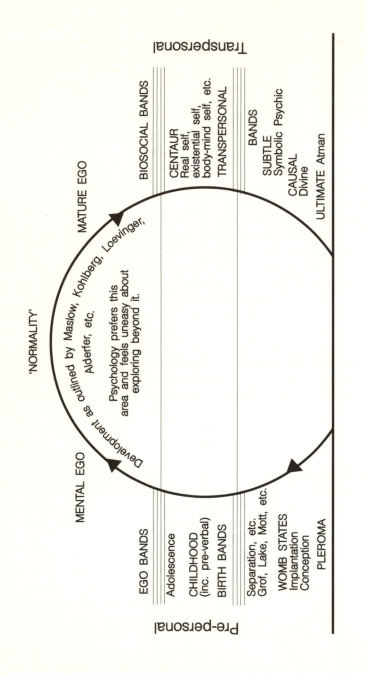

'NORMALITY'

MENTAL EGO   MATURE EGO

Development as outlined by Maslow, Kohlberg, Loevinger, Alderfer, etc.

Psychology prefers this area and feels uneasy about exploring beyond it.

Transpersonal

BIOSOCIAL BANDS

CENTAUR
Real self,
existential self,
body-mind self, etc.

TRANSPERSONAL
BANDS

SUBTLE
Symbolic Psychic

CAUSAL
Divine

ULTIMATE Atman

Pre-personal

EGO BANDS

Adolescence

CHILDHOOD
(inc. pre-verbal)

BIRTH BANDS

Separation, etc.
Grof, Lake, Mott, etc.

WOMB STATES
Implantation
Conception

PLEROMA

Figure 5.1 Ken Wilber's map.
Source: Rowan (1983), p.132. Revised and consolidated by John Rowan in April 1982 and approved by Ken Wilber in May 1982.

thought about very much. It is the stage, usually occurring in the womb (this seems obvious to me, but apparently not so obvious to Wilber), where distinctions start to appear. We start to distinguish a figure from the background on which it stands: in other words, there starts to be a consciousness of something and an other. It may not be at all clear which is which, and fantasy (or in Kleinian terms, phantasy) and hallucination may complicate the picture. Extreme and basic emotions start to appear, and Wilber speaks of 'oceanic-euphoria and primordial fear'. There is a primitive urge to survival, which may become obvious at this stage if life is threatened. There is some awareness of things happening, but no sense of time. There may be the first glimmerings of a desire to hold on to good things and reject bad things, because there is now the tentative beginnings of a sense of division between self and other.

It is a shame that Wilber did not take on board the idea of prenatal experience, because it is now so well attested and understood. There is a great deal of research appearing about foetal experience, and an international interest in pre- and perinatal consciousness, and it appears quite unarguable now that consciousness does begin to develop in the womb, particularly if there are traumas to be faced, such as attempted abortion, accidents to the mother or continued insult to the foetus, such as smoking, drinking, drugtaking, depression and so forth (Verny 1982, Ridgway 1987). The experience of birth is so traumatic (Grof 1979, Lake 1980, Wasdell 1990) that it almost always brings an ego into being, if it has not emerged already. More data on this is emerging all the time, and some important facts are now contained in the big book by Fedor-Freybergh and Vogel (1988).

Body ego

Now with this stage emerging there is a definite feeling self, though emotions are still primitive, such as pain, rage, terror, joy. There is a lot of fantasy, and some ability now to distinguish and identify fantasy images. This is the stage where Melanie Klein's early stages of good breast and bad breast appear. Thinking is very much in terms of wishes rather than reality. Separation anxiety can be very high at this stage.

The object relations school in psychoanalysis (people like Fairbairn, Guntrip, Winnicott and Balint) have done a great deal of work in this area, and it is now much more easy to see what an important stage it is. Also a great deal of developmental research has now been carried out on babies, and it is clear that the very young infant is far more conscious and far more competent than had previously been thought (Stern 1985, Bremner 1988,

Bradley 1989). There is no doubt that a baby has an ego from its first moments of life outside the womb.

Just to give some examples of this, because some people are still not familiar with the recent research, and Wilber never mentions it, consider these items:

Goren *et al.* (1975) found that infants with an average age of nine minutes attended closest to a schematic face compared with a blank head shape, or one with scrambled features. Dziurawiec and Ellis (1986) couldn't quite believe this, repeated the work with improved methodology, and got the same results. It seems that the purpose of this is to aid in bonding.

Wertheimer (1961) studied newborn babies actually in the delivery room, as soon as they were born. He worked only with those where there was no anaesthesia and no apparent trauma. He found that if he presented a series of sounds, placed randomly to left and to right, the baby looked in the direction of the sound source. There was no random looking about, just a direct look in the right direction.

Lipsitt (1969) did an experiment where newborn babies, just a few hours old, had to turn their heads to the right at the sound of a tone, and to the left at the sound of a buzzer. If they turned the right way they got a reward – a sweet taste in the mouth. It took them only a few trials to learn which way to turn their heads. Then the signals were reversed, and it took them only about ten trials to unlearn the old task and learn the new one. Tom Bower, working in Edinburgh, says:

> The newborn can localize sounds. He can locate objects visually. He seems to know that when he hears a sound, there probably will be something for him to look at, and that when an object approaches him, it probably will be hard or tangible.
>
> (Bower 1977, p. 24)

Visually, the baby has size constancy from birth onwards: also shape constancy, form and colour perception, movement detection, three-dimensional and depth perception (Slater 1990). After two days a baby will show a preference for the mother's face when this is shown side by side with a stranger's face (Bushnell *et al.* 1989).

Several investigators in the 1970s found that babies less than a week old will imitate other people. If we stick our tongue out at the baby, the baby will begin to stick the tongue out too. If we stop this, and begin to flutter our eyelashes, the baby will flutter the eyelashes back. If we then open and shut our mouths, the baby will match us at the same speed. If we use a TV split-screen technique, showing the adult's face and the baby's face side by side, we find a very close matching of one to the other, which by five weeks old becomes very accurate and very quick, so that real two-way communication is taking place. Even at 42 minutes old, Meltzoff found the beginnings of this kind of response. An extraordinary book has now come out, detailing all that babies are aware of at birth (Chamberlain 1988).

So this is a very important stage in the development of the person, and a very definite body ego emerges and becomes solidified at this stage.

Membership self

This is the stage of being a family member. There is a clear sense of time now, and language is used quite easily, while logical thinking emerges and becomes stronger. But mythical thinking goes alongside and is not perceived as being contradictory. What is important is to be accepted by the family, and to belong. Moving on from the previous stage, where the self was identified with the body, now the self is identified with the family, or with some other primary group.

When this is generalized later, it means a total identification with the group. I am nothing, the group is everything. This sort of regression often occurs in cults, where the person is encouraged, on the pretext of spiritual growth, to 'drop the ego'. What this really means, however, is to disown one's own centre altogether, and regress to an earlier stage of development where the parents (now the guru, leader or teacher) are always right and know the answers to everything, as Hassan (1988) has shown in detail. So what is healthy and normal at one stage can become highly suspect at a later stage.

What Wilber is saying about these stages is that they all proceed in the same way. They proceed by disowning the previous stage and moving on to the next stage. But the disowned stage is actually retained, though not necessarily in any conscious way. It may be set on one side and put away in a drawer, but it is still there, in the drawer. And it can always be returned to again. This can now clearly be seen as a concept of nesting, where each stage remains nested within the next.

Mental ego

Now at this stage the person is supposed to have a personality and to be able to play roles. One has to give up one's family membership position and take up an independent position. Stepping stones to this (or sometimes alternatives to this) are the peer group and the couple relationship. Emotions and thinking are much more differentiated and sophisticated now. There is a great deal of self-control, and the image of the horse and the rider is often used to represent this. The mind is the rider, and the body and the emotions are the horse. But this is just one of many splits we set up at this stage, between masculine and feminine, intellect and feelings, spiritual and material, and so on. This is all in order to get the control we feel we need at this stage. We need esteem from others at this point, to boost and form our ego. Wilber says rather mysteriously that one of the aims at this stage is 'To conquer death by becoming father of oneself'. The most noticeable feature, however, is the preservation and enhancement of the self-image.

Now from a transpersonal point of view there is something curious to note about the mental ego. It gives us a form of consciousness which, because it is generally socially approved, becomes taken for granted. But what is taken for granted becomes rigid and unquestionable, and what is rigid and unquestionable is not mentally healthy. This produces a fascinating paradox:

> A transpersonal model views our usual consciousness as a defensively contracted state. This usual state is filled to a remarkable and unrecognised extent with a continuous flow of largely uncontrollable thoughts and fantasies which exert an extraordinarily powerful though unappreciated influence on perception, cognition and behaviour...
>
> Viewing our usual state from an expanded context results in some unexpected implications. The traditional model defines psychosis as a distorted perception of reality which does not recognise the distortion. From the perspective of this multiple states model our usual state fits this definition, being suboptimal, providing a distorted perception of reality, and failing to recognise that distortion. Indeed, any one state of consciousness is necessarily limited and only relatively real and hence from the broader perspective psychosis might be defined as attachment to, or being trapped in, any single state of consciousness.
>
> (Walsh and Vaughan 1980, pp. 10–11)

This is really an extraordinary realization: that our ordinary consciousness, which we take for granted – and precisely because we take it so much for granted – removes us from a wider reality. We are just not in touch with this expanded reality which is there open to us. Luckily there is a way out of this, which is simply to carry on with the process of development which has taken us so far.

Yet there is one crucial difference. At each stage of our journey so far, society had been on our side, and had said in effect, 'Yes, go on, you are doing well.' But now there is no such boost from society if we want to carry on. We have to do it from our own intention and our own will. Society will in most cases put up obstacles instead of helping.

Centaur

This is the important next stage of development. The key thing here is the healing of the splits of the previous stage. Wilber speaks of a 'total bodymind being.' There is a conscious emergence of the real self, and a consequent increase in spontaneity and autonomy. The phrase which often comes in at this stage is: 'I create my world'. This is the stage where we start to take responsibility for our own development, rather than allowing ourselves to be moved on as if up an escalator. Symbols may be used deliberately for growth. This is the highest point in the existential realm. Blissful states or peak experiences may be experienced. Again, however, as before, it may be very scary to move on from the previous stage, with all its certainties and all its familiarity. In earlier chapters we have referred to this as the autonomous stage or level or position.

This is an extraordinarily important step, and the concept of the centaur stage is one of Wilber's most important contributions. It represents at one time the end of the process of individual development within the confines, so to speak, of one's own skin; and the beginning of the process of transpersonal development, because it breaks the mould of the mental ego. It is very hard to get to the centaur stage without going through the process of psychotherapy (or the best kind of long-term counselling), because it entails working through the unfinished business of the past, and bringing everything into the present. Only in this way can a genuine existential consciousness be achieved. We cannot have the authenticity which is so crucial at this stage unless there is a whole person there to be authentic.

This is a particularly paradoxical stage, because of this quality of being the end of one process and the beginning of another. It is a spiritual stage which may be totally atheistic. It opens up the possibility of a much deeper sense of community, but it is the most individualistic stage of all. As Wallis (1985) has well argued, this is the home territory of the growth movement, and it is characterized by epistemological individualism.

TRANSITIONS AND BREAKTHROUGHS

I suppose this trip from mental ego to unified bodymind self (centaur) through the biosocial bands is one of the most interesting changes in consciousness, because it is quite close at hand for many adults. It always seems to involve a lot of pain and discomfort, because it means questioning all the roles one has been playing. Like all these transitions, it is dialectical – it involves negating the previous stage of development.

Incidentally, what Wilber means by 'bands' is a set of experiences, possibly but not necessarily traumatic, which follow one another in quick succession, rather like going on a scary fairground ride, or a flume at the water centre, or through the white water in a set of rapids; once the process starts, it seems to take over and to be inescapable (see Figure 5.2). It can be seen that the figure is the very one we used earlier for discussing the different types of meditation, and it is interesting to see the correspondences which emerge from that.

Wilber is particularly interesting on the process of transition from one stage to another. He says that two dimensions are necessary to it – firstly a creative urge or impulse or drive (creative as opposed to destructive) and secondly a willingness or desire to let go (as opposed to holding on). If we have the creative urge, but also a desire to hold on, many good things may happen, but they will all happen at our present level – no development will take place. If we have the willingness to let go, but also a destructive urge, we may actually move back to an earlier level. Real development, he says, always involves incest and castration – incest because we want to hold on to the one thing we have to let go of, and castration because we fear we may have our power cut off anyway, whether we like it or not. By letting go creatively, we can overcome this and move on.

The relevance of all this to social science is that most of us stick to the central, upper part of the map (Figure 5.1). We say, as it were, 'I am only interested in the personal'. But just as in recent years research has shown that there is far more than we thought in the early stages – the baby is far more competent than we thought, the birth process is far more meaningful than we thought, the foetus is far more competent than we thought, and so on – now we have to recognize that there is much to take account of in the later stages too. I have noticed people talking about the transpersonal and about spirituality generally, in a way which was not on even five years ago. People are coming out of the closet, as it were, and admitting or affirming that they have indeed had subjective experiences which fit in with Wilber's objective analysis. Certainly in my own case I have found Wilber to be a very good guide to my own experience, making sense of it all along the line.

One of the things which Wilber makes easier to understand is the idea of a breakthrough in psychotherapy. It has to do with this notion of a transition which we are examining in detail.

One cold Saturday in February we had an all-day marathon and I had

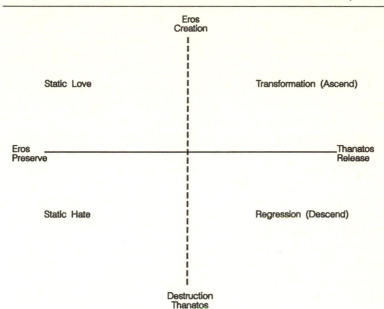

Figure 5.2   The process of transition.

the most profound experience of my life. For on that cold winter day I discovered a whole new world... I experienced my own beauty that day, as a woman, as a person. I really felt it on the inside... I loved everyone as they were... I was seeing differently... I went through a door to a place I could only call whole, clear vision.

This is one example, taken from an anonymous participant, of the breakthrough, this time in a primal group. This particular one seems to me an example of getting in touch with the centaur self, the real self; and I have seen it happen to many other people, in my own and other people's groups. To me it is familiar territory.

And of course there can be smaller breakthroughs, not so fully realized, not so dramatic perhaps, but still marking an important step forward. In the field of therapy, we often say that each such breakthrough must be followed by a period of working through, to integrate the new material into daily life. Before continuing, it seems worthwhile to dispose of one false obstacle. From a feminist point of view, there may be something suspect about the idea of a breakthrough – it sounds rather masculine and cell? When am I going to sleep? Why is it so hard for the officers to tell me anything? A couple people ignore the chairs and sleep on the cement floor. I don't think I'm that desperate yet.

Finally, after six in the morning, I am called by a deputy and asked some basic information like my address, full name, and medical conditions. Then I'm given a red t-shirt, red pants, a red sweatshirt, and worn out underwear and socks. After I've changed, I'm given a mattress and told that I'm being taken to my pod, whatever that means. I've been sitting on a plastic chair for fourteen hours. I attempt to sleep in a sitting position with my knees to my chest, and my head on my knees, but it doesn't really work. At this point, I don't care what happens to me.

I am not taken to a single-person cell; it looks more like a row of military-style bunk beds. It's after breakfast, but everybody's asleep. The only empty bunk is right next to the toilet and shower, and the light is directly above it. I put my mattress on the bottom bunk and some girl rushes to help me. I thank her, but tell her I'll put the sheets on the mattress myself. She refuses and starts doing it for me. After she makes my bed, she asks me where I'm from and tells me that I can use any of her bathroom products until I can get my own from commissary, then goes back to sleep.

I think I should stay awake, expecting the inmates to wake up soon, curious about the new arrival, but I'm too exhausted. It's almost seven in the morning, and I fall asleep within seconds of my head hitting the pillow. I wake up at lunchtime, which is at eleven. The day goes by pretty fast with me napping between meals. Different inmates come to bring me gifts. One gives me a cup, and another one gives me a notebook, a pen, and a soap bar. I am hesitant to accept them, but I don't know how to refuse, either. What could these inmates have done to end up in here?

After midnight, I am violently awakened by somebody ripping the blanket off my face. I knew I should expect a fight eventually, but penetrative. But really this is not so – a birth is a breakthrough, and girl babies are just as good at breaking through as boy babies – and need to break through just as much. Feminists need to, and do, break through established conventions more than most people.

Not long ago I came across a diagram which seems to me to do justice to the idea of a breakthrough. It comes from Ken Wilber's (1977) book *The spectrum of consciousness*, and it looks like Figure 5.3.

What Wilber says – and I am deliberately dropping his labels, because I want to generalize what he is saying – is that we progress in our personal growth, or in our personal or spiritual development, from one number to the next in logical fashion. We extend what we know from 1 to 2, we add more information from 2 to 3, we add new experiences from 3 to 4, we get new feelings and sensations from 4 to 5 – and all these things are interchangeable and additive.

But then we come to the point where the upper and lower cones intersect. This is the point where a complete changeover takes place. Instead of progressing to the next number, we fall through into infinity. All our existing acquisitions become useless at this point, and we cannot use the old approach any more. An entirely new set of rules applies. In

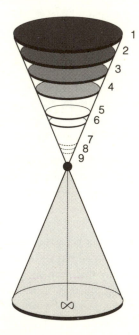

Figure 5.3 Breakthrough.

terms of Figure 5.2, we move off the surface of the diagram on to another similar surface.

This seems to me a very accurate and evocative picture of what happens. And Wilber emphasizes that the only way we can avoid the logical sequence of regular steps followed by a breakthrough is by refusing to let go. All the way down from 1 to 10, it was a question of acquiring more and more, of getting, even of grabbing, perhaps. But now, at the central point, it is a question of letting go, of abandoning our preconceptions, our identity.

I am not at all saying that all breakthroughs are the same thing. All I am saying is that they take the same form. There is more than one break-through, but all breakthroughs have this same pattern, which is put in another way in Figure 5.2.

This is perhaps reminiscent of the recent discoveries in catastrophe theory, but I think catastrophe theory is different in that you can always get back to your starting point. With the kind of breakthroughs we are concerned with in personal growth, there is no way of going back.

What I have found in my own experience is that there is one of these double-cones (Wilber's hour-glass figure) below another, so that there is a continual process of learning followed by breakthrough, followed by consolidation, followed by new learning, and so on. This is something which has certainly been found in spiritual growth by people like Thomas Merton, Evelyn Underhill and James Horne (1978).

So this seems to be common ground between personal growth (the work done in groups and in one-to-one therapy) and spiritual development (the work done in meditation, prayer and ritual). In both cases there is an intellectual element and an experiential element, and in both cases it is the experiential element which is the real heart of the matter, so far as change is concerned.

And in both fields this point, where we have to let go of our previous images and self-image, feels very risky and dangerous. But always we find that it is less dangerous and less different than we thought at first. So the message is that all shall be well: and all manner of things shall be well.

THE MAP CONTINUED: 1 (SEE FIGURE 5.1)

Lower subtle

Here we move on into the ability to question our strict boundaries, our restriction to what is within the walls of our skin. We may now acquire psychic sensitivities or abilities, such as perceiving auras, communicating with the supposedly dead, ESP, clairvoyance, dowsing, healing, out-of-body experiences, etc. This corresponds with what we earlier called the extrapersonal. Wilber says this means going beyond 'meaning in my life'; giving up intentionality and self-actualization; letting go of self-autonomy. My own experience is that these things come in much more a little later, in the higher subtle.

Higher subtle

This is the stage of the 'higher (or deeper) self'. One may speak of inspiration at this level, meaning actual messages apparently coming from a higher or deeper source. One may find affirmations useful at this stage. Some speak of guardian angels, others of the overself, or of high archetypes. Rapture or bliss is common at this stage; compassion is of a high degree, and widely expressed. This is the stage with which we are centrally concerned in this book. Fully getting into this stage demands what Heron (1988) calls 'the great reversal', where our whole set of assumptions at the centaur stage turns round on itself, and surrender becomes more important than assertion.

John Enright, in a discussion of change versus enlightenment, makes a telling point about this, when he says:

> It now seems to us that it is precisely by the tissue of narrow (good/bad) evaluations, both of self and others, that the individual maintains excessive individuality and dampens or cuts out potential Good, 'transpersonal' experiences of oneness and connectedness with others and the universe. If evaluations could be dropped, these so-called transpersonal experiences are right there, waiting to be had.
>
> (Enright 1980, p. 230)

This is an important expression of the great reversal, and leads very naturally on to the experience of the transpersonal self.

THE TRANSPERSONAL SELF

What happens at this stage is that we have an experience of contacting what used to be called the higher self. This is the sense of being in touch with my transpersonal self, my Deep Self. This often comes about in transpersonal therapy or groups, or in psychosynthesis therapy or groups, but again it can happen through meditation or in many other ways. (See Ferrucci 1982, Vaughan 1985, Starhawk 1982.) At first it appears to be outside of us, and may even appear to have a three-dimensional reality.

Essentially it has a touch of the divine – it is a symbolic representation of the sacred. I used to say that there were many synonyms for the transpersonal self, depending on the belief system of the participants, but now I am not so sure that all these things are the same. In the years to come I think we shall see much more discrimination and differentiation in this area.

Edward Whitmont, a Jungian, refers quite clearly to the transpersonal self, and has this to say about it:

> This particular entity of the implicate order has been called Higher Self or Spirit Self in esoteric tradition. I prefer to call it Guidance Self. This Guidance Self is something other than the psychoanalytical self, which refers to the empirical personality and its complexes, to the explicate definable and describable order, and which in esoteric tradition has been called 'lower self'. I propose to call the empirical personality the 'complex self'. The Guidance Self is implicate order; it is of the nature of archetype.
>
> (Whitmont 1987, p. 7)

This seems a very useful and accurate way of putting the matter, because in practice the transpersonal self very often does give guidance or help to choose between alternatives.

John Heron (1988) wants to distinguish between the real self, the transpersonal self and the cosmic self. He says that the real self is self-creating. Contact with it puts us on the road to self-creation, where we can truly take responsibility for ourselves, and say things like – 'I create my world.' This corresponds to what we have been calling the centaur stage. He goes on to say that the transpersonal self is self-transfiguring. The person at this level freely chooses to unfold the higher intuitive self and to go deeper into the prepersonal material of their own history. The cosmic self, however, does not seem to correspond with what we shall call the causal self.

My own view is that the transpersonal self is best represented, in most cases, by a person. But it does not have to be so. I have known cases where the transpersonal self was represented by a dome, or flowing water, or a jewel (Valassis 1989), or a flower, or a light of some kind. For example, Michael Emmons quotes the example of a 20-year-old woman in a therapy session who said this:

> It was as if there were a bright light encompassing my whole body. My body seemed to inflate and balloon out and 'I', the 'me-ness' of my body, seemed to be filled and carried with this light... The light then narrowed into a stream of an intensity I would imagine a laser beam to

have and focussed deep down somewhere, no place physical that I can point to, just deep in my 'me-ness'... After awhile the light seemed to be focussed on the lump in my throat where I'd tried to hold down my tears... The lump in my throat dissolved... I feel great.

(Emmons 1978, pp. 111–12)

This symbol of the laser-beam was used in later sessions as a guide, helping to awaken more of the client's potential. This again is serious introverted mysticism.

After having had such an experience I may follow it up in various ways: I may take religious advice and instruction, and most mystics do (Moss 1981), but even so, I have to decide which instruction and advice to take and which to follow, and there is no way I can put the reponsibility for this outside myself. Even if I say that it is a voice inside me, I still have the responsibility for which voice to listen to. Jon Klimo (1988) has a good discussion of this point in his book on channelling, which we shall come back to in Chapter 11. In that book he quotes from an interview with Jean Houston, where she says:

There's a movement of attention from conscious states to depth states in which an enormous amount of information is stored... I'm willing to say that the psyche is much larger than we think and is engaged at many levels with an ecology of consciousness that is broader than its own local base.

(Houston 1986)

This idea of an ecology of consciousness is important, because of the way in which the whole question of boundaries gets questioned at the trans-personal level.

I don't want to say much more about the deeper self, because I think it is familiar to most of us, but I just want to underline that it is a spiritual experience. More uncommon, however, and much less discussed, is an aspect of the breaking down of barriers which I have called 'the self open to others'.

John Heron (1988) points out that when two people, both of whom have reached this stage, are in close communication with each other, they create a third being, their unity. There is a large overlap between their consciousnesses. He calls this 'dual-unity'. So far it sounds very special and unusual, but interesting things can also happen when only one of the people concerned has reached this stage.

Stan Grof (1988), as we saw earlier, talks about two closely related transpersonal experiences, which he calls 'dual unity' and 'identification

with other persons'. Both of them, he says, involve the loosening or melting
of the boundaries of the ego. But he is referring mainly to the experiences
of the client in therapy; I want to talk about the experiences of the therapist,
too. Grof does in fact hint at this when he gives the story of his wife
Christina identifying with the dying Gregory Bateson: she felt as if she
were inside him, and feeling everything he felt. He says – 'It seemed clear
that experiences of this kind would be invaluable for diagnostic and
therapeutic purposes, if they could be brought under full voluntary
control.'

What he obviously did not know was that several people have now
begun to do just this. In a previous chapter we noticed several different
examples of this in various areas. This work makes it clear that therapists
of several quite different persuasions have all had the same experience and
found different ways of talking about it. I think this is something which
has been very little discussed, and which now must be recognized as a
spiritual experience which can be cultivated or ignored, but which actually
does happen (cf. pp. 54–8).

Some interesting remarks about the way in which we come into this
subtle stage are given by Frances Vaughan, under her earlier name of Clark:

> Three distinct stages can be distinguished in the process of awakening
> to one's transpersonal identity. The first stage could be called the stage
> of *identification*, characterized by the development of self-awareness...
> [This is what we have called the centaur stage.] The second stage of
> transpersonal awakening, in contrast to the first stage of self-identifica-
> tion, is one of *disidentification*... [This is the stage we are at now.
> Psychosynthesis has a good deal to say about this.] The third stage of
> transpersonal awakening is one of *self-transcendence*... At this stage the
> concept of a transpersonal self or witness may also be dropped. [This is
> what we shall be calling the causal stage.] It is important to recognise
> that concepts which are useful at one stage or in particular circum-
> stances, have only relative value and should not be considered as
> defining absolute reality.
>
> (Clark 1977, pp. 74–8)

It is the middle one of these stages which is most characteristic of
transpersonal work as we shall be defining it here. It is a stage which lays
great emphasis on images and symbols, and recognizes that words can let
us down when we try to describe experiences of this kind. We have already
seen how important this is in the actual practice of transpersonal work. Let
us now get back to the map which we left for this digression.

THE MAP CONTINUED: 2 (SEE FIGURE 5.1)

Lower causal

Deity-archetypes condense and dissolve into final-God, the Source of all archetypes. This means that we find ourselves giving up symbols and finding them a drawback rather than an advantage. We also give up gurus or masters, though we may very readily relate to a larger discipline. People who reach this level often speak of perfect radiance and release, not as a glimpse, but as a readily obtainable experience. There is a compassion at this stage which is different from, and deeper than, experiences of compassion which one had earlier. We are in touch here with the ground or essence of all previous stages.

Higher causal

People speak here of formless consciousness, boundless radiance. Final-God self dissolves into its own Ground of formlessness. Buddhists speak of the samadhi of voidness. Both man and *dharma* forgotten. *Nirodh*. Coalescence of human and divine; the Depth, the Abyss, the Ground of God and soul; I and the Father are One; *nirvikalpa samadhi*; *nirguna Brahman*. The Ground of God and the Ground of the soul are one and the same. My *me* is God. This is true self-transcendence, of which all previous versions were merely approximations or substitutes.

The ultimate

Unity-Emptiness. Nothing and All Things. Seamless, not featureless. Transcends but includes *all* manifestation. Identity of the entire World Process and the Void. Perfect and radical transcendence into and as ultimate Consciousness as Such. Absolute Brahman-Atman. *Sahaja yoga*; *bhavi samadhi*, realm of *Svabhavikakaya*. Nirvanic level. *Cittamatra*. Kether.

I have said less about the later stages, though Wilber has a great deal to say about them, because I have found that people have so little experience of them that they go blank or glazed when I talk about them. But perhaps there is sufficient to show that this is a process of psychospiritual development which we are all involved in, whether we want it or not and whether we know it or not.

To sum up, the transpersonal area includes the centaur, the subtle and the causal. When we are working in any of these areas we may be working transpersonally. But the subtle is the heartland of the transpersonal, and the centre of our concerns in this book.

One of the things which bothers people about this account is that it appears to be so hierarchical. The first thing to be said about this is that if we wish we can regard these stages merely as positions which it is possible to take up, without any implication of superiority. But the second thing to be said is that not all versions of hierarchy are oppressive. Let us see what Wilber himself says about this.

SOME CONSIDERATIONS ABOUT HIERARCHY

In an interview originally published in *ReVision* magazine, Wilber goes into this in some detail. He starts off by saying that if we believe in evolution we must believe that the complex includes the simple, in a way in which the simple does not include the complex:

> Each higher level cannot be fully explained in terms of a lower level. Each higher level has capacities and characteristics not found at lower levels. This fact appears in evolution as the phenomena of creative emergence. It's also behind synergy. But failing to recognise that elemental fact – that the higher cannot be derived from the lower – results in the fallacy of reductionism. Biology cannot be explained only in terms of physics, psychology cannot be explained only in terms of biology and so on. Each senior stage includes its junior stages as components but also transcends them by adding its own defining attributes... All of the lower is in the higher but not all the higher is in the lower. A three-dimensional cube contains two-dimensional squares, but not vice versa. And it is that 'not vice versa' that creates hierarchy. Plants include minerals but not vice versa; the human neocortex has a reptile stem but not vice versa, and so on. Every stage of evolution transcends but includes its predecessor – as Hegel said, to supersede is at once to negate and to preserve.
>
> (Wilber 1982, p. 257)

Now that is a very defensible position, and I would go along with it completely. But it does miss something which I think is better dealt with by Riane Eisler. She wants to say that hierarchies have been very dangerous historically, and we have to recognize these dangers. Yet she wants to say that the idea of hierarchy cannot just be dismissed as if it were of no importance or unreal in some way. So she distinguishes between two different kinds of hierarchy – one which is undeniably harmful and to be opposed, and the other, which does justice to the insight expressed by

Wilber, and which is beneficial and must be recognized. This is how she does it:

> In connection with the dominator model, an important distinction should be made between domination and actualization hierarchies. The term *domination hierarchies* describes hierarchies based on force or the express or implied threat of force, which are characteristic of the human rank orderings in male-dominated societies. Such hierarchies are very different from the types of hierarchies found in progressions from lower to higher orderings of functioning – such as the progression from cells to organs in living organisms, for example. These types of hierarchies may be characterised by the term *actualization hierarchies* because their function is to maximize the organism's potentials.
>
> (Eisler 1987, p. 205)

This seems to me to do justice both to the dangers and to the reality of the concept of hierarchy.

PSYCHOTHERAPY

Let us now begin to see how all this mapmaking applies to psychotherapy. In the next chapter we shall be going into this in more detail, but it will be useful here to apply the ideas to all the existing forms of psychotherapy, to see where they fit into Wilber's schema. Firstly let us see how it looks if we take as a dimension the Wilber map just outlined. We can ignore the earlier stages and the later ones, and just concentrate on the middle-to-upper stages which are most familiar and most used in psychotherapy (see Figure 5.4).

It can be seen that there are four columns here. The first one is labelled ego/persona or mental ego. This is the level at which most counselling and psychotherapy is carried out. It has to do with adjustment to consensus reality. The client at this stage is going through some very unpleasant emotional experiences, and wants to get back to the status quo. Or perhaps the client has been experiencing incapacitating feelings for a long time, and just wants to be able to love and to work. The client may be presenting with depression, anxiety, shyness, bereavement, exam nerves, fear of flying, loss of a partner, persistent headaches, any one of the thousand symptoms and problems which plague our daily life.

Virtually all practitioners are able to handle this level of work, because virtually all practitioners are familiar with this level of development in their own experience. Probably the vast majority of the work done in this field is at this level, and the vast majority of the research carried out is also at this level. Language is extremely important for this kind of work, because language embodies the consensus reality which the person wants to get back to.

Psychoanalysis is included in this column because classical Freudian psychoanalysis explicitly says that it is restricted to this level. There are of course some neo-Freudians and groups who are not so restricted, such as Horney, Fromm, Guntrip and so forth, and we shall have more to say about them later on.

The second column is the one which has been of most interest to humanistic practitioners, although of course most of them work most of the time in the first column, just like everyone else. At this level, which Wilber calls the centaur and I call the real self or autonomous stage, the emphasis is on freedom and liberation. There is a great deal of the humanistic literature, which I have tried to sum up in another book (Rowan 1988a), saying that we go from the realm of deficiency (where all the motivation is to repair some deficit) to the realm of abundance (where the motivation comes from a positive urge to explore, create and grow). Some people talk about the move from an emphasis on having to an emphasis on being.

It is very important to note, however, that this centaur, this real self, is still regarded as single and bounded. It has definite limits, a habitation and a name. People at this level often talk about community, but their actions are in fact very individualistic.

What is also important to note is that no one can bring someone else to this level who has not reached it themselves. This is an amplification and extension of Freud's original statement that the therapist can only move the patient to the limit of the therapist's own resistances. What we are now having to go on to say is that as well as resistances, the therapist also has contractions. These contractions are drawings-back, avoidances, distortions of growth. But someone who has never contacted their own real self, because of this kind of contraction, cannot enable someone else to contact his or her own real self.

This is a crucially important point. Each of the Wilber steps requires a move to a new definition of self, and this is a very central and involving move. It affects the whole person in a radical way. It is not something which the intellect can put on and take off. In fact, it is the intellect which does most of the contracting and avoidance which prevents movement further along the scale.

Let us now look at the third column, labelled subtle self or soul. This is the area worked in so thoroughly by James Hillman and many other Jungians, and by Assagioli and his followers. This is the level which mainly

	1	2	3	4
WILBER LEVEL	PERSONA/SHADOW	CENTAUR	SUBTLE SELF	CAUSAL SELF
ROWAN POSITION	MENTAL EGO	REAL SELF	SOUL	SPIRIT
Self	I am defined by others	I define who I am	I am defined by the Other(s)	I am not defined
Motivation	Need	Choice	Allowing	Surrender
Personal Goal	Adjustment	Self-Actualization	Contacting	Union
Social Goal	Socialization	Liberation	Extending	Salvation
Process	Healing – Ego-Building	Development – Ego-Enhancement	Opening – Ego-Reduction	Enlightenment – Questioned ego
Traditional Role of Helper	Physician Analyst	Growth Facilitator	Advanced Guide	Priest(ess) Sage
Representative Method	Hospital treatment Chemotherapy Psychoanalysis Directive Behaviour modification Cognitive-behavioural Some transactional analysis Crisis work Rational-emotive therapy	T-Group method Gestalt therapy Open encounter Psychodrama Horney etc. Bodywork therapies Regression Person-centred Co-counselling	Psychosynthesis approach Some Jungians Some pagans Transpersonal Voice Dialogue Wicca or Magic Kabbalah Some astrology Some Tantra	Zen methods Raja Yoga Taoism Monasticism Da Free John Christian mysticism Sufi Goddess mystics Some Judaism

Focus	Individual and Group	Group and Individual	Supportive Community	Ideal Community
Statement	I am not my body I am not my emotions I am not my desires I am my intellect To say anything more would be presumptuous	I am my body I am my emotions I am my desires I am my intellect I am all these things and more	I am not my body I am not my emotions I am not my desires I am not my intellect I am a centre of pure consciousness and will	Not this, not that
Questions	Dare you face the challenge of the unconscious?	Dare you face the challenge of freedom?	Dare you face the loss of your boundaries?	Dare you face the loss of all your symbols?
Key Issues	Acceptability Respect	Autonomy Authenticity	Openness Vision	Devotion Commitment

Figure 5.4 A comparison of four positions in personal development.

deserves the term transpersonal, and of which we have noticed many examples up to now. Here we are concerned with problems which, as Jung pointed out, often come more in the second half of life, though it is perfectly possible for them to arise at any time.

It is an area where symbols are pursued for the insight and growth they may bring. Words become of lesser value, because we are now moving out of consensus reality. The mental ego is desperately worried about this, because it thinks of words as being the only things which are really safe. Much of the taken-for-granted aspects of the world are now radically questioned: in particular, the boundaries which divide us from the world in general and other people in particular do not seem so important. Because of the dangers of self-inflation at this stage, a supportive community becomes very important, so that one can keep an eye on one's pretensions to spiritual exaltation. We shall be coming back to many of these issues later. Suffice it here to point out again the question of contraction. Many people draw back from this level because it seems too scary and so open to misuse. But the whole of this book will go to demonstrate that this level is not only very important for the average client, but very important for the practitioner to explore.

The fourth column is put in, not so much because it is of great relevance to psychotherapy, but because it indicates that the third column is not the end of the road. Again it is possible to hold back, the familiar contraction ensuring that one will stay at an earlier level rather than advancing to this, the deep water of spirituality. Here at the level of the causal self, the level of spirit, we have to give up all the symbols which were so useful and got us so far at the previous level. This is the realm of religion proper, as we shall see in more detail later on.

Here, then, are the four columns which show how the therapist has to develop himself or herself if the intention is really to be able to handle the whole person who is there in the consulting room. The therapist who does not develop, who gives in to the contraction which prevents progress along the scale, will be unable to help the client move to the next level. Thus the therapist can be a block in the way, rather than a facilitator, helper or guide.

FURTHER STEPS

Now that we have seen how one dimension works out – the psychospiritual dimension – let us add a second dimension and see if that helps even further in making our map of the psychotherapies.

If we make the well-known distinction between those psychotherapies which want to deal only with the conscious mind, and those which in addition wish to talk about and deal with the unconscious mind, this will give us a useful second dimension along which to range the different forms of psychotherapy. Thus cognitive and behavioural therapy will want to deal only with the conscious mind (as will rational-emotive therapy, personal construct therapy and so on), while psychoanalysis, hypnotherapy, Mahrer's experiential therapy and so forth will have an important place for the unconscious mind.

This then, put together with our previous discussion, would give us Figure 5.5.

It can be seen how we have dropped the fourth column, because here we are dealing with psychotherapy rather than religion. But the three columns retained are the same as the first three on Figure 5.4.

Each form of psychotherapy can now be seen in relation to those which come close to it. And the clusters which form are very plausible and meaningful to those who are familiar with them. Those in the centre are the most varied and flexible, and can extend outwards in all directions.

SCOPE AND LIMITS

Let us look at the scope and limits of some of these psychotherapies, particularly in relation to the transpersonal.

Primal integration can be said to be one of the fullest and most complete forms of psychotherapy, because it includes everything a client might need. It works at the four levels Jung talked about – sensing, feeling, thinking and intuiting. It has fewer gaps and untrodden paths than any other approach on the chart. But for that very reason it may not be suitable for the novice client. It may be too much too soon for the client who has done very little therapy before. It is ideal for the person who has been in therapy for five years or more and is beginning to get impatient at the rate of progress. If we think of the whole process of psychotherapy as a course with two phases (Kopp 1977), primal integration is a phase two therapy. Phase one is where the client is gradually discovering through personal experience that there is such a thing as the psychodynamic unconscious and childhood trauma. Phase two is where the client heals the splits which have appeared through that process, and goes on to deal with the more fundamental splits which lie deeper in the psyche. This is doing work at the level of what Michael Balint (1968) called 'the basic fault'. Primal integration is definitely prepared to go into the transpersonal, and the tenth issue of the journal *Aesthema* was entirely devoted to the question of spirituality in relation to primal work. My own article in that issue

operating
potentials
or   psychiatry
conscious
mind   behaviour   existential   basic
                      modification   meditation

                      behaviour
    ↑   therapy

                      cognitive   focusing
                      therapy
                                ret
                      family
                      therapy
                                personal   gestalt
                                constructs   therapy
attention   some ta
explicitly
paid to   person-   psycho-
                               centred   drama

    | hypno-   encounter
                      therapy   co-counselling

                          nlp
                                          some feminist   psycho-
                                                           synthesis
                          Reichian   bioenergetics
                                          biosynthesis   trans-
                                                           personal
                                          biodynamics   psycho-
                               primal   primal   therapy
                               therapy   integration
                      Freudian
                               object   Jung
                               relations
deeper   Kohut
potentials   Klein
    or   Lacan   Mahrer   Hillman
unconscious
    ↓   mind

---

                 mental ego   real self   subtle self

                 Psychospiritual development dimension from Ken
                 Wilber model

Figure 5.5   The therapeutic space.

maintains that going deeper into the primal areas of the psyche actually makes it easier to get into the transpersonal areas of the psyche.

Feminist therapy is a curious label in a way, because it means an attitude towards the whole field, rather than a particular technique or theory. So there can be analytic feminist therapists, humanistic feminist therapists, transpersonal feminist therapists, and no doubt cognitive and behavioural feminist therapists, though the latter may be rare. Feminism seems to be an attitude which can in principle spread to any of the other specific psychotherapies on the chart. In fact, it is important that it should, because it is basically saying that in the past psychotherapy, like every other field, has been biased against the female. In fact, those male therapists who claimed to cultivate and understand femininity were often no better in this respect than those who said nothing about the matter. So if this balance could be redressed, it would be of benefit to all psychotherapists and their clients, of whatever persuasion. Chaplin (1988) has a particularly interesting approach in relation to the transpersonal.

Another interesting feature is that the position of feminist therapy reminds us that this approach brings in an explicitly political dimension which other psychotherapies do not. Perhaps we could think in terms of a third dimension, having to do with conservatism/radicalism. If we made height relate to radicalism, we might see the whole of the middle part of the chart rising into the air, and the edges moving downwards. We should get a sort of arch or tunnel. Co-counselling, encounter, the person-centred approach and gestalt have historically been associated with radical groups and political awareness. Mahrer pays lengthy and explicit attention to social factors. The existentialists have always had a political streak. Transactional analysis, too, has made some moves in this direction. But feminist therapy goes further than any of them, it seems, in very centrally relating therapy to the social context.

Open encounter can be said to be the fullest and most complete approach to group work. It is prepared to go into every area of therapy and life in order to do its work, and is enormously flexible because of that. It is very demanding of the group leader, who has to be exceptionally well-trained and experienced. It is a paradoxical approach, because while on the one hand it is very open and democratic and egalitarian, it does on the other hand give great power and authority to the leader. One of the old school of encounter leaders used to be nicknamed 'the drill sergeant', because he introduced so many structured exercises. But in recent years the trend has been for the leader to be much less charismatic and pushy, and much more open, laid-back and willing to listen. The emphasis is on the existential rather than the spiritual, but Schutz (1989) makes it clear that it is this openness, modelled by the leader and encouraged in the group, which makes it possible for transpersonal elements to come in. I have suggested elsewhere (Rowan 1991) that encounter can be a paradigm for integrative psychotherapy, uniting as it does the regressive, the existential and the transpersonal.

Co-counselling is a marvellous and politically very interesting approach, which has a great deal to offer. It is horrifying to pick up an enormous tome on self-help groups and therapies, with every approach you can think of in it, and co-counselling gets missed out. Presumably this is because it has not been adopted by the kind of people who write academic papers, and so there is not much literature about it, but this is a feeble excuse to ignore something so widespread and important. It is a matter of great pain, also, that the original school (Re-evaluation Counselling) launched by Harvey Jackins has always stayed isolated from the mainstream of humanistic counselling. By keeping so pure and independent, it has missed out on a whole network of connections which could have increased its effectiveness manyfold, in my opinion. There are, of course, drawbacks to co-counselling, simply because it is so well designed to be safe for the novice. It is very easy for a pair of co-counsellors, or even a whole local community, to get into a cosy collusive way of working where nothing very deep or challenging ever gets done. Co-counselling communities are notorious for getting too sweet and sugary all too easily. The incessant smiles and hugs, so warm and delightful at first, can come to seem like a fixed convention just as remote from reality as the put-downs they replaced, and very off-putting to the outsider. But co-counselling fulfilled an important role in my own development, so it certainly can perform very well. Again it can go into the transpersonal area, as John Heron (1974) has shown in detail.

Psychodrama is one of the most approachable of the group methods. It is hard to go to a psychodrama group and not come away feeling – 'I could do that!' But in fact it is much harder than it looks. There was one incident at a conference where a psychodrama leader, who was supposed to be highly trained and experienced, completely lost control of one situation in his group, and had to be rescued by a visiting leader who happened to be sitting in. As in all group work, the group leader (the director in this case) has to be very responsive to what is actually going on in the group – not what is supposed to be going on. Psychodrama is one of the best developed group methods in the field, and it is now becoming written about more than before. It has always been open in the direction of the transpersonal, right from the time in the 1920s when Moreno asked someone to stand on a table and be God, particularly in its emphasis on creativity and spontaneity, two characteristics of the superconscious. Moreno himself certainly had a mystical side, which is generally played down by writers on psychodrama.

Bioenergetics is another of those therapies which we would regard as 'phase two'. It gets people into very deep material very quickly, and is not for the novice or for the faint-hearted. In the film *W.R. Mysteries of the Organism* some of the scenes show Lowen at work in his New York studio, and it is clear that there is a lot of screaming going on. In fact, when Janov wrote his book *The primal scream*, many people pointed out at the time that there tends to be a lot of screaming in all the Reichian and neo-Reichian approaches. It is for this reason that bioenergetics is one of the approaches which tends most of all to get growth centres thrown out of their premises, because the neighbours can't stand the noise. This is particularly true when bioenergetics is used as a group method, as it often is. In a big room with fifty people who all seem to be screaming at once, the noise can be deafening. But done in a one-to-one way it is not so much of a problem. Again in recent years this has extended to studies of the aura (particularly by John Pierrakos) and other areas which are not encompassed within consensus reality.

Biosynthesis is the most complete of the body therapies. It has been patiently honed and put together by David Boadella, who is one of the master therapists of our time. It is very expert-oriented, and requires a great deal from the therapist because of this. But it seems to offer a really well-worked-out body therapy which will no doubt be developed further in the future. Boadella certainly has a place for spirituality in his system.

Psychosynthesis is one of those approaches, like gestalt therapy, which people plagiarize and lift things from unmercifully. Everybody seems to think they can do guided fantasy, just because they once went to a psychosynthesis workshop, or even a workshop somewhat removed from the original. Certainly many of us in the 1970s came across many of the ideas before realizing that this was where they had come from in the first place. The important idea of subpersonalities, for example, comes from psychosynthesis, and is now used by all and sundry. But in its original form it is a very powerful and wide-ranging discipline, which in principle at least can cover the whole gamut of psychotherapy. In practice, however, much of the emphasis tends to be on the higher self and the superconscious, no doubt because that is the missing area in most other therapies. Psychosynthesis in its original form seems to have promise of being a very gentle approach (not many screams in most psychosynthesis work) which can still take people anywhere they need to go.

While transpersonal psychotherapy can be thought of as a derivative of psychosynthesis, it is clear in Gordon-Brown and Somers (1988) that it is much more than that, and has quite different origins. There are in fact a number of ways of carrying out transpersonal approaches, and the one just mentioned owes much to the personal stature of Ian Gordon-Brown and his co-workers over the years. Some people may feel that it is a little technique-oriented, but the authors have created something which is very effective and intellectually defensible, and it is good to have this chapter now available and in print, so that this work can be made known to others who may use it and take it further.

Neuro-Linguistic Programming is one of those American approaches with all the apparatus of certification, levels of training and so forth. It is brash and manipulative, and very unlikeable so far as many British people are concerned, partly because of its cavalier attitude to other forms of therapy or counselling. It is certainly better for specific nameable and measurable problems, rather than for deep personal difficulties. But it does contain some very sharp thinking about the whole process of communication within psychotherapy, and it can only be ignored at the peril of overlooking something important. It is particularly strong in the area of observation – of noticing what the client is doing. And it shows how to use that observation to make better interventions, more accurate and more pointed. We have certainly learned much from it about how to gain rapport with a difficult client, and even if this were all, it would be useful. But there is much more to it than that, and well worth knowing. It seems to have little interest so far in the spiritual, but this is probably not necessary to it, and who knows what may happen in the future?

Some of these approaches may come across as a little technique-oriented, but in fact the person of the therapist is always very important, even in NLP. As has often been pointed out, it is always necessary in psychotherapy to go by the actual person doing the therapy, not by the label on the door.

Some therapies do not touch on the transpersonal at all. These include:

BEHAVIOUR MODIFICATION
BEHAVIOUR THERAPY
COGNITIVE THERAPY
FAMILY THERAPY
JUNGIAN ANALYSIS (London school)
KLEINIAN ANALYSIS
PERSONAL CONSTRUCT THERAPY
PSYCHOANALYSIS (Classical school)
RATIONAL-EMOTIVE THERAPY

Some therapies touch on the transpersonal, but not in any systematic or worked-out way. Some practitioners will include this, others will not. These include:

ADLERIAN THERAPY
BIOENERGETICS
CO-COUNSELLING
EXISTENTIAL PSYCHOTHERAPY
FEMINIST THERAPY
GESTALT THERAPY
OPEN ENCOUNTER
PERSON-CENTRED THERAPY
POSTURAL INTEGRATION
PSYCHOANALYSIS (Object relations school)
PSYCHODRAMA
TRANSACTIONAL ANALYSIS

And some therapies explicitly acknowledge the importance of the transpersonal, and have established strategies about working in this way with clients. These include:

BIOSYNTHESIS
JUNGIAN ANALYSIS (Zurich school, Archetypal school)
PRIMAL INTEGRATION
PSYCHOSYNTHESIS
TRANSPERSONAL PSYCHOTHERAPY

It is hoped this outline will make some of the relationships here somewhat clearer.

Chapter 6

Wilber and therapies

In the previous chapter we found the general theory of Ken Wilber, and again in this chapter Figure 5.1 may be referred to. As we saw, it offers a map of psychospiritual development which is convincing, and gives us a useful way of seeing how psychology is related to spirituality. But what he has gone on to do is to relate this very specifically to psychotherapy. He first did this in a small but very important book (Wilber 1981a) which acts as an excellent introduction to his ideas about psychotherapy. But later on he went much further and gave copious details of how his theory connects with the therapy world. This material seems so important and so shattering to many of the existing views on therapy that I think it is worth summarizing it and commenting on here, so that more people become aware of how exciting this work is, and how relevant it may be to the training of future psychotherapists. So this chapter is based on the three chapters by Ken Wilber which appear in the book *Transformations of consciousness*, edited by him with Jack Engler and Daniel Brown: 'The spectrum of development', 'The spectrum of psychopathology' and 'Treatment modalities'.

FIRST FULCRUM: SENSORIPHYSICAL SELF AND PHYSICAL OBJECT CONSTANCY

The infant (general word used to cover foetus, neonate and very young baby) starts off in a symbiotic relationship with the mother. It has little sense of where it ends and the mother begins. The first task of development is to come out of this closed monadic system, and the omnipotent dual unity which may succeed it, and to become a separate body self. Figure 6.1 shows the form of the process. Here **a** represents the original fused state, **c** represents the stable, differentiated version of the self which emerges at each stage, **d** represents the stable differentiated object world of that c   d

b

a

Figure 6.1   The form of each fulcrum.

stage, and **b** represents an intermediate stage where the whole process may get stuck, as it were.

At the particular stage we are considering here, **a** represents the failure to move away from symbiosis and fusion at all. This results in pathological terms in the autistic type of psychosis, where there is virtually no separate sense of self, and therefore no ability to relate to the physical world or to other people. If, on the other hand, some move away from fusion does take place, but somehow separation is prevented from proceeding, we may get stuck at point **b**, where what may result is symbiotic infantile psychosis, most adult schizophrenia or a depressive psychosis.

In either case, the separate body self does not develop properly, and so the corresponding idea of object constancy also does not develop properly. This dual development, of self constancy and object constancy, is very basic. If it does not happen, the foundations for the types of psychosis we have mentioned are laid.

In my own work in primal integration, I have found that this fulcrum often has to be dealt with by the client in her or his life long before the first year of life outside the womb, which is where Wilber and the authorities he quotes (Mahler *et al.* 1975, Blanck and Blanck 1979, Kernberg 1976) locate it. If a trauma comes in the womb – such as an attempted abortion, an accident to the mother which puts the foetus at risk of its life, a persistent and repeated negative attitude of the mother and so forth – then just because the infant has to deal with it before this separation has had a chance to take place, the most primitive defences may be used. Similarly if there is a trauma of birth, the same considerations apply.

At this stage, as has been pointed out by people working in the primal area (Rowan 1988b), there is only one person present, as it were. The structure is basically monadic, in the sense that there is no relationship involved. We are talking here of what Janov (1977) calls 'first-line traumas' – that is, those which are very physical and survival-oriented and which occur before language can be used by the infant.

The implications of this are twofold at least: one, psychosis is probably much more common than we realized, and maybe we should talk about the normal psychotic as we have already learned to talk about the normal neurotic; and two, psychotherapists need to work through their own psychotic material before they can deal properly with clients who have problems which go back this early.

Wilber thinks that no form of therapy can cope with this level of pathology, and that pharmacological or physical modes of treatment are primary. I would agree with this only where this lesion was so early and so deep that no subsequent experience ever ameliorated it. This may be so, for example, in someone who is so autistic that they just cannot be reached in any way at all. But in most cases this is not so; as Winnicott (1958) and others have pointed out, it only takes some later good-enough mothering to undo most of the harm which such early failures create. So in the majority of cases I would disagree with Wilber, and suggest that the primal approach, used by many of the body-oriented therapies, can get into these spaces and work there. The key to understanding this is to see that first-line traumas are quite common, and not restricted to people with autistic psychoses (Colter 1988, Freud 1988).

This is a point underlined by David Wasdell (1990), who draws out from it the idea that much of our social problematic is derived from very early and primitive projections of a psychotic nature. He also makes the point that the reason why we stop at **a** or get stuck at **b** is usually because some trauma occurs which cannot be dealt with in any other way.

SECOND FULCRUM: PHANTASMIC-EMOTIONAL SELF AND EMOTIONAL OBJECT CONSTANCY

The next task takes for granted and is based upon the successful emergence of the whole sensoriphysical self on the one hand, and the whole world of sensoriphysical objects on the other, which should have happened at the first fulcrum. Once this is done, we can go on to learn how to distinguish between internalized self-images and internalized object-images.

Again we start from a state of fusion (point **a** on the diagram), where these images are not distinguished from one another. And again we have to go on to a point where emotional and phantasmic object constancy, this time referring to structures within the person, have to emerge. This is a much more sophisticated task, and it may take eighteen months to cover the ground between the first and second fulcrum of development.

This second task is qualitatively different from the first. It involves a progressive differentiation of the emotions. Instead of just feeling generally good or generally bad, the infant starts to feel grief, longing, rage, terror, joy and love. It has to learn not only how to distinguish its own emotions from those of its mother and other significant others, but how to distinguish its emotions about itself from its emotions about others. It learns to distinguish between fear and anxiety, guilt and envy. It has to develop a vocabulary of mental pictures and images to go with those emotions, to help to identify and recognize them, in the absence of words.

As people working in the primal area have noted, there are basically two people involved in the issues at this stage, and it is essentially a dyadic structure which is at issue. It is not so much that the self at this stage possesses a libido; rather, the self at this stage simply *is* a libidinal self, as Guntrip (1961) has suggested. And libido immediately suggests some object or person being needed or wanted. This is closely connected with Janov's (1977) description of the 'second-line trauma', which he says is basically emotional and largely pre-linguistic. A severe trauma at this stage may interfere with the normal process of development and result in the sort of primitive splitting of consciousness which produces the so-called border-line personality – that is, someone who we would not call psychotic but who is not really neurotic either, in the terms we shall be considering shortly.

In terms of our diagram, **a** is the state of fusion, **c** is the self image now differentiated out, **d** is the set of object images now separated out, and **b** is again the intermediate state where some arrest or fixation has taken place. So according to Wilber at **a** we get the narcissistic personality disorders, where the person has not surrendered the grandiosity and omnipotence of the fused state. And at **b** we get the borderline personality disorders, where a separate self-image has started to emerge, but its structure is so tenuous or weak that it constantly fears engulfment by the other or abandonment by the other. So for the borderline personality the opinions of others are all-important, making the person all good or all bad alternately. Here Wilber is relying on Kernberg (1975) and Masterson and Rinsley (1980).

Wilber says that therapy in this area has to build up a structure. We actually have to hold the patient until he or she can develop a self capable of having neurosis, repression and resistance. We have to help the individual re-engage and complete the separation–individuation process. This has to do with the selfobject transference which Kohut (1971) refers to. That in turn involves an understanding of the two central defences which the individual uses to prevent separation–individuation from happening – projective identification and splitting. A brilliant exposition of this whole set of concepts has been provided by Hinshelwood (1989).

Again people in the primal field (e.g. Rowan 1988b) would disagree in part with this, and say that we can work with second-line traumas in the uncovering way that Wilber says is ruled out. It is precisely by bringing out the ways in which the dyadic relationship went wrong that the person can be encouraged to move beyond it. Wilber says nothing about the traumas which actually prevent the normal development through these fulcrums – he never raises the question as to *why* normal development should be interrupted or distorted. But people working in the primal area believe that it is through meeting and dealing thoroughly with these traumas that real change in therapy takes place.

THIRD FULCRUM: REP-MIND SELF AND CONCEPTUAL OBJECT CONSTANCY

The next task then takes the stage. Here the child is developing symbols and concepts towards what Piaget calls the preoperational stage of thinking. We are now in the realm of language aned childhood proper, around what Freud called the Oedipal phase. The child moves from having a self-image to having a self-concept. Wilber says that the child at this stage finds it very hard to take the role of the other, to see things from another person's point of view. He does not seem to have come across the work of Donaldson (1978), who showed that children of 3 years old can indeed see things from different points of view.

This is the classic stage of development for the neuroses to appear. But again we must distinguish between the problem of not progressing beyond point **a**, which results in the borderline neuroses, and moving to point **b**, which gives us the psychoneuroses proper, with their major defence of repression. In the former case, we get either neurotic developments burdened with deficiencies coming from inadequate mastery of the earlier tasks, or a part-regression to more borderline states in the face of too difficult Oedipal problems. Blanck and Blanck (1974) and Gedo (1981) are quoted here. In the latter case, we get the classic neuroses of the Oedipal period, which have been written about at length in the psychoanalytic literature. No one argues any longer that Oedipal problems are universal, but they are certainly very common, and need to be understood and taken into account. All we might need to remark is that just as the first fulcrum had to do with a monadic structure, and the second with a dyadic structure, so this stage has to do with a triadic structure – in the first instance, self, mother and father, but also ego, superego and id. Whereas at the second fulcrum most of the conflict was interpersonal, at this stage it becomes more intrapersonal, because it is not so much the actual mother and father who are involved, but rather their internal representations as what Jung (1968) helpfully calls the mother complex and the father complex.

For therapy here Wilber recommends the classic uncovering techniques, including psychoanalysis proper, much of gestalt therapy, and those aspects of Jungian therapy which have to do with integrating the Shadow. To these I would add primal integration, working at the level of third-line traumas, and most of the humanistic therapies, such as psychodrama (Gale 1990) and person-centred therapy (Rogers 1990).

FOURTH FULCRUM: RULE/ROLE MIND AND SOCIAL OBJECT CONSTANCY

The task here is to go on to create a mind that can not only imitate a role, but can actually *take* the role of others. This opens up an entirely new dimension of object relations, with a new sense of self as measuring up to social demands and expectations. Loevinger (1976), Maslow (1987) and Kohlberg (1981) have charted much of this level of development with their notions of conformity, esteem from others and conventional law-and-order orientation.

What develops here, according to Wilber, is script pathology, or what he also calls script neurosis; the kind of thing which transactional analysis (Clarkson and Gilbert 1990) deals with and which the communications theorists who deal with families (Palazzoli *et al.* 1978) also point to. The pre-eminent defence mechanism of this stage is the 'duplicitous transaction' – the individual overtly communicates one message while covertly sending another; if the covert message is mentioned, the individual strenuously denies it. These covert messages and hidden agendas are central to this stage.

Personally I found Wilber's treatment of this fulcrum in the book very thin and sketchy, and I asked him to expand on it. This is what he wrote:

Let me try to specify the points a, b, c, d at fulcrum 4 and fulcrum 5. Fulcrum 4a is simply the beginning of the script self, the beginning emergence of concrete operational thought, and its initial fusion or nondifferentiation from the representational or preoperational mind. The point is that, as Piaget and others have demonstrated, the child at this point (roughly age 7) cannot well understand the role of other or, therefore, clearly grasp its own social role in many situations. The self first has to differentiate from or transcend the preoperational mind; at the same time, it has to learn to take the role of other, to some significant degree, and learn to recognise its own given roles in various situations. Both of these are involved in the overall phase of b at fulcrum 4. The self does not choose these roles. It is not capable of highly introspective/reflexive cognition or choice. Rather, it more or less conforms to the roles as it understands them, or is taught them. It learns scripts. Now, getting to 4c, or the ideal completion of this phase, does not mean the self has differentiated from its roles. What it has differentiated from is its incapacity to take roles. It is now squarely and unreflexively identified with its roles, good or bad, in a belongingness-conformist-conventional sense, and it *recognises* other conventional roles (which are at fulcrum 4d).

A failure in this overall process means one of several things: the self cannot differentiate from the fulcrum 3 mind and its inability to take roles (this is simple arrest at fulcrum 4a); or, more often, it means that the roles it learned are false, contradictory, inappropriate, misleading, self-demeaning – it has bad scripts, it has script pathology. If all goes well, however, fulcrum 4 is completed, and a stable conventional-conformist self (4c), recognising other conventional roles (4d) is formed.

(Personal communication, 28 July 1987)

This seems to help a good deal in making this fulcrum more explicit and more understandable. Wilber says that therapy here is more cognitive than psychodynamic. So cognitive therapy (Weishaar and Beck 1986), social learning approaches, family therapy and communication theorists (Manor 1984) are all relevant here, as well as transactional analysis. The approaches of George Kelly (personal construct therapy, see Fransella and Dalton 1990) and Albert Ellis (rational-emotive therapy, see Dryden and Ellis 1986) are also relevant here.

FIFTH FULCRUM: FORMAL-REFLEXIVE MIND AND REAL RELATIONSHIPS

The task here is to move to a self which truly thinks for itself, and which is able to look over the four walls of the role system in which it finds itself. This is the level which Maslow has called getting esteem from yourself rather than from others; which Loevinger calls the conscientious-individualistic phase; and which Kohlberg calls the postconventional stage of moral development. Erikson (1963) has well described the crisis of 'identity *versus* role confusion' which is often involved here.

Wilber says that the therapy here must involve introspection. By this he means looking inside oneself without the interpretation of defensive operations. The therapist can help in this process by engaging in a Socratic dialogue with the client.

Again here Wilber's treatment in the book is very thin and unsatisfying, and I duly wrote to him to get some further explanation. Here is what he said:

> At this point (roughly ages 8–14), then fulcrum 5 can begin to emerge. Fulcrum 5a is simply the beginning of this process, where the formal operational mind has not yet fully emerged or differentiated itself from the previous concrete operational mind. In other words, the self does not yet possess introspection, hypothetico-deductive reasoning (it cannot understand 'as if' or 'what if' statements), pluralism, nor perspective. But as this mind begins to emerge and differentiate itself from the prior conventional mind, then it can begin to subject all of its previous roles and beliefs to its own logical scrutiny, to experiment, to perspective – this is part of phase b of fulcrum 5. At the same time, it can begin to differentiate merely reacting to others as conventional roles from acting towards others as self-reflexive individuals (for those who are, in fact, self-reflexive). Its own needs switch from belongingness to self-esteem (Maslow), and the self, as a self-reflexive and choiceful entity (that's 5c) begins to recognize and interact with other self-reflexive and choiceful selves (that's 5d). Fulcrum 5 neuroses refer to all the difficult and confusing things that can go wrong here – failure to differentiate from conformist roles, fear of introspection, confusion as to 'who am I?', failures of self-esteem, and so on.
>
> (Personal communication, 28 July 1987)

This again seems to clarify matters a good deal, and I found this very helpful. No named form of psychotherapy seems to be involved here, but I suspect that many therapists engage in the types of dialogue which are indicated here, when it is clear that this is the level which needs to be engaged. For example, if a client said, 'When I criticized my neighbour for her attitude to dogs (she wanted them all shot), she criticized me for my attitude to doctors (mistrusting them all)', one might engage in a Socratic examination of how prejudice looks from the outside, and how it feels from the inside.

SIXTH FULCRUM: EXISTENTIAL SELF AND
ENCOUNTER WITH THE WORLD

The task here is to move to a self which works on a basis of what Wilber calls vision-logic rather than formal logic. It entails the emergence of an integration of many splits in the person, most particularly the split between mind and body. Wilber uses the analogy of the centaur to refer to the difference between the horse-and-rider separation of the previous stage and the unification of the present stage. At this level we have the experience of authenticity; a combination of self-respect and self-enactment. At this level we get what Maslow calls self-actualization, what Rogers calls the fully functioning person and what Perls calls the self as opposed to the self-image.

What may happen at point **a** here is that there is a turning back from the process of self-actualization. Maslow once warned that anyone who deliberately set out to be less than he or she could be would be deeply unhappy for the rest of their lives.

The sort of depression which emerges at point **b** of this fulcrum is existential depression – a thoughtful, steady, concerned, profound depression (often called 'angst') which has much to do with a perception of real meaninglessness and authentic uncertainty in the world. Like so many of the people who write nowadays about this stage, Wilber emphasizes the dark side of authenticity, but I would like to emphasize here that authentic experience of the world does not have to be dark or depressed or anxious – it can just as well be an experience of joy or happiness. As Spinelli says in his discussion of authenticity, 'Many practitioners of contemplative or meditative techniques, for example, claim to experience "altered states" during which authentic uncertainty becomes acceptable and is the means to "spiritual enlightenment"' (Spinelli 1989, p. 114). This is an important point, which will link with our later discussion of the transpersonal level.

Wilber says that therapy here should mainly consist of analysis and confrontation of the various inauthentic modes of the client, and Wilber refers to the work of Koestenbaum (1976), Yalom (1980), May (1977) and Boss (1963). My own suggestion would be gestalt therapy; my impression is that others talk about existential therapy, but Perls actually practised it. And the recent writing on gestalt therapy (Clarkson 1989) makes it clear that it has an existential commitment. Similarly, open encounter, the person-centred approach, logotherapy and psychodrama are all capable of working at this level, as is primal integration.

This is really the heartland of the humanistic approaches, and we saw in the last chapter how so many of them function at the centaur level and help the client to get there or remain there.

SEVENTH FULCRUM: PSYCHIC SELF AND EXTRAPERSONAL REALITY

Here the task is to form a psychic self which will not flinch from entry into the occult field, and the cultivation of psychic qualities of one kind and another. Fixation at point **a** on the diagram might be to do with running away from the occult and the psychic on the grounds that one is not worthy or not brave enough to enter upon this new territory. Arrest at point **b** on the diagram seems often to do with a too sudden exposure to frightening experiences of a psychic or extrapersonal kind, such as the experiences related by Gopi Krishna (1972), John White (1979) and William James (1901). But they may often have to do with psychic inflation – a common affliction of beginning practitioners in this area – the Dark Night of the Soul, split life-goals (spiritual practice *versus* earning a living, for example). Wilber speaks of other problems, such as 'pseudo-dukkha', 'pranic disorders', 'Yogic illness' and other afflictions.

Wilber suggests that therapy at the level of frightening experiences which come too suddenly is simply to engage with the same process in a conscious way, by the adherence to some spiritual discipline. For more psychotic-like episodes, Jungian therapy is suggested. Psychic inflation can be handled by optimal disillusionment, preferably coming from someone who has been there themselves. The Dark Night of the Soul experience is cured by prayer; it hardly ever leads to suicide and is seen afterwards as having had a valuable purpose.

There has recently been a great expansion of work in this area, and the term 'spiritual emergency' has been used to represent failures at this level (Bragdon 1990, Grof and Grof 1989, Grof and Grof 1990). For example, people may cultivate journeys out of the body; but if a journey out of the body happens spontaneously, it may be very frightening for a person, and they may draw back and refuse to have anything to do with such experiences.

EIGHTH FULCRUM: TRANSPERSONAL SELF AND ARCHETYPAL FORMS

Here the task is to develop a new kind of self which can relate to forms of the divine, no matter how conceived in a given belief system. This may be developed perhaps first of all in the area of meditation, and in the cultivation of intuition or healing. Usually the idea of an 'inner teacher' or 'higher self' or 'deeper self' comes in at this point. Such divine forms are at first perceived as being 'above and behind' mental–psychic consciousness. Eventually, as contemplation deepens, the self differentiates from its psychic moorings, and ascends to an intuited identification with that presence. Gradually we realize that the divine form or presence is our own archetype, an image of our own essential nature. This identity arises concomitantly with a stable witnessing of the object relations of subtle consciousness – infinite space, audible illuminations, Brahma realms or intuited identification with a guru or inner teacher.

The failure to move beyond point **a** here is again a failure of nerve, where the person retreats and withdraws into the comfort of the psychic self while having been aware of the possibility of further development. This could be what Maslow (1973) calls 'the Jonah complex' and what Haronian (1974) calls 'repression of the sublime'. This means retreating from any involvement with the transpersonal at all. Getting stuck at point **b** can take various forms, the most basic of which is a fracture between self and archetype due to a fear of letting go of the previous structure. This can result in fragments of an archetypal presence appearing as objects of a still dualistic awareness. One form this can take is the pseudo-Nirvana referred to in Buddhism (Goleman 1977), where the person hangs on to illuminations, raptures, ecstasies, insights or absorptions and mistakes them for final liberation. Another form is to get stuck on the insight that everything is terrifying, oppressive, disgusting, painful and loathsome, and to be unable to let go of that and move on to a fuller realization.

Wilber says that therapy here often has to involve some form of inquiry into the contraction that constitutes the separate-self sense. It is seeing the contraction which is necessary for progress to continue. This contraction at bottom involves an inability to accept the death of the previous self-sense and its attachments and desires. For those painful states which result from meditation itself there is no cure except more meditation. The only thing more painful than meditation is failing to continue meditation. This is another kind of spiritual emergency, and the previously mentioned books on this subject are relevant here, too.

For example, Emma Bragdon says that 'opening to life myth' is very characteristic of this stage:

> The inner world of a person opening to life myth is replete with dramatic archetypal images that portray profoundly significant themes to the person. It is as if they are reworking in their mind the creation of the world itself and social culture in that world. Images of kings and

queens are prevalent, as are ceremonies and ancient rituals, cataclysms and disasters. Performing rituals, actually participating in the myths, is usually essential to a person opening to life myth.

(Bragdon 1990, p. 29)

It is very important, of course, for a person going through this sort of thing not to be incarcerated in a mental hospital, so easy to get into and so hard to get out of. For more on this see Chapter 9.

She also remarks on the way in which therapy and spiritual emergence may be mixed up:

In a period of intense spiritual experience, this same zigzag pattern is often sped up in such a way that a person with a strong sense of self may be opening to Subtle or Causal level experiences and the next minute be working with very regressed states of consciousness. Within this intensity, there is an impulse of the psyche to work through, to release the hold of the earlier stages, to liberate more energy to stabilize at a higher level of development.

(Bragdon 1990, p. 46)

The image of the spiral stair on the mirrored floor, mentioned earlier, seems to be relevant here. People in spiritual emergency need support which has to have these two sides to it: freedom to regress to earlier levels, and freedom to surrender to transpersonal influences. This support can only come from someone (or a group) who respects and understands the process involved.

NINTH FULCRUM: FORMLESS SELF AND THE WORLD OF FORM

Here we have to move from the subtle realm into the causal realm. We have to differentiate between ourselves as formless or unmanifest on the one hand, and the entire world of Forms, or the Manifest Realm. Again to stay at point **a** simply shows a failure of nerve, a fear of further movement into the unknown, a pathological need to hold back even though some awareness of the causal realm has been contacted. At this stage the desire for liberation can block the path leading to liberation. To get stuck at point **b** leads to what Wilber calls 'Arhat's disease'. A sort of blankness arises, which is confused with the kind of emptiness natural to consciousness at the developed stage of this journey. This brings about the holding on to a kind of dualism, a tension between the manifest and the unmanifest realms.

Only as this disjuncture is penetrated does the manifest realm arise as a modification of Consciousness, not a distraction from it.

And again at this stage the cure for the pathology is to persevere on the path, moving on through the deceptions into the truth. For this purpose a guide is essential – someone who has been through this and come out the other side.

DREAMS AND LEVELS

One interesting outcome of all this is that a dream can be interpreted at any one of the nine fulcrums, and might have important meanings at more than one of them. When I did this with a group in June 1989 one person's dream seemed to have a good deal of significance at F–2, F–3, F–4 and F–6, but not at F–1, F–5, F–7 or F–8. I did the same thing again with another group in June 1991, and found that the person's dream this time seemed to have a lot of meaning at F–2 and F–3, some meaning at F–5, F–6 and F–7, but not at F–4 or F–8. This is fascinating work, and very revealing for the person concerned, but it should not be attempted lightly, as it opens up very fundamental areas of the person's psyche, which may need to be worked on further in that person's own therapy. Thus it should only be carried out with people who are already in therapy.

Part III

How it works

Chapter 7

Some practitioners

Let us now examine the people who are now working in this field, to find out what they say and what they do.

JEAN SHINODA BOLEN

Jean Shinoda Bolen has contributed some fascinating material to our field by writing two books about goddesses and gods, and how they can relate to psychotherapy. She again comes from the Jungian camp, like so many of those we are meeting here. Her first book was *Goddesses in everywoman*, and this was followed a few years later by *Gods in everyman*. Here we shall look only at the former, because the latter is not really so interesting, for reasons which we shall be meeting in a later chapter, where we discuss polarities and the male.

There is an Introduction to this book by Gloria Steinem, who says in part:

> At a minimum, these archetypal goddesses are a useful shorthand for describing and thus analysing many behaviour patterns and personality traits. At a maximum, they are ways of envisioning and thus calling up needed strengths and qualities within ourselves.
>
> (Bolen 1984)

What Bolen is saying is basically that women can come under the influence of at least seven different ancient Greek goddesses. Under each one we act differently, think differently, feel differently and relate to other people differently. These goddesses are archetypes who are always there, always active, always available.

The seven goddesses she deals with in detail are the three virgin goddesses (Artemis, Athena and Hestia), the three vulnerable goddesses (Hera, Demeter and Persephone) and the alchemical goddess Aphrodite.

Artemis, goddess of the hunt and the moon, personifies the independent, achievement-oriented feminine spirit; Athena, goddess of wisdom and craft, represents the logical, self-assured woman who is ruled by her head rather than her heart; Hestia, goddess of the hearth, embodies the patient and steady woman who finds comfort in solitude and exudes a sense of intactness and wholeness.

Hera, goddess of marriage, stands for the woman who considers her roles as student, professional or mother secondary to her essential goal of finding a husband and being married; Demeter, goddess of grain and the maternal archetype, represents a woman's drive to provide physical and spiritual sustenance for her children; Persephone, maiden and queen of the underworld, expresses a woman's tendency toward compliancy, passivity and a need to please and be wanted by others. Aphrodite, goddess of love and beauty, governs a woman's enjoyment of love and beauty, sexuality and sensuality, and impels women to fulfil both creative and procreative functions.

Each of these goddesses is examined in detail, and case histories given of how they have shown themselves in the work of clients of Jungian analysts. They are related to parents, adolescence and young adulthood, work, relationships to women and men, sexuality, marriage, children, middle years and later years. The psychological difficulties associated with each archetype are gone into in some detail, and ways to grow are suggested for each one.

There are also some very interesting and helpful ideas out of the story of Psyche, giving four valuable lessons for women.

All in all, this is a most exciting and ground-breaking book, which gives insights which several women I know have said they found inspiring and useful. To a therapist or counsellor this book could be very useful in suggesting different possibilities. It would be nice to see a book which brought in the goddesses of Africa.

SEYMOUR BOORSTEIN

Seymour Boorstein is a great contributor to the field, starting work in the 1970s and editing the biggest book of readings to date. He is particularly good on dreams, and gives this example:

> A 24-year-old computer programmer sought psychoanalytic treatment because the thoughts and feelings about his past continually intruded into his spiritual practices. In spite of an antipsychiatric attitude, he finally came for help because all attempts to work through these feelings

in his meditational practice had been unsuccessful. Although obviously very bright, he had 'arranged' never to go to college in order not to compete with his father, a prominent physician. His father was a harsh and punitive person, and the oedipal rivalry fears dated back to the age of 5 or 6. It also became clear that success in the young man's spiritual practice had come to symbolize an oedipal victory with the following need to undo it. Traditional analysis of the oedipal transferences afforded him the relief from his repeated need to fail in all of his endeavours including his spiritual work.

(Boorstein 1980b, p. 41)

Here we can see what comes up again and again in this work, the way in which spiritual endeavours and therapeutic endeavours are different but complementary. They are not to substitute for one another.

CRITTENDEN BROOKES

Crittenden Brookes is a talented Jungian analyst who has made some valuable contributions to the whole transpersonal approach, though sometimes he restricts himself rather too rigidly to Jungian terminology. He has a particularly striking example, however, of working with a client where he is clearly stepping out of the usual Jungian mould:

A 30-year-old woman in the latter stages of an extensive analysis had become increasingly dissatisfied with what she felt to be slow but steady progress and too much attention to 'details' in her life. She felt that she had worked-through some difficult problems, and that she was now ready to make some rather drastic changes, including change of career and return to school. This feeling had come up increasingly during her analytic sessions.

The analyst felt that there was indication for caution in regard to this attitude, but admitted to his analysand that he himself was not entirely clear on the issue. He suggested, and they mutually agreed, that she should consult the I Ching (The Book of Changes) – or 'throw an I Ching' – as a way of obtaining both an 'impersonal reading' and some perspective on the question. The analysand threw the coins during an analytic session and obtained hexagram 62, 'The Preponderance of the Small'. This hexagram cautions against 'attempting large things', indicating that 'one should not strive after lofty things but hold to lowly things...since the requisite strength is lacking.' The instruction seemed to speak quite directly to the question, but the analysand was dissatisfied with it, feeling that perhaps she had not followed the correct procedure in obtaining the hexagram.

Upon her return home from the analytic session, she consulted the I Ching again on the same question, and again obtained hexagram 62 (one chance in 64). She found the repetition of the hexagram very convincing and decided to continue to work slowly on herself, making no large changes in her life for the present.

About a year later she was referred to another analyst, a woman, for the completion of her analysis. Again, she had been feeling quite restive with her life and considered the possibility of making some extensive changes. Again she consulted the I Ching and for the third time obtained hexagram 62.

Finally, about two months later, again restive with what she considered to be the slowness of changes in her life, she consulted the Book of Changes for the fourth time on the same question, and for the fourth time obtained hexagram 62. This final event precipitated an extensive examination with her analyst of her tendency to throw herself impulsively into ill-considered actions, a tendency that included magical thinking and other aspects of a hysterical personality-formation, which had hitherto gone unanalyzed.

(Brookes 1980, pp. 65–6)

This seems a good example of where the openness of the transpersonal therapist brought about a very good result.

JAKE CHAPMAN

Jake Chapman is one of many people in different countries now who run a specialized workshop called the Enlightenment Intensive. Unlike most of the people who run them, however, he has written a book about it, called *Tell me who you are*. It is divided into two parts. The first part is a fictionalized account of a three-day Enlightenment Intensive, as seen by one participant, who discovers his Real Self; the second is a run-down and explanation of some of the background of the Enlightenment Intensive, to make it more understandable.

The first part is very well written, and gives a colourful and convincing picture of what it might be like to actually go through an Enlightenment Intensive.

The second part gives interesting historical details of the origins of this workshop and of the personality of Charles Berner, who created the format which is used in it.

So for most purposes this is a good book, which carries out admirably the task which was presumably set for it, of publicizing and educating people about the Enlightenment Intensive, what it is and what it does, and why.

But it does commit the one glaring sin which seems to me unjustifiable, of perpetuating what I call the 'one-two-three-infinity' account of spirituality. What this does is to say that we have the body and its sensations ('one'); the emotions and feelings ('two'); the intellect or mind and its thoughts ('three'); and everything is spirituality or enlightenment – just one thing, just one all-pervading massive Unity.

I have to disagree with this, for reasons given earlier. There are actually many mansions within the realm of spirituality. We saw in Chapter 1 how this can be described by many different authors. What we are all saying is that there is not just one thing called enlightenment, and either you have got it or you have not got it. But in this book that is precisely what Jake Chapman does say, over and over again.

This may be because he relies a great deal, as Charles Berner did, on the ideas of Zen Buddhism. Now Zen Buddhism has a lot to answer for, in my opinion, in leading people up the garden path in this respect. All the Zen people seem to go on about this same idea – that enlightenment is a once-for-all, all-or-nothing thing. And they are just wrong about this. It is an oversimplification to say this, and an oversimplification which appeals a great deal to those who want things to be quick. And three days is quick, even though the process may be painful.

What I believe is that there is something which I call 'a breakthrough experience'. This is the subjective experience you get when you break through into a qualitatively higher state of consciousness than the one you are usually in. Ken Wilber has a nice diagram of this, which looks a bit like an hour-glass, and we discussed this in Chapter 5.

Now the Enlightenment Intensive aims at a breakthrough in this sense. This is perfectly valid and useful; but I think it misleads by suggesting that this is the final and only breakthrough, as though there were only one Truth, final for all time.

Some of the best Masters do not do this: for example Jeff Love, in his chapter on the Enlightenment Intensive in his book *The quantum gods*, made it clear that there were levels and degrees of enlightenment, and this seems to me much better. But this present book is dumb on this point, and I think this is really misleading. However, the Enlightenment Intensive is a very good experience for getting at an experience of the Real Self, and anyone who is struggling with (or avoiding) this issue in therapy would be well advised to go to one. It could save them a lot of time.

DINA GLOUBERMAN

Dina Glouberman says she has chosen a new word 'imagework' to refer to the self-help process she has used herself and taught to many others, because 'visualization' suggests visual images, which not everybody can do. Images can be sensed, felt, heard, smelled and even tasted as well as seen. She has now written a book on imagework which exemplifies many of the concerns of this book.

There is in her book a real respect and awe for the strength and depth of imagery, and there is no sense of images being used lightly or unthinkingly as a device or gadget. Glouberman speaks movingly of the images of death which a child had and committed to paper just before her accidental death from a shark.

The book is full of examples, both from the groups which Glouberman leads and also from her own life and her own experiences. She is not prescribing something which is good for other people, but sharing a great deal of her own process and her own discoveries. For example, she says:

I was hoping to study with Frank Lake, a pioneer in helping people to re-experience their own birth, when I read in a journal that he had just died.

Instead of wallowing in frustration and regret, I decided to talk to him in my mind, and ask him to help me do in spirit what I could no longer ask him to do in person. With 'his' help, I went through an unforgettable experience of feeling myself regressing to the moment of conception, and experiencing that moment as a brilliant flash of light and as a kind of whole-worldness in which I was the world.

(Glouberman 1989, p. 274)

There is a discussion of the unconscious, and the way in which there is more than one unconscious realm. There is a good chapter on dreams. This is a very practical book, with a lot of information about making decisions and choices in life. Glouberman tells how she became slim and fashionable by using imagery.

What I also like is that this book is not all positive. There is a good discussion of resentments, rejections and mourning, which to my mind is much needed and very well done. It does justice to the transpersonal. She says:

A world view that includes the transpersonal also often involves a belief that we are not struggling alone in an indifferent world. We live, rather, in the context of a universe, or a higher being or beings, or a higher self, that can be trusted to be essentially benevolent and that is protecting us, guiding us, or in some sense acting for us and for others, at least in the long run. If we are going to deal with images in a transpersonal way, it is safer to do so within such a framework, so that the power of images is not seen to be our own personal power, and thereby misunderstood and misused.

(Glouberman 1989, p. 273)

The book contains a number of exercises for the reader to carry out, and group leaders will find these exercises very useful in their work.

JOHN HERON

As far back as the early 1970s, John Heron was writing about transpersonal psychology, in a way which directly referred to counselling. He brought meditation into counselling, and showed how it could be an important resource. He pointed out how meditative techniques could be used in interpersonal relating, and in group work. He drew attention to catharsis as being important both in individual depth counselling and in inducing altered states of consciousness. He made a list of transpersonal states, not as complete as that given by Grof (Chapter 1 of the present work), but good for its time (Heron 1974).

More recently Heron has been interested in rewriting psychology completely, in line with insights coming from a group of people who he says are on the other side of death.

When I am working, they will gather round on my right side, and affect the way my mind operates. It is rather like being on the receiving end of a chain of influence, which does not interrupt or suspend my own creativity, but kindles it. I shape the words, I monitor the coherence, I control and select, I judge what is fitting and what is not. And at the same [time] there is a massive influx of thoughts which set my mind alight.

(Heron 1988, p. 5)

His suggested structure is actually not very different from Assagioli's, though there are a number of additional details. His 'transpersonal self' is much like Assagioli's; his 'infrapersonal self' is a kind of deep spirituality which Assagioli never mentions, a sort of depth equivalent of the 'height' of the transpersonal self; his 'autonomous self' is much like Assagioli's 'I'; but his 'higher intuitive self' is between the 'I' and the transpersonal self; and his 'atavistic psyche' is a sort of combination of the personal unconscious and the collective unconscious. These are interesting distinctions, but because Heron resolutely refuses to refer to any other investigators in any detail, it is hard to assess the validity of these new ideas. At the moment I am inclined to think that his 'higher intuitive self' corresponds with the lower subtle, the psychic, the extrapersonal. He himself speaks of ceremonial magic in this connection.

He distinguishes between the self-creating person, who is the person who is working at the level of the autonomous self (what we have called the centaur level), and the self-transfiguring person, who is working at the level of the transpersonal self. He recognizes that there is an important breakthrough at the level of the autonomous self, but says that the Great Reversal really only comes at the level of the transpersonal self, where we see that all our early efforts to build up the ego were illusory and need to be radically questioned.

So Heron is more theoretical than practical, and his actions have sometimes been controversial, but he has many useful insights, and it would be wrong to ignore him.

JEAN HOUSTON

Jean Houston has been to this country many times, and tends to work in large workshops rather than in one-to-one therapy. But many of her ideas can be adapted to individual work, and her approach is sophisticated, wide-ranging and inspiring. In 1965 she and her husband, Robert Masters, formed the Foundation for Mind Research in New York. Since then they have issued many reports and explored the nature and range of human capacities, and the nature and range of methods for extending those capacities.

She has written two major books in this area, one called *The possible human* and the other *The search for the beloved*. In the former, she starts off by saying that any real therapy must involve the body. So all her work is grounded in the body and in taking the whole unity of body–feelings–intellect–soul–spirit seriously. She also has a terrific sense of humour, and is grounded in that important way, too.

Her books largely consist of exercises, and the main text is fairly small by comparison, which makes for a very practical approach. Here is one which she says specifically appeals to the symbolic–mythic level of consciousness which we have been exploring all through this book:

> Again, close your eyes and breathe deeply. Feel the inspiration ascending to your brain, giving it a great and wondrous life. Exhale and feel the wash of new invigoration, a marvelous energizing. Continue this

for one minute, sensing as you do so a deepening within yourself as you allow yourself to travel to an excitement and clarity of adventure such as you have not known before.

You are walking in a forest and you hear behind you the sound of slow measured hoofbeats. You turn and see a majestic black horse approaching you. Its rider is a distinguished and benign-looking skeleton in armor. He bows to you with great dignity and presents you with a golden chalice.

You have three minutes of clock time, equal to all the time you need, for this experience to unfold.

Open your eyes now, share what you have found on this journey with others or by writing or drawing in your journal.

(Houston 1982, p. 173)

Never judge an exercise like this until you have tried it yourself, using if necessary a cassette recorder for the instructions. Incidentally, Jean Houston has some interesting remarks about using recorders, including the advice not to sound too lugubrious.

Some of her ideas have been taken up by others, and there is a very interesting book by Jay Earley (1990) which has exercises in the areas of developing a relationship with yourself, opening the heart, social transformation, life purpose, empowerment and the spiritual realm.

Houston talks about her work as sacred psychology, and says that in our day this must involve some element of initiation, as it runs so counter to the general conditioning we have been subjected to all our lives: she says that is why 'the ritualization of rebirth plays so key a role in sacred psychology.'

What we have referred to as the transpersonal self, or the guidance self, she refers to as the entelechy self – the self which has to do with our ends, our aims, our purposes on this planet. And she sometimes refers to this as the 'operant angel' of our everyday lives. By getting in touch with it, we become more aware of what we are here for.

> As we become more and more person/planet, there is less and less distinction between the questions, 'What do I want from the universe?' and 'What does the universe want from me?'
>
> (Houston 1987, p. 32)

But always she has her feet on the ground, agreeing with those who say that there is a danger in all this work of becoming too inflated and too eager to go higher and higher. She agrees with most other psychologists that the brain is extremely important in all this. But she thinks we underestimate the brain and do not do it justice.

She lays a good deal of stress, as we have in this book, on imagery and the importance of cultivating it. And when it comes to the brain, she does not hold back, but approaches that in the same way. Some of her exercises on this are quite elaborate, but work very well, as for example this one:

LEFT BRAIN/RIGHT BRAIN

Find a chair and sit upright, with your spine as straight as possible. Close your eyes and direct your attention to your breathing. Allow the rhythm of your breath to become regular. As you do this, allow your consciousness to rest in your solar plexus... and gradually move up through your body, passing through your lungs and then your heart... moving up the left carotid artery to the left side of your brain... Move your awareness forward now to your left eye. Keeping your eyes closed, look down with your left eye... Now up... Look to the left... and to the right... Keeping your awareness in your left eye, allow that eye to circle clockwise... and counterclockwise. Which direction is easier? You may find it easier if you imagine you are looking at a clock and follow the numbers of the clock as you move your eye. Now shift your attention to your right eye. Keeping your eyes closed look down... and then up... Repeat this several times... Now move your eye from right to left... Allow your right eye to circle to the right... and then to the left... Let it go clockwise... and counterclockwise... Is this easier with the right eye than the left? Relax your eyes, feeling them get soft and releasing the muscles around the socket. Rest for a minute...

Keeping your eyes closed, direct your attention to the right side of the brain... and now to the left... Shift back and forth easily a few times, noting any differences between the two sides of your brain... Does one seem more accessible than the other? Keeping your eyes closed and relaxed, imagine the images that will be suggested as vividly as possible. Don't strain as you do this.

On the left side of your brain, imagine the number 1, and on the right side the letter A...

On the left side the number 2, and on the right side the letter B...

On the left the number 3, and on the right the letter C...

On the left the number 4, and on the right the letter D...

On the left the number 5, and on the right the letter E...

Continue with the numbers on the left and the letters on the right, going toward the number 26 and the letter Z. You don't have to actually reach 26 and Z. Just continue for a minute or so. If you get confused or lost, go back to the place where the letters and numbers were clearly together and begin again... Rest for a minute, relaxing your attention as you do so...

Now reverse the process you have just done, putting the letters on the left and the numbers on the right. On the left image the letter A, and on the right the number 1...

On the left the letter B, and on the right the number 2...

On the left the letter C, and on the right the number 3...

Keep going toward the letter Z and the number 26... Stop and rest for a minute... Note whether it was easier on one side than the other, whether numbers or letters were more clearly imagined...

Continuing with your eyes closed, on the left side of your brain imagine a festive outdoor scene with a big picnic and fireworks. On the right imagine a couple getting married...

Let that image go and, on the left, imagine a procession of nuns walking two by two through a lovely medieval cloister. On the right there is a hurricane sweeping through a coastal town...

On the left is an atom. On the right is a galaxy...

On the left are fruit trees bearing new blossoms. On the right the trees are weighted down with frost and snow...

On the left is the sunrise. On the right is the sunset...

On the left is a green jungle forest. On the right is a snow-covered mountain in the Alps...

On the left is a three-ring circus. On the right is a thick fog...

On the left is the sensation of climbing rocks. Try to capture the feeling and sensation of the rocks and breathe easily as you experience it. On the right, image how your hand feels caressing a baby's skin...

On the left, the feeling of plunging your hands into warm sloppy mud. On the right, that of making snowballs with your bare hands...

On the left you are pulling toffee. On the right you are punching a punching bag...

Now, on the left you hear the sound of a fire engine. On the right the sound of crickets chirping...

On the left the sound of a car starting up. On the right somebody is singing in a very high voice...

On the left the sound of ocean waves on a beach. On the right the sound of your stomach growling...

Now on the left the smell of a pine forest. On the right imagine smelling freshly brewed coffee...

On the left the smell of petrol. On the right the smell of bread baking...

Now on the left brain, the taste of a crisp, juicy apple. On the right the taste of hot buttered toast...

On the left the taste of a lemon. On the right the taste of nuts...

Now on the left side of the brain, experience as fully as you can the following scene. You are riding a horse through the snow and sleet, carrying three little kittens under your coat, and you are sucking on a peppermint. On the right side of the brain you are standing under a waterfall singing 'You are my sunshine' and watching a nearby volcano erupt... Rest...

Now, eyes still closed, with your left eye look up toward your left brain. Move the eye so that it circles and explores this space... Roam around for a while... Now do the same thing for a while with your closed right eye on the right side of the brain...

Now with the left eye trace some triangles on the left side of the brain... Now make some rectangles... Now make some stars... With the right eye trace some triangles on the right side of the brain... Now make some rectangles... Now draw some stars...

Now make many overlapping circles at different angles on the left side, leaving spirals of light streaming from these circles into the left side of the brain. Imagine the brain as charged with energy by this light... Make many overlapping circles at different angles on the right side with the right eye, leaving energizing light streaming from these circles...

Now, with both eyes, circle vertically just in the middle of the head. You should circle along the *corpus callosum*, the ridge where the hemispheres of the brain come together... With both eyes together, circle as widely as you can inside your head...

With both eyes, create spiralling galaxies throughout your brain. Fill the whole of your brain space and the inside of your head with them... Stop and let your eyes come completely to rest...

Now much more slowly and deliberately make horizontal circles with both eyes just at the level of your eyes, and circling as widely as possible inside your head... Now make those circles smaller, still horizontally at the level of your eyes... Make them smaller... and smaller... and smaller... until you get down to a space that is too small for circling and then you will want to fix on that point and hold it... Continue to breathe freely with your muscles relaxed as you do this...

If you lose the point, make more large circles, letting them become smaller and smaller until you get back down to a point, staying fixed on that point for as long as you can easily... Rest for a moment...

Then, in the middle of your forehead, imagine a huge sunflower... Then erase the sunflower.

Simultaneously, imagine a sunflower on the left and some green damp moss on the right... Let them go.

Imagine that there is a big tree growing right in the middle of your forehead... Let go of that.

Imagine that there is a golden harp on the left, and just a little to the right of the harp is a drum. Hear them as they play together... Let them go.

Imagine on the left an eagle, and on the right a canary, both of them there together at once... Let them go now, and imagine the canary now on the left and the eagle on the right... Let them go, and imagine two eagles on the left and two canaries on the right... Let them fade away... Breathe easily, and if you need to adjust your position to be more comfortable, do so.

Now, in the middle of your forehead, imagine a small sun... Then imagine the sun just inside the top of your head... Roll it back round the inside of your skull to the inside of the back of your head, so that if your eyes could turn completely around in your head, they would be looking at it... Now raise the sun along the back of your head to the top and then forward down to the forehead... Now raise it along the inside of the head from the forehead back to the top and then to the back of the head, and then to the top of the head and back to the forehead... The sun should be making vertical semicircles on the inside of your skull...

Now let that sun move out in front of you and see it setting over the sea... From somewhere in the direction of the sunset a sailing ship is coming on to the scene... From what direction is the sailing ship coming? From the left, from the right, or from some other direction?...

Let that image fade away, and imagine an elephant walking. Become more and more aware of him as he walks... He stops and eats something, pushing his long trunk into his mouth... then he walks some more... then he sees you and breaks into a run... He slows down and then he stops and eats some more...

Let the elephant go, and imagine seeing Father Christmas in a sleigh pulled by reindeer... Observe the sleigh and watch it accelerate... then slow down and stop... then start up again, going faster and faster as it circles around and down a spiral track that is inside of your head... Starting from your chin, the sleigh spirals up and around and around and around until it reaches to the top of your head... Then it spirals down and around and around and around to your chin... Then it rushes up and around and around and around to the top of your head... Then it circles down and around and around and around to your chin... Circling now up and around and around and around to the top of your head... Let it stop there poised on the edge of the front of the top of your head... Now yawn and let Father Christmas and his sleigh and reindeer drive down over your nose and into your mouth... swallow the sleigh, and forget all about it!

Now focus attention on the left side of your brain for a while. Concentrate on it and imagine what your brain is like on the left side. Be aware of the grey matter and the convolutions of the brain... Concentrate in the same way on the right side of the brain... Pay attention to the thick bands of fibres that connect the two hemispheres of the brain...

Now sense both sides at once, the whole brain... Sense its infinite complexity, its billions of cells intercommunicating at the speed of light... Meditate on it as a universe in itself, whose dimensions and capacities you have only begun to dream of...

Now, breathing very deeply, imagine that by inhaling and exhaling you can expand and contract your brain. And do this for a while, expanding your brain when you inhale slowly and deeply, and contracting your brain when you exhale slowly and completely...

Let your brain rest now and, holding its image, speak directly to your own brain, suggesting, if you wish, that its functioning will get better and better... Suggest that you will have more brain cells accessible to you and that the interaction of the cells and all the processes of the brain will continuously improve as time goes by... Tell it that the right and left hemispheres will be better integrated, as will older and newer parts of the brain... Advise your brain that many of its latent potentials can now become manifest and that you will start working together with your brain in partnership to allow these potentials to develop in your life...

Listen now and notice if your brain has any messages for you. These messages may come as words or images or feelings. Give the brain time to respond, withholding judgement... Does your brain want something from you?... What does your brain want to give you?...

Again being aware of the whole of the brain, begin to feel a real sense of both communication and communion with your brain. Think of it as a new friend and of this friendship as a profound and beautiful new fact in your life. In the weeks to come, spend time nurturing and deepening this friendship so that the two of you (your brain and your consciousness) can work together in useful ways. But now, spend some minutes communing with your brain. Images may come to you, or feelings, or words, as together you move into a more complete partnership and friendship...

If you wish, while you do this place your hands about half an inch above your head and have the sense that you are caressing the 'field' around your brain, in the same way that you might pat or stroke the hand of a dear friend...

If you have some special intention for your brain, offer it now...

Continuing to feel a communion with your brain, open your eyes and look around. Observe whether there are any changes in your sensory perceptions. How do you feel in your body? What is your mood and your sense of reality? Do you feel that your possibilities have changed? Observe these things...

As you do this, stretch and move around the room. When you wish to, suggest to yourself that you are becoming more and more wide awake... Find a partner, and for the rest of the time, discuss your experience during this exercise.

(Houston 1982, pp. 64–70)

ARNOLD MINDELL

Arnold Mindell is a native New Yorker, trained in Jungian analysis and with degrees in physics and psychology. He works in Zurich, and has lived there for more than twenty years. His way of working, however, goes far beyond what most Jungian analysts would consider proper.

His emphasis throughout is on process. 'The therapist's only tool is his ability to observe processes.' This enables him to see the importance of nonverbal communication, and to pay attention to the body and the actions of the client.

An important concept for him is the dreambody. 'The dreambody is a term for the total, multi-channeled personality. It expresses itself in any one or all of the possible channels I mentioned. It can also use the telepathic channel and can manifest itself in dreams.' He says that with the discovery of the dreambody, dreamwork and bodywork become interchangeable. 'I find that if I start working on the dream, it invariably switches to the body problem and vice versa.'

Perhaps his best book is *Working with the dreaming body*. This could be a key book for the transpersonal psychotherapist working today. It exemplifies a way of working which the practitioner can aim at, and gives copious examples of how the author actually does it in practice. The quotes above come from this book.

It is a delight to read the stories in this book of how Mindell works with people. He keeps on creating or recreating different forms of therapy – for example on page 53 he speaks on behalf of a deeper potential within the person, a technique developed by Alvin Mahrer (1989b), whom Mindell does not seem to have heard of. It seems that adopting this process approach enables him to invent afresh whatever needs to be invented.

It also enables him to work with dying and psychotic people. But he cautions that working in this way needs a lot of training, and a lot of knowledge about body processes and mythology, 'usually more than is available at our medical and psychological training centres'. The reason for this is that caution is needed as often as bravery, and to use both well requires wisdom.

He has a good discussion of double messages, how important they are and how to deal with them. He also goes into the importance of countertransference in this area, and how the therapist's body, and the therapist's dreams, can be involved in the whole process. In other words, he sees that the process can include both client and therapist, and can even go beyond that two-person relationship.

This seems to me a brilliant book – one of those books which can inspire the therapist, and encourage the therapist to know more and do more and use his or her imagination more. It should be on the reading list of every course on psychotherapy which does not want to be too narrow and limited.

Mindell has written many other books, and some of them are much better than others. Proceed with caution.

WILL PARFITT

Will Parfitt is an active group leader and an inventive and effective person in this field. He has written a book with the provocative title of *Walking through walls*, which could lead to disappointment if someone went literally by the title. The walls in question are internal rather than external.

This is a good self-help book with a lot of exercises to do. I would make the usual warning noises about such exercises being really more suitable for people leading groups or workshops, but there is a good selection here.

It includes ideas from Assagioli, Gurdjieff, Alice Bailey, Fritz Perls, Chris Griscom and many others. Here is one of them:

> Relax and centre.
>
> Sit on a chair or cushion with a second chair or cushion conveniently placed in front of you, facing in your direction. Imagine that your soul sits on that chair. Without trying too hard, engage your soul in a dialogue. Start by telling it something about what you think, feel or sense.
>
> When you feel ready, move positions, sit on the chair or cushion opposite and become your soul. Look back at yourself as a personality in the original position, and answer back. Say whatever comes to you.
>
> At your own pace, allow a dialogue to happen between your personality and your soul. Do not try to make it anything special, or force it in any way, but simply see what happens. And watch for non-verbal messages that might come from the soul chair, such as particular body postures, facial expressions, gestures and so on.
>
> (Parfitt 1990, p. 122)

This book takes a New Age stance, and emphasizes several times that we are not our bodies, we are not our feelings, we are not our thoughts, and so forth. It has quite a lot in it about the soul, and about how the soul relates to the personality and the subpersonalities.

This is not a scholarly book, because there are few indications of where the various things come from: it is a practical book for wide use. It is as if the author were saying: I have been working in this field for some time, and here are some of the best things I have come across and used myself.

ANDREW SAMUELS

Andrew Samuels is one of the brightest of the British Jungians, and everything he does is interesting in some way. He is still developing and changing, and it is fascinating to see the twists and turns along the way. From the point of view of our purposes here, the most interesting thing he has written is a book called *The plural psyche*. I don't think the title is very good – Samuels is obviously much more attracted to the dual than to the plural – but let that pass.

In one chapter he has some very good things to say about time. We tend to fall for the idea, he says, that things cause each other in a strict linear sequence. But maybe there is a simultaneity as well as a succession to be thought about. 'Adult potentials are not caused by childhood – they are present within it... We can avoid a split between child and adult by conceiving them on a two-way continuum' (Samuels 1989, p. 23).

In another chapter he has some fascinating ideas about multiple interpretations of dreams and other material. He is explicitly not in favour of offering the client a choice between conflicting explanations, but rather suggesting that several meanings can all be true at the same time. We have already come across this idea in the work of Ken Wilber, who is saying the same thing rather more fully.

Chapter 6 is entitled 'Beyond the feminine principle', and is a stirring re-examination of Jungian ideas about gender, which as we saw earlier tend to be quite sexist. He says that in the present time there is a good deal of gender confusion, and that this is healthy and right and inevitable, because we are in an historical period when the old gender certainties are being challenged by feminists. In such a period – 'Inadvertently, those who propound a "feminine principle" play into and replicate the dynamics of unconscious gender certainty, denying gender confusion' (Samuels 1989, p. 97). And from this point of view he even questions many of the things which Jungians often say about the two great archetypes involved in gender: 'The difference between you and your animus or anima is very different from the difference between you and a man or woman' (Samuels 1989, p. 104). This is similar to the point I have made myself that a *yin* man is very different from a *yin* woman, and a *yang* woman is very different from a *yang* man.

In Chapter 7 he goes on to the question of the borderline, and makes it clear that he thinks the borderline is where most of us live. This is very stimulating stuff, and he says things like: 'Just as there needs to be movement between ego and unconscious, so there needs to be movement between the neurotic and psychotic parts of a personality' (Samuels 1989, p. 110). This cool assumption that we all have psychotic parts is something which I have urged myself, but which I have not often seen elsewhere.

Chapter 9 introduces the notion of the *mundus imaginalis*, a very useful concept which we have looked at in detail in earlier chapters of this book. It arose for him in a project he was doing on countertransference, and he came to notice that as well as the ordinary countertransference which refers to what is going on in and about the therapist's ego, there is another kind of countertransference in which the therapist seems to get inside the client, and to experience directly the internal objects of the client. This he calls *embodied* countertransference, also because the bodily sensations of the client and of the therapist seem often to be involved in such transactions. There is an image (which may be visual or otherwise) and a body sense at the same time.

He then makes quite a leap, which I think is justifiable and certainly worth thinking about, via the concept of intuition, to saying that:

In the countertransference experience, the image is being made flesh. Where that means that the Other (the patient's psyche) is becoming personal (in the analyst's body), I would conclude that an analyst's countertransference may be further understood by regarding it as a religious or mystical experience.

(Samuels 1989, p. 165)

It is a visionary experience. Images that turn out to be shared, he says, generate an archetypal power.

Links are made in this chapter between this thinking and the views of Corbin and of Winnicott, who talks about the 'third area' between the conscious and the unconscious. In this area the usual separation between people does not exist in the same way, perhaps. 'Images pertaining to one person crop up in the experience of another person because, on the imaginal level of reality, all images pertain to both' (Samuels 1989, p. 170). They are located in the *mundus imaginalis*, the imaginal world. This imaginal world is a place where the concrete and the imagistic are intermingled, and Samuels suggests that we are talking here about the 'subtle body'; he quotes Goodheart and Schwartz-Salant along similar lines, the latter saying: 'This space, long known as the subtle body, exists because of imagination, yet it also has autonomy' (Samuels 1989, p. 172).

LISA SAND

One of the more unusual and little-known approaches in this area comes from Lisa Sand, who has developed something she calls soul-directed therapy. She calls this a spiritual psychotherapy, but it would more accurately be called spiritualist therapy. She states that experienced psychotherapists who have died are eager to help less experienced psychotherapists who are still alive. She says:

On a deeper level the goal of treatment in the end is the clearing away of all blockages in the psyche to a perfectly free flow of energies. Expressed differently, one can call it a centering of the individual or a harmonization of all his constituent abilities in a multi-dimensional whole. It is a synchronization of the lower self with the higher Self so that they form a unit, a one-ness.

(Sand 1984, p. 8)

Although expressed in a naive way, this is fairly compatible with most of the other approaches mentioned here. There is a fair emphasis on the law of karma, that one's difficulties in this life may result from actions performed in previous lives.

There is also quite an emphasis on the importance of analysing dreams for the light they may shed on the process which the client is going through. She tells about 'a patient with ample black hair' who had a dream about:

> an encounter with a beautiful black panther who obviously loved him very much. The animal nipped him in the hand once. The patient told it not to do that any more and go out of the house and not come back; but the panther kept returning through special openings in the doors, behaving most lovingly. Upon analysis it was clear that the patient saw his own higher Self as the beautiful big cat. Because of a misconception, namely that letting it govern his actions and attitudes meant being 'holy', he was resisting its takeover, didn't trust it.
>
> (Sand 1984, p. 13)

This reminds us of some of the points made in the Introduction, about the confusion which often surrounds the transpersonal, and is a good example of the way in which this confusion may be resolved during the course of the therapy.

More unusual is the way in which this therapist will enlist the services of a medium, clairvoyant and clairaudient, in the process of therapy, actually in the session with the client. This person she calls the 'mediator', and says:

> The mediator is used to transmit most valuable information and counsel from 'dead' relatives or advisers of the patient... Many times, in these special sessions with the mediator, I have seen strong resistance or rebellion in the patient vanish after a major emotional release.
>
> (Sand 1984, p. 15)

This is of course a very unusual procedure, and I am not sure whether to salute it or not. Of course it does not seem so outlandish after the careful work of Roger Woolger, and it certainly might be worth trying in suitable cases. Lisa Sand does not use hypnosis at all.

JACQUELYN SMALL

Jacquelyn Small is a transpersonal therapist who has taken a particular interest in addiction. Her first book, *Becoming naturally therapeutic*, was very interesting, but her next book, *Transformers: The therapists of the future*, was even better. In it she gives quite a usable model of the transpersonal, and uses it to good effect. Like the other good authors we have met and shall meet, she insists that the spiritual approach is no substitute for psychotherapy or counselling, and says: 'The ego will continually draw us backwards, toward the level where the unmet need exists, until the need is met' (Small 1982, p. 60).

She has some good remarks about time, suggesting that we stand all the time at a junction between the horizontal dimension of time, where our personal life takes place between past and future, and the vertical dimension of timelessness, where our transpersonal life partakes of the nature of Being, of the eternal now. We have it in our power to pay attention to both, or to one or the other exclusively. A complete human being has the power of choice to move into one or the other as necessary.

She has some good exercises, including the one following, which is called going into the silence:

An exercise in mindfulness.

'Sit in a quiet place, pleasant and warm. Close your eyes and begin feeling yourself relax... Let go of the tension in your body... Realize that gravity will hold you up... Just sit... Just be...

'Take a few quiet, even breaths.' (Long pause)

'In your mind's eye, imagine you are going inward toward the centre of your being. Deeper and deeper... inward... inward... down into the centre... where all Truth resides...

'Everything is totally still... stillness... complete silence... silent stillness.' (Long pause)

'Be here now... absorb the silence... feel its weight...'

(Allow two minutes to pass with no sound.)

In a low, calm, quiet voice say the following:

'Now allow the Silence to speak... to show you who you are... what you need to know.'

(Allow another two minutes to pass, or however long your intuition says your client needs. Do not allow your own anxiety or impatience to rule you. Stay tuned in to your client's experience, and you will know exactly when to speak.)

'Now slowly allow yourself to ascend back out to the surface of yourself... Slowly come back here with me.'

(Small 1982, pp. 247–8)

As usual, time will be needed for processing whatever came out of that experience, and helping the client to digest it.

HAL STONE AND SIDRA WINKELMAN

Hal Stone and Sidra Winkelman come from a Jungian background, but have now broken away to found their own school. The main book written by these two authors, who are married to each other, is *Embracing our selves*, published first in 1985, and then in a revised edition in 1989, which is perhaps the most ambitious and well-worked-out approach to the use of subpersonalities in psychotherapy yet devised. They call their approach Voice Dialogue.

They say it is important to recognize that there is more to life than subpersonalities or the Aware Ego. They talk about a self that simply *is*, rather than *does* or *has*. And they suggest that a useful move at a certain point in the process of therapy is to ask to talk to that self – 'the part of you that just likes to be, not do anything, just be.' If the person then says they can't do that, or don't know how to do it, the therapist can offer to help. The way this is done is to face the client and make eye contact.

> Assuming the ability to make eye contact, the facilitator must now contact her own being energy. This particular energy brings with it a feeling of great peace and quiet, a sense of being centered and grounded. Once the facilitator makes this contact with herself, she then simply sits with the subject, speaking little, if at all. By holding the energy for the subject, the facilitator gradually induces it in the subject and that is why we call the process *energetic induction*. It can help bring through any energy that is not available to the subject.
>
> (Stone and Winkelman 1989, p. 220)

This is an interesting idea, which fits very well with our earlier discussion of the self open to others. Of course it would have to be done at the right time, not in an attempt to cut corners. They also make an interesting point about our relationship with certain of our inner characters, those whom we might despise and put down most:

> The Children of our inner world know how to 'be'. Most of the rest of our personality knows how to 'do' and how to 'act'. The gift to the facilitator in working with these patterns is that he must learn how to 'be' with them; otherwise they cannot emerge. When dealing with the Inner Child, the dictum is: 'There's nowhere to go and there's nothing to do.'
>
> (Stone and Winkelman 1989, p. 150)

This seems a wise and deep thing to say, and if therapists could take this more seriously they could perhaps avoid the pitfalls which Alice Miller more than anyone else has pointed out.

They also seem to be on the side of the angels, so to speak, in relation to the question of power. A combination of strength and vulnerability, to some people exact opposites, seems to be a good way of looking at empowerment. And once we have seen it in this way, we can appreciate how particularly relevant this concept is to women:

> In a way, women are more likely to seek empowerment than men. Because they do not have equal access to traditional power, they are forced to work from an empowered position (power integrated with vulnerability) rather than a power position (identification with archetypal power energies).
>
> (Stone and Winkelman 1989, p. 196)

This again is a question hardly touched on by other writers in this field, who often seem to assume that women are going to have just the same types of subpersonalities as men. But this is not necessarily the case at all, and it is good to be reminded of this.

There is in fact in the work of Stone and Winkelman a good appreciation of the special problems of being a woman in the patriarchal society of today. They talk a good deal about the types of subpersonality which it would be most useful for women to cultivate and make familiar. One of these is the Warrior. Not the kind of warrior which may spring to mind with a spear and shield, stamping and grimacing, but the kind of warrior we have become acquainted with through the work of Carlos Castaneda, Hyemenyosts Storm and others:

> Until recently, warrior energy was considered unfeminine, castrating, or worse yet, some form of devilish possession. We can now clearly see how necessary it is for self-protection, and how powerless a woman can be if this energy is disowned.
>
> (Stone and Winkelman 1989, pp. 194–5)

The Killer Who Protects... Men and women alike need warrior energy to protect themselves. Needless to say, women are seen as life-givers and healers, and the thought that they might have any destructive energies is intimidating... To deny our destructive energies, whether male or female, is to deny a major power source. Sadly, such denial often causes destructive energy to be projected onto men... Interestingly, this voice has been so thoroughly repressed in women that it rarely assumes the form of a female as a subpersonality. It is far more likely to be a jungle cat, a graceful feline killer.

(Stone and Winkelman 1989, p. 198)

So we have here a good awareness of the way in which we are living in a particular historical epoch, in a particular part of the world, with a particular subculture. They are telling us that we have to take into account the social context within which all therapy is done.

FRANCES VAUGHAN

Frances Vaughan is a pioneer of transpersonal psychology, and has been involved with transpersonal conferences and other events for many years now. She has also been elected President of the Association for Humanistic Psychology, thus demonstrating a wide range of sympathies. Her most influential book is called *The inward arc.*

This excellent book has ten chapters: 'Healing the whole person'; 'Evolution of self-concepts'; 'The transpersonal self'; 'Healing awareness'; 'In pursuit of happiness'; 'Mapping the spiritual path'; 'Guidance on the path'; 'Creativity and dreaming'; 'Healing relationships'; and 'Transpersonal vision'.

It is a very sophisticated book, using the recent work of Ken Wilber and others, and would be useful to anyone who might be interested in these matters. There are many good quotes scattered through it, as for example this one from Ken Wilber: 'A person is neither a thing nor a process, but an opening or a clearing through which the Absolute can manifest' (Vaughan 1985, p. 39). How challenging this is for anyone who is still trying to make sense of people through ordinary psychology! But this is also a very down-to-earth book, giving chapter and verse for many of the assertions made, and always relating the ideas to practice.

The chapters which stand out for me are the ones on the self and on healing. The author deals with the body self, the emotional self, the mental egoic self, the existential self and the transpersonal self, and has the best discussion I have seen of the relationship between self, soul and psyche.

The chapter on healing awareness deals with physical, emotional, mental, existential and spiritual healing, and the chapter on healing relationships has some very good material on psychotherapy, and the similarities and differences between therapy and healing.

And in her discussion of these desired directions, Vaughan deals with Christian metaphors, the Chakra symbolism and the ten ox-herding pictures. In her discussion of leaders and followers, she points out that there are many different leaders and many different kinds of followers: the sycophant, the devotee, the student, the seeker and the disciple.

Many of the chapters have experiential exercises, and in general this is a very usable book, interesting for any therapist or counsellor.

ROGER WOOLGER

Roger Woolger was born in England and trained at Oxford in behaviourism and linguistic philosophy, which some would consider two of the most boring and inadequate disciplines known to humanity. While still there, he discovered meditation and Jung, in that order. He then went to work in Vermont. It was there that he had his first, and very dramatic, experiences with past life recall.

His best-known book is called *Other lives, other selves*, subtitled 'A Jungian psychotherapist discovers past lives', which expresses quite succinctly what the book is all about.

This is one of those first-rate books that not only covers a specialized area fully and memorably, but also illuminates the whole field of psychotherapy. I can't think of a single therapist who wouldn't benefit from reading this book. It also makes one think of the scope and the limits of transpersonal psychology. Woolger is familiar with the work of Stan Grof and Morris Netherton, and started, with his wife Jennifer, by leading workshops in the area of past lives. He then went on to use the same approach in his individual psychotherapy practice.

He makes it clear that he does not use hypnotism, but simply encourages the person to follow some feeling, phrase or bodily sensation back to its origins in the past. This is what many other therapists do who work with regression; it is just that Woolger explicitly encourages the client to go back into previous lives if that seems relevant and possible. He deals with the objection that it might be fantasy.

Almost in passing, Woolger acknowledges that we are multiple beings, that our past-life selves can be treated as subpersonalities. Like other subpersonalities, they can be worked with through active imagination, and can be very useful for us to contact and deal with.

He discusses four main ways of looking at past-life phenomena: the psychic, the parapsychological, the religious and the psychotherapeutic.

Woolger is beautifully clear about working in a psychotherapeutic way, and not otherwise. It is not his job, he says, to make his client feel better, but to deal with painful realities:

While there are some psychotherapists who believe that the summoning of beautiful and transcendent imagery – spirit guide figures, gurus, angels, the Higher Self, etc. – is sufficient to alleviate psychological distress, I must confess I am not among them.

(Woolger 1990, p. 86)

And he quotes Jung as saying – 'We do not become enlightened by imagining figures of light but by making the darkness conscious.'

However, he regards himself as really a transpersonal psychotherapist, prepared to go into any of the six realms of the person's life: the body; the here-and-now everyday life (including the relationship with the therapist); the biographical; past lives; the archetypal; and the perinatal. He arranges these diagrammatically not as levels or stages, but as the petals of a lotus. This enables him to say that whichever of these realms seems to be most reachable at the moment is worth working with: 'The psyche is following its own chain of resonances to release feelings and images that will take us closer and closer to the core of the complex' (Woolger 1990, p. 271). And he gives many interesting case histories to show how this works out in practice.

Woolger makes the point that one of the effects of working in this way is to take the emphasis off the parents. The mother of a client in therapy often feels that she is being singled out as being responsible – consciously or unconsciously – for all the neuroses of her child. But if, as Woolger believes, the baby arrives with all the scars of its previous lives upon it, all ready to produce effects in its new and current life, the mother cannot be to blame for these. So this theory is politically interesting as well as being practically efficacious.

CONCLUSION

Of course there are many other names we could mention, but this is perhaps sufficient to give a sense of the range of this field, and some of the types of work which are being done within it.

Chapter 8

Group work and education

It will be useful at this point to turn aside for a moment and look at the question of transpersonal group work and education. This is so for three reasons: firstly there is a teaching element in all psychotherapy, though it is often not mentioned; secondly psychotherapists often get involved in running groups and workshops of various kinds, which may or may not have an educational element; and thirdly therapists and counsellors some-times get involved in public lectures or courses which are educational in nature.

A good deal of work has been done on transpersonal group work and education, and the emphasis is on opening up the territory of the imagin-ation and the spiritual both for children and for adults.

DREAM SHARING

One area which can be fruitful is to work with dreams. The very act of dream sharing is unfamiliar in our culture generally, and it gives quite a feeling of doing something off the beaten track. If we want a group to share dreams it is often necessary to start off by sharing a dream of our own.

As soon as the idea of dream sharing comes up, or in fact working with dreams in any way, the question gets raised – what if I don't have any dreams? Many people in our culture do not remember their dreams and the whole area is a blank for them. In some cases there are psychological reasons for this, and because of that it is important to respect the person who cannot produce any dreams. But for most people it is permission and encouragement which are needed, and these are quite enough to elicit quite a crop of dreams to work with.

Some hints which people have found useful are:

1   On going to sleep, imagine your mind as an empty TV screen, waiting for a programme to be projected on to it.
2   Suggest to yourself that you are going to have at least one dream and remember it.
3   Don't open your eyes straight away when you wake up, but let the dream images come back, and go over them.
4   When you feel that this recall is complete, move to another position in which you normally sleep, and more images may come back.
5   Have a paper and pencil handy, and jot down what you can remember straight away. Some people like to use cassette recorders instead of pen and paper.
6   Be sure not to miss out any unusual scenes and any words, particularly unfamiliar words or phrases, which might have come from a dream. These can be particularly important and revealing.
7   It is better not to open your eyes, and it is possible to learn to write with your eyes closed. Some people have even bought boards with wires across, as used by blind people, to make sure they write in straight lines.
8   Record dreams in the order in which you recall them. Don't try to work out which came first in the night.

A good source of hints on dreams and dreaming is Patricia Garfield (1976), though what she says about the Senoi has to be taken with a pinch of salt. It may be worth saying something about the Senoi, because this story is so persistent (like the untrue story of the hundredth monkey and the statement that Don Juan was a Yaqui Indian) and so seductive that many people still believe it to be true.

The story is that the Senoi of Malaya, a primitive group living in a crimeless, violence-free society, used dreams as psychological forces that the dreamer can learn to control through a process of dream education. It goes on to say that Dr Kilton Stewart, the first psychologist to live with the Senoi and study their dream theories, translated their system into a methodology applicable to our Western society. Clara Stewart Flagg, his widow, trained under his personal guidance for twenty years, and continues his work as the only dream educator claiming to practise Senoi Dream Education.

This seems clear enough, and most of us have heard of the Senoi and their dreams – how they held a community meeting every day, at which dreams were brought in and discussed, and the whole community was guided and lived by these dream discussions. The whole of Chapter 5 of the well-known book *Creative dreaming* by Patricia Garfield is devoted to describing how this was supposed to work: Garfield says, for example: 'The question "What did you dream last night?" is actually the most important question of Senoi life.' And you may have seen in the shops a workbook showing how this Senoi practice can be linked to Jungian ideas on dreams. The whole idea is that the Senoi learned how to control their dreams, so as to use them for community purposes. 'Perhaps the most striking characteristic of the Senoi is their extraordinary psychological adjustment. Neuroses and psychoses as we know them are reported to be nonexistent among the Senoi' (Garfield 1976, p. 83).

Unfortunately none of this is true. There is not, and has never been, any such Senoi practice. It was all an invention of Kilton Stewart, who wanted to turn people on to his own ideas about dreams, and found this the easiest way of doing it.

The people who discovered this deception were known to some of us quite well in the early 1970s. John Wren-Lewis was the first Chairperson of the Association for Humanistic Psychology in Britain, and Ann Faraday, his wife, was active in London speaking and writing on dream work. Her two books, *Dream power* and *The dream game*, can still be seen in the shops.

In the 1960s and 1970s a couple of anthropologists and some film makers visited the Senoi and failed to find any of the phenomena which Kilton Stewart had written about. However, there was some dispute as to whether they had talked to the right people, and even of whether they had been deliberately deceived by a Government which wanted to hide the harmonious Senoi because such things would upset the Army.

So in 1982 Ann Faraday was asked to write something on dreams, and since she was already in India with her husband, they both decided to visit the Senoi and see for themselves. In Perak they met educated Senoi who invited them to stay in their jungle villages. During the next year the two of them visited dozens of Senoi villages, living with the people and joining in their trance dance sessions. They found no practice and no recollection of the type of dream control which Garfield and others had talked about. And when asked directly about it, the Senoi were horrified at the idea of coercing their dreams in any way – their whole attitude was passive and accepting rather than active and masterful.

The Senoi are a very peaceful and gentle people, Ann and John found, but Stewart's claims about their extraordinary mental and physical health were simply not true. They die as young as most people in primitive tribes, which is not what we would expect if the health story were true.

So how did all this happen? Kilton Stewart was an American psychologist who met an anthropologist named Pat Noone, who was very taken with the Senoi and later married a Senoi wife and lived with her in the jungle. Noone took him for a three-month visit to the Senoi in 1934, and Stewart fell in love with the people too. Noone's account of this trip does not mention dream control at all, and neither does Stewart's unpublished manuscript written at the time. Stewart then took a brief Rankian psychoanalytic training in Paris in 1935, and this turned him on tremendously – he got very excited by his own dreams and their analysis. In China later that year he wrote a whole theory of dream control.

A year later he and Claudia Parsons visited Noone and the Senoi again, and Parsons wrote up the experience in a book called *Vagabondage*. They spent seven weeks in the jungle, where they did not live with the Senoi but stayed in separate huts outside the village. Stewart then came back to England and again took up psychoanalysis. It was not until after his death that his ideas came into prominence.

John Wren-Lewis says that Stewart was once described to him as a 'proto-hippie-guru'. He was a charismatic man, especially to women; everybody liked him. He was a creative thinker and had a gift for seeing in things what he wanted to see in them.

This is an interesting story because it is yet one more instance of how easy we find it to believe what fits in with our own ideas and interests. Like the story of the hundredth monkey, or the tales of Carlos Castañeda, we hang on to fiction because it fulfils our needs and helps us to do what we wanted to do anyway. But it is important to know the difference between truth and lies, even if we find the lies more useful than some of the truths with which we are presented. The full story of the Senoi is now written up in Domhoff (1985).

Dreams can be used in a number of ways in education. The first way is just to share them, and there is a good standard way of doing this, outlined by Ullman (1989) and by Shohet (1985). It goes like this:

1   *Stage 1.* A dreamer volunteers a dream, and the group may ask questions to clarify the dream and to grasp it as clearly and completely as possible. Any real characters in the dream are briefly identified.
2   *Stage 2.* Now each person speaks of this dream as if it were their own, and what they offer to the whole group will be their own projections or imagination. The dreamer is asked to listen without actively participating. He or she is free to accept or reject anything that comes from the group.

Group members share with one another any feelings or moods that the imagery conveys. They might start off: 'In my dream I felt...'

The imagery is addressed and explored imaginatively. The task of the group is to attempt to link the images in the dream to possible life situations or concerns suggested by the imagery. This is offered in the hope that some of the group's responses will have meaning for the dreamer. They might start off: 'In my dream...' and explore the meaning of the images for them.

3   *Stage 3.* The dream is returned to the dreamer who is then invited to respond and share an understanding of the dream. This can be done in any desired manner, taking as much time as needed without interruption.

    If further work is necessary, it proceeds in the form of a dialogue between the dreamer and the group. It is important not to restrict this in any way.

4   *Stage 4.* The dreamer reviews the dream between the time the dream was presented and the next meeting of the group. The dreamer is invited to share any additional thoughts about the dream at the next meeting of the group.

This a good and well-tried method of using dreams in the group, and it will depend entirely on what kind of group it is as to how much of the interpretation moves into transpersonal material.

Dreams can also be worked on in a psychodramatic mode, with the dreamer taking various roles in turn.

Some dream images make striking posters or paintings. These can be worked on in the group; or alternatively at home, and brought into the next group meeting.

It is possible to dramatize the continuation of a dream which seems unfinished. The possibilities are endless.

Patricia Permantgem (1976) makes out a good case for all of these being part of transpersonal education.

MEDITATION

Something which can be used in education is meditation. Experience has shown that it is best to take this in stages, starting with stilling. Stilling is simply sitting in silence, and listening to whatever may come from inside. Specimen instructions may run like this; the parts in square brackets are not read out loud:

What I am about to ask you to do is not easy although the instructions sound very simple. In a moment I am going to ask you to be silent for five minutes. [This length of time can be varied up or down, depending on circumstances.] First of all, make sure you are sitting in a comfortable position. [Pause five seconds.] Sit as still as you can. Now close your eyes if you can. If you find you can't, for any reason, just look down so that you can't see anyone else. And just pay attention to your own experience, whatever is going on for you. There is no need to check your watch as I will call time at the end of the five minutes. OK, the period of silence begins NOW.

(Hammond *et al.*, 1990, p. 73)

Make sure that any distracting noises are reduced to a minimum, so as to give the best chance for this to work. At the end of the five minutes get people to form into pairs and discuss what the experience was like and what happened for them. If the group is small, and there is enough time, it may be best for the whole group to discuss together. The rough rule of thumb is that each person should have four minutes to themselves, so a group of two will need eight minutes, a group of four will need sixteen minutes and so on.

People can also be asked to draw their experience, or to write down what they thought or felt.

Sometimes, with very naive groups, it is a good idea to teach relaxation before doing the exercise on silence.

Another step towards meditation can be done by teaching various methods of clearing the mind of chatter and jumble. One way which has worked well recently is this:

Sit still or lie down in a comfortable position. Imagine that your mind is a computer screen, and that you have a key on your keyboard which clears the whole screen. This is called the CLEAR key. Now you are watching the screen, and you see coming up on the screen all your thoughts, all your words and pictures and feelings and messages. Just watch them for a while. [Pause fifteen seconds.] You may notice that they change and you can key in new thoughts which will then appear on the screen. [Pause fifteen seconds.] Now reach out for the CLEAR key. OK, press the CLEAR key. Now all you can see is a blank screen. [Pause fifteen seconds.] The screen is clear. Just watch it. [Pause fifteen seconds.] If more pictures or anything else appear, then you can press the CLEAR key again. [Pause fifteen seconds.]

(Hammond *et al.* 1990, p. 81)

Again people can discuss the experience, as before. If people have been discussing in pairs, it is always important for the whole group to come back together and tell anything they want to share with the whole group, or with the facilitator, because occasionally some deep feelings can be stirred up by these simple exercises.

We can go on from here to various types of meditation proper, which is now much easier because the groundwork has been laid.

ENCOUNTER GROUPS

It is not always realized that encounter groups and marathon groups are well suited to the emergence of transpersonal material.

At first this sounds very unfamiliar and unusual, until we realize that virtually all group leaders rely on their *intuition* a great deal. As we have seen already, intuition takes many forms, but can be one of the faculties of the higher unconscious. Intuition, then, can often take us into the realm of the transpersonal.

Let us move on to take up another, similar, point about imagination. Again, many group leaders use *imagery and fantasy*, and these too can be part of the transpersonal realm. When we ask a participant to bring to mind an image of his or her inner conflict, or suggest that they imagine what their opponent might turn into, or invite them to bring to mind a certain scene, we are invoking the imaginal world, which is the realm of the transpersonal.

So when Schutz tells the story of a British woman in one of his groups who was asked to become very small and go inside her own body (Shaffer and Galinsky 1989, p. 218), he was working in a transpersonal way. We can see from this that imagery very often involves playing with the normal limitations of time and space. (In his more recent work, Schutz (1989) explicitly uses meditation, prayer, chanting and Arica spiritual exercises.)

James Elliott, another important writer on encounter, does not say as much as Schutz about the spiritual aspects of his work, but he does say that human beings are not just physical objects but are best characterized by such words as freedom, choice, growth, autonomy and mystery. He also refers to *creativity* and liberation (Elliott 1976, p. 58).

Another phenomenon noted by Elliott is the Fusion Experience, which often happens after primals and similar cathartic experiences. The whole person is involved, and seems often taken outside their ordinary world. 'Looking back on the experience, [one has] the feeling that one was outside time and space. Typical comments are "The world fell away"...' (Elliott 1976, p. 198).

Elizabeth Mintz, who wrote the classic book on the marathon group, does not say much about spirituality in her 1972 book, but makes up for it by a later book which is all about it. In *The psychic thread* she gives an example where a young man's impotence was cured, not by the usual process of therapy, but by a group ritual in which he symbolically castrated each of the other men in the group. This arose quite spontaneously in the group, and she says of the event: 'It was an enactment of a mythic ritual, a primitive ceremony, which tapped the deep levels of the collective unconscious; it was a transpersonal experience' (Mintz 1983, pp. 153–7).

In the same book, Mintz talks of countertransference of such a kind that the group leader actually feels inside her own body the next thing which needs to happen for the participant. This links directly with the research on countertransference mentioned by Samuels (1989) in his recent book, which again links this with the transpersonal, and with the Jungian idea of the imaginal world.

It is my strong impression that the climate has changed considerably in recent years, in the direction of more open acknowledgement of the importance of the transpersonal. It was always important in encounter, but it is only more recently that people have said so very much.

Let me give an example of something which happened in a primal encounter group a few years back. A woman said she had never felt like a woman, always a little girl. She wanted the group somehow to give her a rite of passage:

> We always asked, 'What do you already know?' She knew she wanted flowers and water. All the women gathered in the pool with music, candles and flowers. We had flowers in our hair. The men were kept out. We all made a line in the pool and she swam between the legs of all the women. The music changed when she became a woman. I think someone was there to receive her. She changed the colour of her flower from white to red. We dressed her in her finery and brought her to show to the men, and she danced for the men and women. That affected the others who felt that they hadn't had a transition rite. They didn't need to do it too; hers was powerful enough for everybody.
>
> (Rockman 1984, p. 38).

This is mythical work, archetypal work at the level of symbol and image. The change from white to red of course comes from the three phases of the Great Goddess, who goes from maiden to mother to crone. This corresponds to the three phases of the moon, waxing, full and waning, and to the colours white, red and black. In Hindu religion this is called the *trimurti*.

In this particular group it was common to organize funerals in a ritual manner to mourn losses which are often unrecognized in our culture: this might include abortions, or the loss of a partner, or the loss of a subpersonality which had been prominent up to its loss in the process of therapy.

Funerals had set props – a corpse, a sheet, candles. Music, usually Fauré's Requiem. Often a recital of the Kaddish, regardless of whether or not people were Jewish. Usually an object had to get buried, the knife that had killed the person, or some symbol of rage or fear or whatever emotions were being buried. There was a procession to a hole outside. The person was asked to say everything he wanted to say to the dead person, speaking directly, as in gestalt therapy. We repeatedly asked, 'Is there anything you need to do before you say goodbye, or in order to say goodbye?' Often a candle was left burning on the grave. There were post-funeral rites – placing a branch, or flowers daily, or three times a day on the grave.

(Rockman 1984, p. 39)

Rites of healing and rites of rebellion were also enacted in these groups, particularly when they were led by a therapist who was also an Anglican priest, who seemed to have a gift for this sort of thing, and whose status seemed to help the process.

The people who went through these experiences seemed to become not only more individual, as in the ordinary encounter group, but also more connected with others, more overlapping with others. This is one of the distinguishing features of work at the transpersonal level.

Some might feel that this is all quite ordinary, and that there is no need to mention the transpersonal, but I don't agree. I think we can get a much more accurate sense of what we are doing in group work by recognizing that we are working on many different levels all the time.

Mintz cautions that it is also possible to go too far in the direction of paying attention to the extraordinary in the group. The group leader can actually start to feel like a psychic, and can indulge in activities which are basically ego-inflating, such as telling participants what they are thinking or feeling before they are aware of it themselves.

This can work the other way round too: group members can try to get close to the leader by significant anticipations of what she or he wants or needs. This is particularly likely to happen when there is a strong transference to the leader. And of course it has to be treated with caution like any other transferential phenomenon.

When this happens in a group between group members, it is almost always beneficial, however. Here it comes under the heading of what is called in psychodrama 'tele', which is regarded as a healthy and desirable phenomenon. Two or more group members may have an uncanny awareness of one another's deepest needs and feelings. This often comes out in exercises where people have to pick up partners. If the choice is allowed to be as free as possible (e.g. asking people to stand up and mill around before choosing) people very often choose each other in an extraordinarily appropriate way.

Jung has discussed this sort of thing under the heading of synchronicity – the meaningful co-occurrence of things which can be dismissed as coincidence. But these group phenomena are so common that it is hard to dismiss them in this way, any more than one would dismiss the phenomena of transference.

Mintz even describes at some length how these transpersonal matters can be used in supervision. One thing which can be done is to ask, in a supervision group, for people to produce an image of a client, or of the client–therapist relationship, and this often produces fascinating results. For example, in one group where a therapist seemed to have a stuck position in regard to a client called Angela, the group was asked to produce an image of Angela, and one person produced an image of Angela thrusting a knife into the neck of the eldest of her young brothers, whom she had experienced as unbearably difficult. Angela's presenting problem had been fear of having a baby, with no objective difficulties in the way. The therapist now tactfully raised with the client the possibility that she had actually wanted to kill her brother. Now the fear came to the surface: 'If she had a baby boy, might she not hate him as she had hated the obnoxious brother? Might she not even want to kill the baby?' The deadlock was broken; Angela could now make her decision about motherhood without being haunted by murderous feelings from the past (Mintz 1983, pp. 130–1).

Many more details about transpersonal work in education are given in the excellent books by Hendricks and Wills (1975), Hendricks and Fadiman (1976), Hendricks and Roberts (1977) and Gloria Castillo (1978).

Part IV

Critical issues

Chapter 9

Issues in transpersonal theory

In this chapter we shall look in more detail at certain issues which have arisen from time to time in our discussion so far.

WOMEN'S SPIRITUALITY

It is perhaps cheeky and asking for trouble for a man to write about women's spirituality, but this amazing literature has had so much effect on me, and has affected this book so much, that it would be churlish in my opinion not to at least indicate what is there.

The basic case is a feminist one: that for many centuries a specifically female tradition of spirituality has been suppressed and denied by the male establishment. This is a tradition which worships a Great Goddess who came before any of the male gods.

It is a tradition in which the flesh, instead of being subordinated to the spirit, is recognized as the basis for life, love and worship. Sexuality and spirituality are not opposed but reconciled.

It is a tradition where men are seen as perfectly OK so long as they recognize female power and relate to it with respect and do it honour. But the moment that men move away and try to be self-sufficient or competitive with women, the trouble begins.

There are some classic works where all this is laid out. One of the most striking of these is Barbara Walker's *The women's encyclopedia of myths and secrets*, where she runs the gamut of mythology and a good deal else besides, looking at it all from a feminist point of view, and often going back to earlier sources to find illuminating origins for many of the dubious ideas in later classical mythology. This is a pioneering work, and like all such not entirely reliable in all its ramifications; but it is a huge eye-opener.

One of the most impressive books is by Monica Sjöö and Barbara Mor, entitled *The great cosmic mother: Rediscovering the religion of the earth*. This beautifully illustrated book not only contains much information about the ancient religion and how it is relevant today, but also has striking and revealing applications of the thinking which emerges from all this to topics like politics, abortion, the machine, war and much else. I think it is the most politically aware of all the books on the Goddess.

Also very good from this point of view, and even more precise, objective and scholarly, is Lucy Goodison's *Moving heaven and earth: Sexuality, spirituality and social change*. This takes immense trouble over the fine detail, and makes no sweeping statements or unfounded generalizations. Based on a Ph.D. thesis, it breaks some new ground and makes many fascinating new points, for example about the symbolism of the sun. There is a long section on the body as a subtle energy system.

More beautifully produced, but equally serious in its approach, is Elinor Gadon's *The once and future goddess: A symbol for our time*. The emphasis here is on how the Goddess has inspired women artists to produce new and striking works which have a bearing on our lives today. The full colour illustrations make one think at first that this is a coffee-table book, but they are all there for a serious purpose which is fully spelt out in the text.

Another book which is strong on art is Judy Chicago's *The Dinner Party: A symbol of our heritage*. This is based on an art work – a huge three-sided table with thirty-nine plates on it. Each symbolic plate, and its embroidered runner, is designed to honour a particular woman or goddess. The book not only explains how important each of these women is, and why, but also introduces us to nine hundred and ninety-nine other goddesses and 'women of achievement' and tells us why we should know about them. The whole thing amounts to an extraordinary paean of praise to women, most of whom were ignored, put down, demonized or destroyed by male power. It is at one and the same time inspiring and shaming to see so much female power and genius, so much of it denied and disallowed.

Another extraordinary book is *The politics of women's spirituality*, edited by Charlene Spretnak, who has more recently been so active in the Green movement. The section headings tell the story: Part One – discovering a history of power (What the Goddess means to women; Mythic heras as models of strength and wisdom); Part Two – Manifesting personal power (Consciousness/Energy/Action; Self-images of strength and wholeness); Part Three – Transforming the political (The unity of politics and spirituality; Applications of spirituality as a political force). This is a magnificent book, and the list of authors reads like a roll-call of the most influential writers on these topics.

I don't want this just to be a booklist. I want to say that in my opinion anyone who ignores all this material is going to be seriously lacking in their appreciation of women in the transpersonal realms. But if one tunes in to these voices, one is going to be much more likely to be able to make transpersonal interventions which are not simply infected by patriarchal assumptions, in a quite unaware way.

Some people, of course, have specifically addressed the issues within psychotherapy and counseling from this point of view. Jean Shinoda Bolen touched a nerve for many therapists when she brought out her book *Goddesses in everywoman*, which gives specific instructions for recognizing seven goddesses when they come up as archetypes in therapy: Artemis, Athena and Hestia (the virgin goddesses), Hera, Demeter and Persephone (the vulnerable goddesses) and Aphrodite (the alchemical goddess). Then later came the book by Jennifer Barker Woolger, *The goddess within*, which deals with the archetypes of Athena, Artemis, Aphrodite, Hera, Persephone and Demeter in a more systematic way, linking them with the Great Mother, and saying that each one represents one aspect of her original strength.

A very famous book is Nor Hall's *The moon and the virgin*, which deals with four important archetypes for women, first outlined by Toni Wolff and Carl Jung: the Mother, the Hetaira, the Amazon and the Medial woman. She goes into each of these, and their relations, in some detail.

One of the most recent books is one of the best: *Shakti woman* by Vicki Noble. This gives an inspiring Tantric vision of the woman as warrior, as power. It shows how the way of the shaman can be very important for women.

Of course Jung and his followers are often not good guides in this area, because of his sexism, spelt out in detail in Demaris Wehr's book *Jung and feminism*. This infects a surprising number of his followers, as for example Erich Neumann's *The great mother*, which is full of misogyny. Even the book *The fear of women* is full of the fear of women.

However, Radmila Moacanin makes it clear that the *dakinis* of the Tantric tradition, particularly in Tibet, have much to teach all of us, in ways which are directly applicable to Jungian psychotherapy:

> The *dakini* of the highest rank is Vajra Yogini. She is the divine figure of the inspiring muse who 'redeems the treasures of aeons of experience, which lie dormant in the subconscious, and raises them into the realm of higher consciousness, beyond that of our intellect' (Govinda). Tibetan Buddhists say that Vajra Yogini has always existed deep within ourselves, in our unconscious, but is suffocated by the ego. When the concept of the ego is pierced we allow Vajra Yogini to appear... In the context of Jung's psychology, Vajra Yogini would be a primordial

image, and as such can act as a mediator 'proving its redeeming power, a power it has always possessed in various religions' (Jung). Vajra Yogini in Tibetan iconography is depicted with a curious expression that is simultaneously loving and smiling, but also wrathful, thus revealing the essential ambivalence of every archetype.

(Moacanin 1986, p. 62)

In this she is like Hades, and it has been said in the Jungian tradition that Hades is the god of soul, and the underworld, and therefore the god of psychotherapy, which spends so much of its time probing what is beneath the surface. So we are not saying in any way that the Jungian tradition is irredeemable.

In any case, not only the Jungians are guilty: Robert Graves' *The white goddess* is quite unaware and anti-woman in many places, and so are the works of Briffault and Bachofen. Something seems to come over men when they try to write about woman, even when they think they are helping. So perhaps I will stop at this point, having at least pointed in the general direction of what needs to be said.

THE MALE POLARITY

Men have been slow to catch up with all this: it is no accident that Lynne Segal's excellent account of the men's movement is called *Slow motion*. But more books on men have come out in the past five years than in the previous five thousand, so men are catching up gradually. And some of this catching up has been in the realm of spirituality.

In his book *Iron John* Robert Bly says that men have lost their way. They have seen through the nonsense of the traditional male chauvinist man (made more conscious recently in the form of the so-called Free Men), and have in some cases taken on the almost equally misleading notion of the New Man, whom Bly renames the Naive Man, who is supposed to be gentle, caring, nurturing and involved with child care, etc. Bly wants to offer instead the mythopoetic model of the Wildman, who is in touch with the original deep masculinity which is his birthright. And he gives a parable in the form of a fairy tale, illuminating the points he wants to make about the wildman.

This is very promising. Bly is a brilliant writer, who does have some very original and striking things to say. He opens up the whole archetypal side of things very well for men. But there is a snag, because in this fairy story there is no information about how the wildman relates to women. He is apparently alone. In the first part of the story he lives at the bottom of a lake, and in the latter part of the story he is a wealthy king followed by a retinue. But we never hear anything about a queen, or any other female in relation to the wildman.

In today's world I am suspicious about any model of the male which does not include some explicit account of how he is to relate to the female. That does not mean, by the way, that the male is defined in relation to the female, just that the relationship is spelt out in some way. Bly says, quite correctly, so far as I can see, that male energy is different from female energy, and that one cannot substitute for the other. Men cannot get their models of masculinity from women. But if a man gets in touch with his deep masculinity in a context which is patriarchal, it is gong to be just as much influenced by that as any other model might be. What we have to question is the patriarchal context, and Bly says not a word about that. In fact, what he does say about the goodness of the father, and the importance of the father to men, actually cuts right across the notion that we live in a patriarchal culture. Bly thinks we live in a 'Disneyland culture', and he is wrong about that. His follower Robert Moore (with Douglas Gillete) has written a much worse book called *King, warrior, magician, lover*, which also denies that patriarchy exists, and says that we live in a 'puerarchy' (rule by boys). Sam Keen's book *Fire in the belly* does at least mention the relationship between men and women, but again completely ignores the power relations between the sexes in society.

Patriarchy is really there, and really hurtful. It is an historical structure, which came into being and can go out of being, and has internal dynamics which are changing all the time. At present it is quite degenerate, and retains many of the old drawbacks without most of the old advantages. It is nothing to do with biological determinism, as some critics suggest. It is about socially and historically defined gender. Recent analyses of it, such as the excellent book by Bob Connell called *Gender and power*, show with a wealth of detail just what an oppressive system it is.

So 'patriarchy' is essentially a unifying term, which enables us to see the single pattern underlying many apparently separate struggles. Riane Eisler (1987) suggests the term 'dominance culture' instead, and this may be a good phrase to use at times.

How then does a male begin to question such a system, which on the one hand gives him a privileged position, and on the other encases him in a rigid role which is hard to escape from, and from which one line of escape leads to frustration?

The Horned God

I think we have to move to a different model again, which is similar to Bly's wildman in being mythological, and to Moore's heroes in being archetypal, yet does have an explicit relation to the female.

The Horned God is a consort. As a son, as a lover, sometimes even as a husband, he relates to the Great Goddess. If we imagine a stone circle with a tall stone in the centre, we have an image of the healthy relationship of the male with the female. The female circle forms the matrix or context in which the male pillar can be filled with power. As long as that male power is contained within the circle, it is safe and usable; but if it tries to be self-sufficient, to roam outside the circle, it comes to grief. (The story of Inanna and Dumuzi, as told by Perera (1981), is relevant here.) Of course the female can also be the pillar in the middle, particularly when pregnant, and then can in the ideal case accept a stone circle of maleness to hold, guard and support her. In the present culture, degenerate as it is, this seldom happens.

Or put it another way. If we hold a guitar string between our two hands, so that the hands are very close together, then the string will hang loose and if anyone tries to pluck it, no note will emerge. This is what Robert Bly has argued very well. If, on the other hand, we pull the hands apart so far that the string snaps, again no music can come out of this. And this is the possibility which Bly has not ruled out – indeed it may be that his formulation makes such an outcome hard to avoid.

But if we hold the hands in tension, so that the male hand is in a strong relationship with the female hand, the string can be plucked and a musical note will emerge. This is the range of creative tension – not too slack, and not so tight as to snap the string. In this way the relationship between the female and the male can be safe, because the continuing dialogue is guaranteed. This kind of alive difference, as the feminist Audre Lorde tells us, is:

> a fund of necessary polarities between which our creativity can spark like a dialectic... Only within that interdependency of different strengths, acknowledged and equal, can the power to seek new ways to actively 'be' in the world generate, as well as the courage and sustenance to act where there are no charters... Difference is that raw and powerful connection from which our personal power is forged.
>
> (Quoted in Kramarae and Treichler 1985)

We do not find answers by seeking one-sided truths which then have to be defended, but by engaging in the creative tension of dialogue.

Another way of putting this point about the relationship is to turn to the Eastern discipline of Tantra. Here is a quote from Arthur Avalon:

> The fully Real, therefore, has two aspects: one called Śiva, the static aspect of Consciousness, and the other called Śakti, the kinetic aspect of the same. Kālī Śakti, dark as a thundercloud, is represented standing and moving on the white inert body of Śiva. He is white as Illumination (Prakāśa). He is inert, for Pure Consciousness is without action and at rest. It is She, His Power, who moves.
>
> (Avalon 1978, p. 42)

This again is clear about the relationship. All power is first of all female power, and the God can only act by relating to her and being with her. But this God is male without a doubt – there is no question about his phallic masculinity, which goes to the very depths of his being. Avalon remarks one of the basic Tantric beliefs is that honour should be paid to women; even female animals should not be sacrificed. If a man in that tradition speaks rudely to his wife, he has to fast for one day. To ill-treat a woman is a crime. And women can be gurus or spiritual directors.

Western paganism can be just as good as this, because it holds firmly to the primacy of the Goddess and the essential relationship to the Horned God. Particularly in the work of Starhawk (1982, 1989), a feminist witch who has written a good deal about this, we find some very strong and valuable suggestions about this relationship. But also in the work of the Farrars, who are much more orthodox pagans, we find this sort of statement: 'Woman is the gateway to witchcraft, and man is her "guardian and student"' (Farrar and Farrar 1984, p. 169). I have gone into this difficult matter at much greater length in my book *The horned god*.

Three levels

Let us see if we can now draw the threads together and knit them into a pattern. It is as if there are at least three models of maleness and how to work with it. Firstly there is the standard social model, where the male has to be a proper man, and not effeminate or cowardly. If one strays outside it in the macho direction it is acceptable or winked at. If one strays outside it in the feminine direction it is much more suspect and condemnable. We need not say too much about this model – it is too familiar, and the Free Men represent it and idealize it.

Secondly there is what one might call the monistic model, which is usual in personal growth and the kind of psychotherapy which is most common in humanistic circles, where we say that the man has to go down into his depths, finding perhaps first a 'good' layer of clichés, then a 'bad' layer of self-put-downs, and then a layer of pain, and then a layer of deeper truth which is OK – or whatever model of layers is being used here. It is OK to be male, and just a question of finding the deeper, truer version of it. This is the model which Robert Bly is using, in a fresh and sophisticated way.

Then thirdly there is a transpersonal model of the male, where we say that the 'bad' layer is found to be bad or harmful only because separated from female energy and female power. Connected up again in a proper relationship with that energy and that power, that which formerly had to be defined as bad transforms into a deeper truth which is OK.

Now these three levels of understanding of the male are not necessarily contradictory. They correspond to the three different levels of work in this area which we noticed in Chapter 5.

The one level, which uses the model of adjustment to social reality, is the level of most of the counselling and psychotherapy which is generally available. The highest aim is to be able to play one's roles in society properly, that is, conventionally.

The second level, which takes the monistic approach, is the level of personal growth. Here the aim is not adjustment but authenticity and real change. At this level of working, one is interested in the personal unconscious, in the healing of the splits, in filling in the holes in the personality, and generally in the integration of the person as a social and psychological being. This is what we have been calling the centaur level, the level of the existential self or the real self. Robert Bly goes no further than this.

The other level is the transpersonal (sometimes called the subtle level). It says that the male and the female must be related through the *hieros gamos* (the sacred marriage) if the male is not to be destructive. This is not about healing the split between the male and the female, but about enabling them to relate together as polarities in an appropriate way – a way that actually works in today's world. And this, by the way, refers also to what goes on within the person – the internal male and female energies. It includes and embraces the gay, the lesbian, the bisexual. The politics of this has been spelled out in the magnificent book by Monica Sjöö and Barbara Mor already mentioned, which contains so much original material.

Again there are some interesting books. Jean Shinoda Bolen has also done one for men, under the title *Gods in everyman*, which deals with Zeus, Poseidon and Hades (father gods) and Apollo, Hermes, Ares, Hephaestus and Dionysus (the sons). Janet and Stewart Farrer have produced *The witches' god*, which is all about the Horned God in his forms of Pan, Osiris, Tammuz, Thoth, Cernunnos, Shiva, Dagda, Loki, Zeus, Eros, Ra and

Wayland Smith. Ly Warren-Clarke and Kathryn Matthews, from Australia, have produced *The way of Merlin*, which has some good material on Llugh, Artu, Beli, Hu, Lancelet, Merlyn, Cernunnos, Gwydion, Manannan, Diancecht, Taliesin and Math, linked to positions on the Kabbala. I have to say, however, that none of these has anything at all to say about politics. This is really a terrible indictment of male interest in this area, and testifies to the way in which patriarchy paralyses men, when it come to facing up to real change. There is one recent book which does have at least something to say about social change, and that is *Celebrating the male mysteries* by Bob Stewart, but I have to say that I find this book quite superficial and really quite inadequate. One or two of the chapters in *Choirs of the god*, edited by John Matthews, also have at least a glimmering of what is needed. The same is true of *New men, new minds*, edited by Franklin Abbott.

Eugene Monick is a Jungian with some interesting ideas, and his books *Phallos* and *Castration and male rage* are worth reading.

> Physical phallos has become a religious and psychological symbol because it decides on its own, independent of its owner's ego decision, when and with whom it wants to spring into action. It is thus an appropriate metaphor for the unconscious itself, and specifically the masculine mode of the unconscious.
>
> (Monick 1987, p. 17)

Monick goes on in his second book to discuss the way in which the phallos as such a symbol has been affected by the changes of recent years in the rise of feminism and the expansion of women's spirituality.

> In psychoanalytic thinking, reflecting Western culture generally, the feminine has been considered dominant in the unconscious, the masculine in consciousness. With the feminine emerging as a force in consciousness, a radical shift in contemporary awareness has taken place. Men are being pushed into an investigation of masculinity in the *un*conscious even as women are discovering feminine consciousness.
>
> (Monick 1991, p. 11)

This is an important insight, and one that is obvious as soon as stated, like all the best insights.

THE BODY

What is the relationship between the spiritual and the body? In transpersonal therapy we are very clear about this. The body is not opposed to or inferior to the intellect or the mind. Again it is the question of boundaries. We have the power to open the boundaries or to close them. If we want to enter into our bodies and become them we can do that. If we want to visualize parts of our bodies or conflicts within them, we can do that. There is a magical relationship between ourselves and our bodies, such that all things are possible.

One of the most important bodily activities is breathing. And it is interesting that the word for breath, and the word for spirit, is the same in many different languages: *pneuma, ruach, anima, animus, prana, ch'i, ki* – all these are words for breath, which are also words for spirit.

It is so much worthwhile paying attention to breathing because it works on four levels:

1   Physical – exchange of gases with the environment.
2   Emotional – we cannot change our emotions without changing our breathing.
3   Intellectual – when we start thinking we stop breathing.
4   Spiritual.

So it connects up all the levels of our being, and in Yoga it is possible to extend this quite consciously so as to link all the chakras in line from the base to the crown.

> The most important result of the practice of 'mindfulness with regard to breathing' is the realization that the process of breathing is the connecting link between conscious and subconscious, gross-material and fine-material, volitional and non-volitional functions, and therefore the most perfect expression of the nature of all life.
>
> (Kapleau 1967, p. 12)

In therapy there are many different kinds of breathing: the deep fast breathing used in regression work; the belly breathing used in relaxation and Yoga meditation; the connected breathing used in Leonard Orr Rebirthing; the lion breathing used in some Sufi work; the provocative breathing used in some neo-Reichian work, and so on.

There is a definite relationship between Yoga as a schema of psycho-spiritual development and the kind of work we do in psychotherapy:

> The royal, or *raja yoga* outlined by Patanjali entails *ashtanga*: eight key practices or limbs. The first two, *yama* and *niyama*, are moral training for purity. The next two are *asana*, the development through physical exercises of a firm and erect posture, or 'seat', and *pranayama*, exercises for controlling and stilling the breath.
>
> (Goleman 1977, p. 76)

Stanislav Grof has made a special study of breathing, and uses it very carefully in his work, which he calls holotropic therapy. He points out that specific techniques involving intense breathing or withholding of breath are a part of various exercises in Kundalini Yoga, Siddha Yoga, the Tibetan Vajrayana, Sufi practice, Burmese Buddhist and Taoist meditation, and many others. More subtle techniques which emphasize special awareness in regard to breathing rather than changes of the respiratory dynamics have a prominent place in Soto Zen Buddhism, and in certain Taoist and Christian practices. Indirectly, the breathing rhythm will be profoundly influenced by such ritual performances as the Balinese monkey chant or *Ketjak*, the Inuit Eskimo throat music, and singing of *kirtans*, *bhajans* or Sufi chants. He also has some interesting remarks to make about hyperventilation or over-breathing, where we breathe faster and deeper than usual for a period of time:

> In some instances, continued hyperventilation leads to increasing relaxation, sense of expansion and wellbeing, and visions of light. The individual can be flooded with feelings of love and mystical connection to other people, nature, the entire cosmos, and God. Experiences of this kind are extremely healing, and the individual should be encouraged to allow them to develop; this should be discussed during the preparation period.
>
> (Grof 1988, p. 171)

Grof also tells us that in Siddha Yoga and Kundalini Yoga, intentional hyperventilation (*bastrika*) is used as one of the meditation techniques, and episodes of rapid breathing often occur spontaneously as one of the manifestations of Shakti (or activated Kundalini energy) referred to as *kriyas*.

It seems clear from all this that breathing is a bodily phenomenon which is symbolic of the body generally in its breadth of inclusion of so many psychospiritual elements. One of the people who has made a special study of this is Magda Proskauer, who emphasizes that the breath forms a bridge between the conscious and unconscious systems. She tells us that:

> The diaphragm dividing the body into an upper and a lower cage can be seen as the organ which divides our two worlds. The lower animal or instinctual world is represented by the abdominal organs, the vegetative life of the earth; and the upper, more conscious world is represented by the lungs, a symbol of the spiritual life. [Lowen (1976) says much the same thing.] Embedded between them is the heart, the seat of our feelings. In order to feel whole we need to bring these two

worlds together. In Greek semantics the word schizophrenia means to be split (schizo) in the diaphragm. The word for diaphragm being phren, also mind.

(Proskauer 1977, p. 60)

These are fascinating ideas, and it is quite possible to get carried away with them. Sometimes, however, the danger is that we lose the distinction between the transpersonal and the extrapersonal here. The test is whether we are in touch with the divine somehow, or whether we are slipping into a kind of spiritual materialism. Goodison (1990) has a long and interesting chapter on what she calls 'the luminous body', but much of it seems to me a kind of reduction of the transpersonal to the extrapersonal.

I have come to feel that in the working of such laws the 'divine' is no more – and no less – present than in the workings of gravity, light, heat and the seed that grows into a plant.

(Goodison 1990, p. 373)

To say this is to expose one to the danger of simply using all sorts of discoveries about the luminous body to feed the mental ego. We have seen in all our work so far that the transpersonal essentially goes beyond the mental ego, first of all into the real self, and then into the subtle self, the transpersonal self, and from there perhaps even into the causal self. The danger of reducing the luminous body to a series of exercises is that we plunge into the dangers outlined by Chogyam Trungpa:

Walking the spiritual path properly is a very subtle process; it is not something to jump into naively. There are numerous sidetracks which lead to a distorted, ego-centred version of spirituality; we can deceive ourselves into thinking we are developing spiritually when instead we are strengthening our egocentricity through spiritual techniques. This fundamental distortion may be referred to as *spiritual materialism*.

(Trungpa 1973, p. 3)

But perhaps the person who has had most to say about the connection between the body and the transpersonal realms is David Boadella. It is very interesting to see the way in which he has developed from a basic Reichian into the much more well-rounded therapist that he has become today. He says:

We can see it whenever someone succeeds in making the transition from hysterical acting out and over-emotionalizing, to the being-filled with the depth of oneself that transforms the breathing. When this happens the breathing loses all panic, all contractedness, all pressurisation and self-torture. I can hear the ocean in it. It moves through the body like tides... The task of all true therapies and the aim of the core teaching in all true religions is to re-connect us with the depth of ourselves... Religion has used the word 'God' for the inexhaustible depth and ground of being... We need to help the person to find his inner ground, his *essence*, the source from which his own healing energy wells up with the power to integrate him anew in spite of whatever he learned about how not to feel alive.

(Boadella 1987, pp. 169–72)

In spite of the sexist pronouns, it seems hard to put it better than that.

CREATIVE VISIONS

As we have already mentioned, the autonomous stage brings with it a vision-logic which relies a great deal on images and symbols. Creativity becomes much more a part of us at this stage. But it is very much a creativity which seems to come from us, and which we own.

At the transpersonal level, we have to move to the type of creativity where something seems to come to us from outside ourselves. We experience ourselves as just a channel or pathway through which, or along which, the vision comes. Again, however, we have to look closely at visions and not take them too uncritically. Discrimination is needed. The same is true with inspiration.

When I have a vision it inspires me. It makes me want to go out and make it happen. Some people have only had one vision. In some cases this came to them in a very authoritative way, as if it were the voice of Spirit or Deity, and of course this is very powerful. They feel divinely inspired or at the very least filled with the power to fulfil their purpose. And obviously great things can come of this – people can be energized to great achievements. The world would be a poorer place without such inspired efforts. But there are great dangers here, too. If my vision is so strong, I can easily get a sense of rightness about it.

In my own personal case, I have had several different visions of how a future society might be, and they have been very important for me. But because I have had more than one vision I know that there are some crucial questions to be asked about this. What happens when I meet someone with one of the other visions?

How can you argue with someone who says they have had a vision? There is no right or wrong, correct or incorrect, about a vision – either you have it or you don't. And you may choose to pay attention to it or ignore it. Equally, if you have two or more visions, there is no way in which you can say that they are consistent or inconsistent, because they occupy different universes, so to speak. Each one has its own logic, rather than subscribing to a common logic.

But you could still evaluate a vision or an intuitive insight in certain ways, if it seemed that there was some question about it. So in practical terms, what we have to do when we meet this kind of apparent disagreement is to take five steps:

1   The first task is to identify whether the other person has a thesis that is derived from a vision. Is it really a vision that forms the backing for a statement?

2   The question then arises – is the visionary locked into some other logic, to be located in some social historical background? This is what is very characteristic of visions. Each one depends on a particular logic, which may be different from the ordinary everyday logic, or the scientific logic, which is often shared more generally.

3   To reinterpret the thesis in its contemporary social nexus, by examining the point of origin of the vision. To see where the vision comes from, and establish the relevance of the connection between that world and the present one. Usually there is a sort of heartland for each vision, where it lives and prospers and has great credibility and usefulness. When taken outside this territory, the vision might not necessarily be so useful or credible.

4   To spell out the strengths and weaknesses of the original vision. What is it good for? What is it perhaps less good for? In its own terms, how does it work in various situations? This is to evaluate it in practical terms. Where does its usefulness come to an end? Where might it be actively dangerous?

5   To follow the vision through to its end. To see where it led, in terms of its own logic, particularly in relation to other visions and other ways of being in the world. If you follow it through, spell out the further scenario, carry the dream forward, does it become self-contradictory or otherwise confusing? What does actually happen if we pursue it through a good number of its ramifications and implications?

The phrase 'locked into' (in point 2 above) seems particularly appropriate. Visionaries, just because their vision is so compelling and so vivid, do seem usually to be locked into it, and all that flows from it. It seems to me that visions cannot be evaluated according to the methods of the empirical sciences – neither old paradigm science nor new paradigm science. This is because visionaries are unwilling to enter into the kinds of relationships necessary for good research to take place. A vision is a vision – it is something I saw in my imagination, in my mind's eye. I might have a vision of a flying unicorn. But there is in that no claim that flying unicorns exist, or that unicorns can fly, or that there are such things as unicorns at all.

But it also seems to me that visions cannot be simply subjected to the kind of political process which has been used historically to settle religious questions – there is insufficient common ground for this process to take place in any meaningful way. So we have to find some other approach, and I think it is precisely to follow the five points mentioned above. And ultimately I hope we can come to the realization that no one single vision is going to do for every situation.

Human beings are rich and complex creatures, operating on many levels and in many contexts. It would be strange if a single vision of a future society or a way of being could encompass all that. Human beings and human societies change and develop over time. It would be strange and unexpected if a single vision could be independent of history and economics and geography and transport and all the rest. It is human to yearn after perfection, but not to achieve it – and certainly not to achieve it for everybody at once.

Some people have criticized this view as a kind of relativism. I do not think that labelling something as 'relativism' helps very much in clarifying the argument. We are trying to talk here about visions, and visions do not make truth claims. Relativism is all about truth claims. Visions may be useful or useless or harmful, they may be inspiring or depressing, they may be illuminative or obfuscating, but they cannot be true or false.

I think actually that visions are rather dangerous as a source of attitudes to the world. As I have been saying, they tend to be very narrow and strongly held, and most of those who have had them have had only one. And it becomes even worse when the person who has had the vision starts to gather followers. Eric Hoffer some years ago wrote an excellent book called *The true believer* about the dangers of followership. And of course the narrower the vision which is being followed, the more potentially dangerous it becomes.

I think visions become somewhat less dangerous when the person has had more than one, and can begin to see that there is a problem about what the relationship between different visions is to be. But even so, I am very suspicious of visions, and think that they need to be handled with the kind of tongs which I have been trying to provide.

Visions can be inspiring and energizing, and on the other hand they can be dangerous. I don't see anything surprising about this. It reminds me of what Hegal says about passion: 'Nothing great in the world was ever achieved without passion.' And yet passion is quite clearly and almost proverbially dangerous.

It is just the same with the question of consistency and coherence. Two visions can be inconsistent, and yet at a different level one may be able to see the coherence between them. In every court of law up and down the land, magistrates and judges are continually day by day meeting with inconsistent accounts of the same events, under the pressure of different interest, different perceptions, different assumptions and the rest. And day by day they are *making sense* of these inconsistent accounts, and arriving at some coherent judgement about how to take it all. All I am saying is that visions may be wildly inconsistent one with another, and yet if we approach them in the right way, we may be able to disentangle the matter enough to arrive at a coherent position which does justice to them all.

RHYTHM AND DIALECTICS

Jocelyn Chaplin (1988) has made out a good case for saying that our every-day consciousness (what we have been calling the consciousness of the mental ego) runs in fixed polarities which exclude one another. The Goddess consciousness which she is interested in, however (which is part of what we would call the transpersonal), sees things as in a dancing rhythm of transformation. So instead of seeing male as opposed to female, we see male and female as dancing, interweaving, crossing over and back. We switch on the TV in a 'masculine' way, then we prepare breakfast in a 'feminine' way, then we read the paper in a 'masculine' way, then we take the children to school in a 'feminine' way, and drive back in a hurry, in a 'masculine' way – we could go on.

So in therapy it is important not to let the client persuade us that things are thus and so, this way and not that way. Maybe they are today, but do they have to be tomorrow? If we want to work genuinely transpersonally, we have to question all the assumptions of rigidity and of fixed boundaries.

POLYTHEISM AND MONOTHEISM

David Miller (1981) has pointed out that all the usual definitions of psychotherapy, including most of the Jungian formulations, seem to take it for granted that there is just one self, just one ego. The whole implication of concepts such as 'individuation' is that there is just one individual who is to come to completion.

The idea of superior monotheism, and progressive stages towards it, has been instrumental to the notion of a superior self, attained through the progressive stages of individuation. Now since monotheistic superiority is questionable, so the superiority of monotheistic models for the self should as well be questioned.

(Hillman 1981, p. 112)

Humanistic psychology is just the same in this respect, with its notion of 'self-actualization' – the obvious assumption being that there is just one self to be actualized. Freudian psychotherapy of all types agrees that there is just one ego, or in the case of rebels like Horney or Reich, just one self. This reveals an unconscious devotion to monotheism.

But what if we questioned this? What if we felt that polytheism were more appropriate? After all, if we have a transpersonal self, and if this is not necessarily separate and distinct from another person's transpersonal self, then in a sense we must have more than one higher self, or at least a share in many.

What does polytheism say? Firstly it says that there are many gods and goddesses, not just one. Or if there is just one, it comes to us in many forms and with many names. And this makes for tolerance. How can we say another person's God is all wrong? It is just another name, another way of seeing the divine.

Secondly it says we ignore gods and goddesses at our peril. It is the ones we ignore, the ones we do not even know about sometimes, which can trip us up, can cause us trouble.

Thirdly it says there is no one right way to talk about the gods and goddesses. Tolerance again. 'There is no orthodoxy in polytheistic theology' (Miller 1981, p. 90).

In a way it corresponds to some of the thinking which is called postmodern. One of the key ideas in postmodernity is that there is no one right answer to anything, certainly not anything fundamental. This is what polytheism says, too, in its own way. So it is right in line with, and in some respects ahead of, this new thinking:

At base we are such beings that only a polytheistic consciousness will account realistically for our lives, and that such a polytheistic consciousness is emerging on the tips of our newest sensibilities.

(Miller 1981, p. 98)

Of course, polytheism fits in very well with the idea of subpersonalities, which I have written about elsewhere (Rowan 1990).

THE MYSTICAL AND MEDITATION

Therapy is a process of giving up our assumptions. So in therapy the best, final, ultimate approach is to encourage and enable the client to question all his or her assumptions without exception. As Levin says:

> *All* conceptual constructions of the experiential process are *defence mechanisms*, to the extent that they solidify into patterns of response that obscure a clear perception of one's situation and block an appropriate, effective and spontaneous involvement.
>
> (Levin 1981, p. 248)

The ideal therapist is someone who can approach the client in a mood expressed by the phrase 'emptily perfect and perfectly empty'. There is then no distortion of the client's experience, no twisting of it to suit some theory. This enables the client to move in the same direction: that is, towards more openness, less restrictiveness. Levin says:

> The therapist thus prepares a spacious clearing, a comfortable openness, for the other... to open out into... We might call this quality 'spaciousness': the gracious hospitable spaciousness we need to grow, to live, open up.
>
> (Levin 1981, pp. 254–66)

There is no statement here of any stages or levels of development, nor of any person or system by which change takes place. The emptiness in the therapist allows the client to move towards her or his own emptiness. But this, as Suzuki (1970) says:

> does not deny the world of multiplicities; mountains are there, the cherries are in full bloom, the moon shines most brightly in the autumnal night; but at the same time they are more than particularities, they appeal to us with a deeper meaning, they are understood in relation to what they are not.
>
> (Quoted in Wilber 1981a, p. 41)

These things do not make us unhappy unless we see them as denying us, frustrating us or unattainable by us. The constant thing in all unhappiness and distress is that it is 'I' who am unhappy or distressed, and all therapy is based on the premiss that it is the 'I' which needs to change, to be worked on. But from our new point of view we can now see this differently. As Wei Wu Wei put it:

> Why are you unhappy?
> Because 99.9 per cent

Of everything you think and
Of everything you do
Is for yourself –
And there isn't one.

(Quoted in Wilber 1981a, p. 53)

This is the equivalent in therapy terms of the statement I made once about
Harold Walsby's ultimate ideology, the ideology that enables us to describe
and account for all ideologies (Lamm 1984). I said that 'the ultimate
ideology must be understood and accepted by nobody', simply because
there is absolutely nothing to understand or accept. I went on to point out:

In fact, the metadynamic level [the ultimate ideology] can have no
expression at all, except the negative one of showing that all basic
assumptions are self-contradictory, each in its own distinct way... We
have seen through all other basic sets of assumptions, and we have
nothing to put in their place.

(Rowan, unpublished manuscript)

Similarly in therapy, as we reject false self after false self in the search for
the true self, we discover that there is no end to this process. When we
realize that, there is nowhere for unhappiness or suffering to belong to or
connect with. To put it in another way, you behold your original face on
all sides. Ken Wilber puts it like this:

The more I look for the absolute self, the more I realize that I can't find
it as an object. And the simple reason I can't find it as a particular object
is because it's *every* object! I can't feel it because it *is* everything felt.

(Wilber 1981a, p. 58)

This is the sort of empty paradoxical talk to which one is reduced when
one tries to talk about what cannot really be talked about. But we have
said enough to make it clear that from such a point of view the idea of
measuring therapy, or of specifying the outcomes of psychotherapy, is
absurd.

This is all very well, and very true. I could actually live up to it at times.
But when I tried to do this and only this in therapy, I found that I usually
could not do it. Always there seemed to be something needed first, some
more immediate aim which had to be carried out before we could get on
to the real emptiness. This now seems to me the essential paradox of
psychotherapy; we can hardly ever do what is the best thing to do because
there is always something better to do first.

If we just do the real therapy, the ultimate therapy, we restrict ourselves
to the clients who are ready for that, and clients are hardly ever ready for

it. This is not in any way to blame the clients: it is merely to recognize that the process of development is long and slow. When I am the client, I am no better than many of my own clients.

It seems that both therapists and clients are equally adept at avoiding the real issue, and perhaps this is necessary. Maybe the periphery is just as important as the centre. Maybe to concentrate on the centre all the time is too pure, too obsessive, too rigid, too arrogant; but at least it seems worth knowing the difference between the centre and the periphery, the ultimate and the proximate.

Perhaps in the final analysis there are many levels of therapy, and we need to work on all of them at different times with different clients. If so, the sooner we know more about how many levels there are and how to work on each of them, the sooner we shall get out of empty arguments as to which level is best. Wilber (1986) has some marvellous ideas about this, which we examined in Chapter 6.

SPIRITUAL EMERGENCE

A very important issue which has come to prominence in recent years is the appreciation of the difficulties which can arise when people move into the transpersonal area. This is particularly difficult when people are suddenly exposed to spiritual experiences which they are not ready for. Christina and Stanislav Grof (1990) have outlined ten specific problems which can come out of such events.

1　Peak experiences. These can be so overwhelming for someone who has never been ecstatic before that there can be fears of going crazy. To be out of touch with ordinary reality, even for a short period of time, is for some people an impossibly worrying event. It is important at this point not to get into the hands of a psychiatrist or a mental hospital.

2　Kundalini energy awakening. Sometimes through yoga, body work or even quite spontaneously, the energy of the chakras can combine to give an overwhelming experience. Again this is worst for people who have no conception of such a thing, and who live in a social context which is unsympathetic to it. The whole body can be affected, and people can assume that they are epileptic or suffering from some physical disease. Emotional upsurges and sudden accesses to memories may occur. This is essentially a healing experience if it can be contained and lived through.

3　Near-death experiences. These are the experiences which are had when people are declared physically dead, and are then revived later.

Even an approximation to this, through an accident for example, can result in a full-blown near-death experience. This is normally a good experience, which can be very positive in the person's life. The difficulty may come from the people around at the time, who may be very worried by what the person says, and perhaps later for the person involved, in owning it and in talking about it.

4   Past-life memories. If a person has, for any reason, a vivid memory which appears to refer to a previous life, this may be very disturbing for the person, particularly if they do not believe in reincarnation. Often such memories have a life-or-death quality to them, which may make them hard to take, at the same time as they make them very meaningful. It seems best to take them seriously, as if they were the product of active imagination, and just work with them in quite an ordinary way. If this is done, they can be as healing as can be the working through of any other trauma.

5   Opening to life myth. Here the person seems to go on a journey to the centre, to the central meaning of life. But because it takes place on a mythic level, the whole process can be dramatic and overwhelming. The person may feel that they are at the centre of global or even cosmic events. Death and rebirth, masculine and feminine energies – these can be central concerns on a grand scale. There are here great dangers of inflation, and this state needs to be handled very carefully and with real understanding, so as not to fall into the error of assuming that it is a manic episode. It can be healing and very positive, if handled correctly.

A good example is given by Steven Hendlin, who helped the client through such a crisis:

> Robert presented as severely depressed with suicidal ideation, complaining of poor sleep and strong currents of energy through his body, especially in the head area... He reported many positive and negative emotional, perceptual and physical experiences, all of which were framed in a spiritual context...
>
> We met four times the first week with added phone contacts... The second week we met three times and continued three times weekly contact until the 33rd hour at which time we cut back to twice weekly... While supporting Robert's framing of issues within a spiritual context, I made it clear to him that I believed basic *psychological-developmental* issues had been neglected which were now causing great conflict and which needed attention... By the sixth hour he was feeling stronger and getting some sleep and by the 15th hour we began to experiment with cutting back his

medication, which he did after informing his psychiatrist... I could
relate to his search to find 'oneness' with God *and* I could see he
also was trying to become *one* with his father.

(Hendlin 1985, pp. 82–5)

The details are given at greater length in the original paper, but the
outcome was good.

Emma Bragdon (1990) makes the point that with these experiences,
they usually last no more than forty days. Interestingly enough, they
often last exactly forty days.

6 Shamanic crisis. This is an initiatory crisis often involving a visit to the
   underworld, where annihilation takes place, followed by a rebirth and
   perhaps an ascent to heaven. Power animals are often involved,
   sometimes in quite horrifying ways. But if the person can be encouraged to stay with the experience and work through it, it can be
   genuinely initiatory, taking the person to a new level of consciousness.

7 Psychic opening. This is the arrival of psychic powers of one kind or
   another, perhaps quite suddenly and surprisingly. All sorts of paranormal phenomena may be involved here, including poltergeist
   phenomena. Out-of-body experiences are quite common – apparent
   journeyings through space, leaving one's solid body behind. Loss of
   identity may be experienced, and this can be frightening, too. There
   may be experiences of synchronicity, which may be confused with
   delusions of reference. Dangers of inflation are great here, as the mental
   ego is all too ready to claim glory and money for faculties like
   clairvoyance and so forth.

8 Channelling. The arrival of spirit guides or discarnate entities offering
   to use one as a channel for communication can be very disconcerting.
   This can be a healing and transforming experience for the recipient,
   and other people may also feel benefited. The dangers of inflation are
   large here too.

9 UFO encounters. Contact with UFOs can be frightening and challenging, and such an experience often carries with it, as do many of
   these other experiences, the feeling that one cannot talk about this.
   One might be regarded as crazy, or at least as self-deluding. Yet such
   experiences can be genuinely illuminating for the person involved.
   They can partake of the nature of initiations. Again ego inflation may
   result, and has to be watched out for.

10 Possession. Here there is a sense that one has been taken over
   completely by an entity which may be good or evil. If it is voluntary,
   as in some religious rituals where the participant is supposed to be taken

over by a god or goddess, there is usually no problem. But if it is involuntary, and particularly if the entity seems to be evil, then it can be very frightening, both to the person and to those around at the time. But 'when the person is given an opportunity to confront and express the disturbing energy in a supportive and understanding setting, a profound spiritual experience often results, one that has an extraordinary healing and transformative potential' (Grof and Grof 1990, p. 99).

There are some very good hints on this from Lynn Breedlove, a psychic with much experience of possession:

> Trust the validity of your experience. Do not deny what you see, feel or hear may be true. Talk to someone you trust about your experience, someone who can accept the validity of possession... Almost anything can work. The most important thing is to believe it may work. It could be an exorcism by a Catholic priest, or a bath in salt water, a prayer to Mother Earth, and/or psychotherapy and centering exercises like meditation or martial arts.
>
> (Quoted in Bragdon 1990, p. 43)

The same hints could be applied to many of these spiritual experiences in one way or another.

There is now a worldwide network of therapists who are willing and able to handle such states, and this is something which all those involved in the transpersonal may be able to help with.

PSYCHOSIS

We have seen that spiritual emergence can be confused with psychosis, but what about psychosis itself? What are we to say about that? My own opinion is that all or most of us are psychotic, just as all or most of us are neurotic, but obviously some people are far worse affected than others, in terms of being able to lead a happy life. The great classic on the question of psychosis is of course John Weir Perry. Starting in the 1950s, he has made great contributions to our understanding of psychosis as a process of self-discovery. His first book (Perry 1953, rev. ed. 1987) has an introduction by Jung, who was fascinated by Perry's work. In the 1970s Perry opened a centre called Diabasis, where people could go through their psychotic episodes without medication, and this was written up in his second book (Perry 1974, repr. 1989). Unfortunately Diabasis no longer exists, due to the withdrawal of funding, but it taught us a great deal.

Someone who has been writing about the distinction between transpersonal or spiritual experiences and psychosis is David Lukoff. He says that if we ask some very simple questions we can distinguish very readily between pure psychotic experiences, pure mystical experiences, and three or four different mixtures of the two. He says: 'Because of its cross-cultural perspective, attention to unusual experiences and positive attitude towards altered states of consciousness (Grof 1985), transpersonal psychology can play an important role in re-visioning the psychopathology of manic psychosis' (Lukoff 1988, p. 136).

In an earlier paper in the same journal (Lukoff 1985) he shows that the questions we have to ask are these: (1) Does the person fall under any of the standard psychotic definitions as used by psychiatrists? If not, then there might still be some non-psychotic psychiatric diagnosis, and this would need to be looked at in the ordinary way. But if there is a psychiatric problem of any kind, we go on to the next question: (2) Is there an overlap with mystical experience, or with some other transpersonal crisis? If not, again there is no problem: the person can be referred for suitable treatment, which Lukoff argues is rarely hospitalization. But if there is, the next question is: (3) Is a positive outcome likely? If not, Lukoff suggests a new diagnostic category: 'Psychotic with Mystical Features', involving careful medical treatment including transpersonal psychotherapy. But if so, the next question is: (4) Is there a high risk or a low risk involved, of harm to self or others? If high risk, Lukoff suggests that diagnosis be deferred, and that hospitalization or placement in a crisis centre is indicated for 24-hour observation. But if the risk is low, he suggests another new diagnostic category: 'Mystical Experiences with Psychotic Features'. In this case hospitalization would be avoided, and transpersonal psychotherapy seen as the main form of treatment. This seems a great clarification of the field, and a much more sensible way of tackling these problems. So this is not only a useful area for therapists, it may be necessary if they are to be able to help individuals who are genuinely puzzled about their personal experience and what it means.

Lukoff's work makes it possible to escape from the romanticism of the saying which sounds so good but which I believe is quite misleading – 'The psychotic and the mystic are in the same sea; but the psychotic is drowning while the mystic is swimming.'

At this very moment Michael Jackson of the Alister Hardy Research Centre in Oxford is working on this area, but has so far not published anything. Some fascinating case histories are presented by John Nelson in his recent book (Nelson 1990) which tries to bridge the gap between psychiatry and the transpersonal.

All in all, this area is a fascinating one, which I feel sure will lead to some important changes in the way in which we think about and treat mental disturbances of one kind and another.

Chapter 10

Critiques of the transpersonal

It is time to look at some of the ways in which all that has been said so far in this book can be looked at as misguided nonsense. There is no shortage of such critiques.

BEHAVIOURISM AND MATERIALISM

Our culture today is generally materialist, so far as the educated leadership is concerned. It tells us that the mind is a function of the brain. And the mind includes everything that we have called spiritual or transpersonal. There is often some lip-service in our culture to the idea of a God, but little in the way of acknowledgement of spiritual experience. It can always be reinterpreted as some kind of illusion due to brain errors.

One of the classic nineteenth–century versions of this was to liken the mind or soul to the lap. The question 'What happens to the soul when we die?' becomes no more complicated than the question 'What happens to the lap when we stand up?'

We shall look in more detail at the question of the brain in a later section.

COGNITIVE PSYCHOLOGY AND COMPUTER ANALOGIES

More specific, though broadly similar, is the current explosion of cognitive science. The whole idea is to show that everything cognitive can be rendered in software and hardware. Now since cognition covers all types of thinking, previously thought to be the distinguishing mark of the human, there then appears to be no place for anything spiritual.

It is amusing to reflect how everything mental was relegated to the scrapheap by the original materialists and behaviourists, but as soon as it became possible to talk about software and hardware — as soon as some physical analogy could be found – it suddenly became respectable to talk about things mental again.

Perhaps the turning point came in the 1950s, when Norbert Wiener uttered the memorable phrase – 'Information is information, not matter or energy.' Before that, to suggest that there was anything which was not matter or energy, or some direct function of matter or energy, was very much taboo. But we obviously have to go further than this if we want to have a place for the transpersonal. What cognitive science does is simply to ignore the whole issue as if it did not exist.

NEUROPHYSIOLOGY AND THE BRAIN

Of course if you are going to deny that there is such a thing as spirituality, there has to be some explanation of how such ideas could emerge. It is here that neurophysiology comes in, with its promise of explaining how such things could happen.

The theory is that the mind is a function of the brain in general, and the cerebral cortex in particular. No brain, no mind. This is a simple equation, but it does not make sense. Ronnie Laing used to take pleasure in showing round a brain-scan, made on one of the latest machines, of a lecturer in mathematics in some Scottish university. The scan showed quite clearly and unambiguously that there was no brain to speak of at all. A sprinkling of cells around the periphery of the inner skull, but that was all. Yet this person was functioning quite normally, to the satisfaction of all concerned. This is a curiosity, but perhaps nothing more.

There are two classic objections, however, to the view that the mind is a function of the brain. One is that there is consciousness in the foetus before there is a brain to have that consciousness. This suggests that consciousness uses the brain, but cannot be identical with the brain. Wilhelm Reich was I think the first Western thinker to suggest that memories could be held in muscle tissue, and that if the muscles were stimulated, the memories would return in the form of body movements and the associated affect. More recent writers like Peerbolte, Mott, Laing, Lake, Emerson, Chamberlain and Farrant have extended this idea to other cells, and have written about cellular consciousness. So even within the borders of materialism there is room for argument about the way in which memories can be held without the brain having been well enough developed to register them. It is not uncommon, for example, for psychotherapists specializing in regression to find clients remembering abortion attempts which failed, at an early point in the pregnancy of their mothers. There is sometimes enough circumstantial detail for this to be checked, and when it is checked, the details do seem to be correct.

The other classic objection is the near–death experience. Many experiments have now been carried out (and there has even been a film called *Flatliners*) to show that people whose brains are not functioning at all can be having complicated and extensive experiences at the same time. There is now so much research on this, conducted by investigators in many different countries (Ring 1984), that it seems the basic point cannot be gainsaid. If the brain were the same as the mind this would be impossible.

FREUD AND THE AVOIDANCE OF THE OEDIPUS COMPLEX

A completely different critique of the transpersonal comes from the Freudian camp. Freud felt that all attempts to explore spirituality were simply motivated by a desire to avoid looking at more basic and important matters such as early experience and in particular the Oedipus complex. People would do anything, he felt, rather than face the unpleasant aspects of their own natures.

So he concentrated on the lower regions, so to speak, and left the higher regions alone. That was his considered choice. But the fact that he and his followers feel uncomfortable about these things does not mean that we have to reject them. No doubt it is true that many people try to avoid the truth about their own Oedipus complexes; but it is equally true that many people try to avoid the truth about their own superconscious.

JANOV AND THE AVOIDANCE OF PAIN

A very similar critique comes from Arthur Janov. In his books he consistently denies any value to spirituality, and regards any interest in it as an avoidance of primal pain.

His only understanding of spirituality is as a religious belief system, and he then says:

> One can imagine that there is someone watching over, that 'I am in his hands', that he will take care and help, etc... That is the function of belief systems; they manufacture a fulfilment that doesn't exist to balm the unconscious need. They attempt to normalize.
>
> (Janov 1990, p. 230)

And so he says that one of the functions of psychotherapy is to get rid of religious ideas – the cured patient simply does not need such things:

why not during the day? I am shocked to see an officer standing by my bunk, instead of an inmate ready to jump me. She grabs my arm to check the name on my plastic bracelet and tells me to get ready for a bus soon. I ask her what bus she's referring to and where she's taking me. She leaves without responding. Two hours later, a different C.O. comes in to take me to the booking area, where I had previously spent fourteen hours on that plastic chair. I see a long line of men already shackled, and I'm told to join the only female inmate on the opposite wall from men. A female officer puts handcuffs on me. When I complain about how tight they are, she tells me they're for the officer's safety and not for my comfort. She puts her finger inside the handcuff to show how much room there is. I tell her that my wrists are not circular and that the handcuffs are digging into my skin. Unfortunately for my wrists, she doesn't understand what circumference is.

———◦•◦•◦———

Another bus ride, not at all like the one from the day before. It's a smaller bus and there are fewer people. It's too dark to see anything, and everybody's sleepy. Hardly anyone speaks. Forty minutes later, it seems like we have reached our destination. The bus stops and the door opens. When I ask where I am and why I'm there, the officer says he doesn't know.

———◦•◦•◦———

It must be around four in the morning and I am alone in a cell with a cement bench. I manage to lay down in a fetal position on the bench and eventually fall asleep. A loud banging on the door causes me to jump up. An officer storms in and tells me I will see the judge now. I ask him what judge; I wasn't supposed to have court today. He says he doesn't know and yells at me to hurry up. I was sleeping on a cement bench just two seconds ago, not knowing why I was there, and now I'm supposed to talk to a judge?

I am led to a little room that looks like an office. There's a computer with a big screen, a printer, and a phone. I see the judge already on the screen, waiting.

"Good morning, your Honor," the officer says, and sits down.

And all of this takes place, I might emphasize, without any ideas being inculcated into him. He loses his religious ideas without one word about religion being discussed in his therapy.

(Janov 1977, p. 455)

So really one has to say that there is no discussion and no recognition of anything spiritual of any kind in Janov's thinking. Yet others working in the primal area find just the opposite. Michael Adzema has written well about this, saying:

Some long-term primallers with whom I have contact have talked of receiving love, helping, strength or bliss that seem to be coming from a place beyond the scope of their current physical existence, to be emanating from a 'higher power' of some sort. Their descriptions have many parallels to some descriptions of spiritual experience.

(Adzema 1985, p. 95)

Unless we regard Janov as infallible, we have to take seriously the experience of others working in the same field.

WASDELL AND THE AVOIDANCE OF THE BIRTH TRAUMA

Another similar critique comes from David Wasdell, a very acute and eminent British thinker. He holds that what people are trying to avoid is the real acknowledgement of the defences arising out of their early experiences, and particularly their experience of birth. One of these defences is to erect fantasies of rebirth, regeneration, ways of rising above these mundane unpleasantnesses.

NEHER AND SELF-DECEPTION

One of the most thorough examinations of this whole area is that of Andrew Neher, who questions a very wide gamut of experience. Like most of the people who explicitly question spirituality, he includes within his definition all sorts of occult practices.

Now right at the start, of course, we made a distinction between the transpersonal and the extrapersonal, between the spiritual and the paranormal. So we may ignore what Neher says about telepathy, faith healing, psychic surgery, out-of-body experiences and so forth. What does he say about transpersonal experience as we have outlined it in this book?

Firstly meditation. Neher wants to urge that many of the experiences found in meditative practice are nothing more than very ordinary and well-described psychological processes, such as habituation and inhibition. These can produce sensory withdrawal and hallucinations. The person may feel that they are levitating or having an out-of-body experience, but this is sheer illusion. I would not argue with this particularly.

Another common psychological process which can be set in motion by meditation is dishabituation. This means that objects which once looked familiar now look unfamiliar and fresh. Neher points out that this is a not too uncommon experience in daily life.

> Dishabituation can result from almost any change, almost any new, different or unexpected stimulus. Perhaps you can recall when a vacation, a new lover, a move to a new home, or even a change in the weather served to 'wake up' your senses and produce a feeling of 'aliveness'. Even illness, shock, pain and risky situations evidently are sometimes valued because of their dishabituation effects.
>
> (Neher 1980, p. 27)

This freshness of perception is sometimes so marked as to be ecstatic. I don't think this is a transpersonal experience as we have described such things, because there is very firmly an 'I' experiencing these things. We have not necessarily left the mental ego behind in what Neher is talking about.

Neher then talks about nonconceptual attention. Here the meditator is able to give up rational, conceptual thought, as well as worries and disturbing fantasies in general. I would regard this as a transpersonal experience proper, because to the extent that it is thoroughly done, it involves the giving up of any idea of self to relate to, and this is genuine subtle-stage material. So how do I react when Neher tells us that:

> Similar effects can be achieved, of course, in a wide range of endeavours – sports, hobbies, martial arts and so on – that require total attention and concentration.
>
> (Neher 1980, p. 28)

My response is that this is a very interesting fact, which has been referred to at some length by Gallwey (1974), Czikszentmihalyi (1975), Spino (1976), Murphy (1978) and Leonard (1977). What these people are saying is that there is an experience of 'flow' which can take place in sporting activities, mountain climbing, etc., which is a genuine subtle-stage experience where the self is radically questioned.

Secondly Neher talks about dreams and imagery. He seems to recognize many of the points we have made here about this, and does not try to dismiss them in any way, though he does not go into the whole question of imaginal space which we have seen is so important to understand.

Thirdly Neher discusses mystical experience. In this book the position I am taking up is that the transpersonal constitutes the foothills of mystical experience, and that the causal stage is the major source of true and deep mystical experiences, as experienced by the great historical mystics described in Underhill's classic. Neher does not dismiss mystical experiences, and ends his discussion by saying:

> Thus mystical experience can be more than a temporary respite from the cares and worries of our everyday lives. Sometimes, in revealing a whole new order of things, it profoundly transforms a life.
>
> (Neher 1980, p. 130)

That seems a good statement to me.

THE CHRISTIAN CRITIQUE

The Christian critique of the transpersonal comes from the other end, as it were, and says that by dwelling on symbolic and lower-level experiences, which it doubts very much are truly spiritual, it takes away the real concern which people need to feel for their own salvation. In other words, people are being offered a sort of substitute spirituality, which misleads them and turns them away from the truth.

What they are really saying, it seems to me, is that the transpersonal is centauric and subtle rather than causal. At the causal level they speak with authority: that is the heartland of Christianism at its best. There is a very useful list of things to watch out for from a causal point of view which has been laid out in recent years.

DANGERS OF THE SPIRITUAL PATH

The dangers of the spiritual path at this level are many and can be treated only summarily here. Among them are the following:

1 *Delusion.* Deluded people, most often without any kind of teacher or support group, believe their experience is causal mysticism when it is not. Ego inflation or lack of humility may be responsible.
2 *Hyperintrospection and self-consciousness.* The self-conscious person searches in the sanctuary of the soul, looking for kicks, trips, trouble and experiences, not self-oblivious delight in the Divine.

3   *Quietism.* The quietist becomes purely and totally passive in contrast to the intelligent action of the wisely receptive mystic, who responds to the Superactive Vitality within.

4   *Privation and pride.* Individualists are so caught up in their own mystical experience that they forget the larger world of people and events outside of themselves. They think they can do without a teacher or support group.

5   *Fakirism.* These fake causal mystics forget the love which inspires a constructive asceticism and are concerned with the destruction rather than the surrender of the body-person. They falsely believe that they must annihilate a nature which is evil or rebellious. There is also a psychological fakirism which blunts and dulls the spirit.

6   *Contempt for the world.* The fakir is also guilty of disdain for the world, which is falsely viewed as a contemptible obstacle. The true causal mystic, on the other hand, who possesses all in the All, loves the whole of creation.

7   *Attraction to psychophysical phenomena.* The somatic marvels which accompany subtle mystical experience do not express the essence of causal mysticism; they are only accidental and secondary and must be neither sought after nor clung to, should they occur. In general, these phenomena are neither purely subjective nor purely objective, but in principle there are three possible levels: (a) Pure subjectivity; here there is no real contact with any spiritual power; (b) A natural effect coming out of spiritual contact; (c) An effect caused by the spiritual contact itself. It is better to reject all three of these as being essentialy limited images.

8   *Fixation and fanaticism.* The fanatic forgets the end and multiplies the means. He hangs around the teacher long after the lesson has been given and is over. This means fixation at one stage of growth and prevents movement on to greater heights or deeper dimensions.

9   *Presumption.* The presumptuous 'mystic' does not fixate on a particular step like the fanatic does but instead skips them, being falsely preoccupied with the end without having become sufficiently and suitably disposed through the discipline of the growth process.

10   *Psychopathology.* Finally, mystics, because they remain in continuity with physical-biological-psychological life, are as susceptible as the rest of us to both ordinary neuroses and full-blown psychoses.

People assume that to be spiritually inclined is to transcend the neurotic traps of life, but this is not true.

(Adapted from William McNamara in Charles Tart (ed.) *Transpersonal Psychologies* [Routledge, London, 1975]. Refers to Wilber's *causal level* of development.)

CONCLUSION

What are we to make of these criticisms? There seems no way of proving them wrong, though we have found fault with some of them, but the weight of all the experience outlined in this book shows that there must be something here to be seriously considered, and not dismissed in any cavalier way.

Part V

The future

Chapter 11

The future of the transpersonal

It is time now to consider the possible directions for future development in this field. What are the ways in which the transpersonal might go in the next few years?

THE SPREADING OF THE TRANSPERSONAL

First of all it seems that the understanding and use of the transpersonal is going to grow. There are many signs of this, particularly in the number of books which are becoming available on different aspects of the matter. More informally, I find that one can talk about spiritual experiences much more readily than was the case even ten years ago. So it seems that at the very time when many other trends are going the other way, into more violence, more crime, more exploitation, there is a strong trend towards acknowledging that we have a spiritual side, a spiritual nature which needs to be taken care of.

One great problem, however, is that while on the one hand the number of good books and good workshops, etc., is increasing, on the other hand the number of bad books and bad workshops is also increasing. And much of the bad stuff seems to be associated with the term 'New Age'. It seems to be one of the marks of the New Age that it is undiscriminating. Everything might be true, everything might be worth pursuing, who is to say what is valid and what is invalid? And this leads to the mixing up of the excellent with the dreadful in such a way as to put off the ordinary sincere enquirer.

If one is tactless enough to remark that Castañada is a liar (Don Juan was not a Yaqui Indian, if indeed he existed at all, and many of the events described could not have happened where and when they are said to have happened), that the Senoi of Malaya never had a system of telling their dreams and controlling their dreams, that Lynn Andrews' work is faked, that Shirley Maclaine recounts many events which never happened, that Hyemenyosts Storm is not presenting authentic Native American traditions at all, that the story of the hundredth monkey never happened in the miraculous way described, that ordinary physics is quite enough to account for people walking on fire and not being burned, that the psychic surgeons of the Philippines are excellent conjurors, the average New Age person reacts by simply not wanting to talk to you any more – you have the wrong attitude and probably the wrong vibrations.

Yet in this area, as in every other, it is important to be discriminating. Let us take as an example the phenomenon of channelling. Channelling is popular nowadays, and some channellers are much in demand for the deep insights which they get from their sources. The idea is that a channeller is somehow in touch with a source, a being of some kind who has access to much wider and deeper knowledge than the person does themselves. The best-known channeller is Jane Roberts, who channelled until 1984 a 'fifth dimensional entity' called Seth. Seth wrote a number of books through her, dictating them in a voice which is unlike the voice of Jane Roberts herself. Some of these are genuinely impressive and contain material which is well worthy of attention. Other famous channelled entities include Lazaris, Ramtha, John, Michael, Ashtar, Spectra, Koot Hoomi, Raphael, Mentor, Emmanuel, Hilarion, Maitreya, Ramala and many others. What are we to make of this? Jon Klimo, who has written the best book I know on this phenomenon, says that more than 80 per cent of the material received comes straight from the channeller's unconscious, or imagination, and there is no particular reason to give that part of it any more importance than that.

But some of it comes, he suggests, from the person's higher self, or what we have been calling the subtle self, or the deep self.

> From this perspective, channelling one's higher Self is not so much a case of self-transcendence as of expanded self-awareness. The greater Self, which is separately conscious of that lesser self as part of it, seems to lend some of its own consciousness to the consciousness of the less-aware component. Furthermore, the awareness of the higher Self is said to be more connected to and in communication with other levels of reality and with ultimate truth than is the lower self.
>
> (Klimo 1988, p. 170)

This now seems very much in line with the view taken in the present work, that the superconscious is a very helpful part of our being, and if taken seriously, has much to offer. It is genuinely spiritual, and genuinely ours, at one and the same time. We can all tune in to it at various times: it is just that the channeller makes a speciality of doing this.

Judith Skutch, who is well known as the publisher of *A course in miracles* (written by Helen Schucman as a channel), which has been one of the most popular books in this area, says this:

> To me channelling is the receptivity of the particular person to suspend judgement and willingly allow the Self that knows more, that is one with the eternal and limitless knowledge, to give its message in whatever form is applicable.
>
> (Skutch 1986)

This does seem, then, to be an important part of the truth. We have seen all through this book that the subtle self does not have the same sense of boundaries as the centaur self or the mental ego, and that therefore the distinction between what is us and what is not us becomes harder to keep neatly drawn.

> Some take the perspective that, rather than channelling a separate group being, the channel (and indeed each of us) is by nature part of such a group being. The individual then channels a hitherto unknown alter personality of his or her larger subsuming self.
>
> (Klimo 1988, p. 176)

This is certainly a possibility worth thinking about, and quite consistent with the view taken here. In the end, Klimo quotes the view of Alice Bailey that 2 per cent of the material comes from masters to their disciples, 5 per cent is from more advanced disciples in training on the inner planes, 8 per cent is from the channels' own higher Selves or souls, and some 85 per cent is from the personal subconscious of the channels. But in any case it is important, say all the best authorities, to be just as discriminating in relation to channelled communications as one is toward any other source of information. Test it, check it, use it if it fits.

It is this discrimination which is so important in the field of the transpersonal, and it is this discrimination which we have been trying to pay attention to throughout this book.

RELATIONSHIP WITH HUMANISTIC PSYCHOLOGY

As this spreading occurs, it will be more and more obvious that there is a boundary question with humanistic psychology. And I think it will become more and more clear that there is a spectrum of things here, rather than just one or two. The exact boundaries may change depending on the purpose involved and the actual practice of the people concerned.

One useful distinction we can make is between realist and idealist philosophies, which enables us to look at these questions in a new way. On the realist side we might say that the person would tend to think that the question of evil should be given a rather high priority; from this point of view evil is a very real force in the world. From this standpoint it seems that people are constantly underrating the extent and brutality of evil, and that consequently they end up caught in evil by their very denial of its pervasiveness. A degenerate form of this attitude is the cynic, who denies that there is any real good anywhere, and all we have is a variety of evils.

Distinct from this is the idealist position, which assigns a lesser import-ance to the question of evil. From this position it seems that although evil may occasionally play an important role in human affairs, it is subordinate to an overall good, which ultimately has already overcome it. From this standpoint it appears that evil is not an actual ontological presence with equal power, but rather something temporary which is always in principle overcome by good. This also has a degenerate form, which says that evil is merely the absence of light, an absence that is ended with higher growth. This is the New Age position which can very easily result in what the Americans call the flake or goof – the person who speaks very high-minded stuff but is not earthed in reality.

If we make this distinction between realist and idealist, this makes it possible to see that it operates within the humanistic camp, and also within the transpersonal camp. In both disciplines there are great names who fall into these categories. Wilber (1989) suggests that they come out in the way suggested in Figure 11.1.

We just need to be sure what the other headings mean. In this particular context, Humanistic means being primarily interested in the human being, soul or psyche, whereas Transpersonal means being primarily interested in the human soul and divine spirit (psyche and pneuma). There are then three headings we will need for the humanistic group, and two headings for the transpersonal group.

The Atheist group, found among the Humanistic people but not among the Transpersonal people, say that there is no divine spirit, whether supposedly immanent or transcendent. Such people are sceptical about many of the claims of the Transpersonal group, and even about those of many of their own colleagues in the Humanistic group.

The Theists hold that the human soul and the divine spirit exist and may commune with each other, but they are ultimately separate ontologi-cal entities. Each has its own nature and its own destiny, and is studied in

| | Realist | | | | | Idealist | | | | |
| | Humanistic | | | Transpersonal | | Humanistic | | | Transpersonal | |
Atheist	Theist	Mystical	Theist	Mystical	Atheist	Theist	Mystical	Theist	Mystical
Sartre	May	Tao		Wilber	Perls	Rogers		St John of the Cross	Later Maslow
Mahrer	Tillich	Zen		Jung					Shankara
Feuerbach	Marcel	James						Ramanuja	Eckhart
		Nietzsche							

Figure 11.1 Wilber's Realist/Idealist chart.

psychology and in spiritual studies respectively. The relationship is important, but it is a relationship and not an identity.

The Mystics hold that at the summit of human growth, there exists a supreme identity of soul and spirit. There is a oneness which at that point becomes visible and evident.

I think this is a very interesting set of distinctions, and that in particular there has been very little discussion of the Realist and Idealist division. But Wilber has made out a good case for saying that these writers do mostly seem to go for one or the other.

What this figure does is to say that within the humanistic camp there are six divisions, and that eminent writers within it may fall into any one of the six. Of course one could quarrel endlessly about exactly who falls into which division, or whether some of the divisions really make sense: for example, is there really room for the 'Humanistic Mystical' division? Most of the occupants of this division look a bit strange. Yet it could be argued that Ronnie Laing did come into the 'Humanistic Mystical Realist' bracket. I don't know what he would have thought about this suggestion. I would put myself now into the 'Transpersonal Mystical Idealist' bracket more than anywhere else, but it seems hubris indeed to put myself into the same bracket as Eckhart and Shankara!

Evil is of course something which inevitably comes up from time to time in the experience of all psychotherapists and counsellors.

THE QUESTION OF EVIL

Charles Hampden-Turner has a useful contribution to make on the question of evil. He sees it as the opposite of good, and therefore subject to the general law of opposites, which is that any opposite taken to the extreme becomes distorted and harmful.

> Evil is unreconciled divisive urges split from direction, action split from emotion, spirit from instinct, I from the other, and repression itself.
> (Hampden-Turner 1981, p. 126)

He goes on to urge that the creative energies of human dialogue must perpetually wrestle with the contradictions of our existence, rather than avoiding them. Good and evil, despair and hope, the power of destruction and the power of rebirth dwell side by side. We need a divine force that penetrates the demonic in life, not one that hovers above it.

This is to say that evil is not so much evil as other – an other which has become detached from its complement, the complement which would redeem it. But since this overcoming of difference is the engine of all real change and development, evil is necessary and desirable. How could I change, and proclaim thereby the power of Good, without being evil? My evil is precious – if it were not there, I would have to invent it. In fact, I am inventing it at every moment. An unwritten book is evil, because it lacks the good of existence. Equally a written book is evil, because it only states a partial truth. The best I can do is to produce interesting evil, fruitful evil, evil which is prepared to meet and deal with its opposite.

This is intellectual flimflam, unless I can feel it in my body. To talk about being evil is one thing, to fully experience it can be very uncomfortable, as if I hadn't worked it out at a body level at all. That is where a companion, a therapist, a group can be very useful, to enable that genuine and thorough working through to take place.

When faced with deep questions like this, I often find that Hegel has something to say which helps. In his lectures on the philosophy of religion, he starts off by agreeing with us:

> In the abstraction of finitude and infinitude – in that general opposition – the finite, as such, is reputed to be evil. That separation which is originally inherent in man has to be annulled... the evil element is the aspect of separation and estrangement, and this estrangement is to be negated... in worship a man creates this assurance for himself, and lays hold upon the potentially completed reconciliation. It is, however, already perfected in and through God, and it is this divine reality which man is to take to himself as his own.
>
> (Hegel 1974, Vol. 1, p. 244)

What Hegel is saying here is that the opposition can be redeemed, that the divine can overcome the evil which has come into being. If we renounce, give up the separation from the complement, we can attain peace. But we cannot do it, as some of the New Age people would like to say, by holding to the Light, and renouncing the Darkness. This is the one-sided resolution to have only half of the matter, and to give up the other half – but this, we have now seen, is exactly what evil is. Light needs darkness, darkness needs light; each without the other is nonsensical:

> Light is an infinite expansion, it is as rapid as Thought; but in order that its manifestation be real, it must strike upon something that is dark. Nothing is made manifest by pure Light; only in this Other does definite manifestation make its appearance, and with this, Good appears in opposition to Evil.
>
> (Hegel 1974, Vol. 2, p. 76)

So good needs evil, and evil needs good. They are related, says Hegel, in our own subjectivity. It has often been remarked that psychotherapy is not objectivity, but a disciplined subjectivity. What Hegel is saying is that this subjectivity in itself can reconcile good and evil, and create something which goes beyond this simple opposition.

> Subjectivity is this negativity which relates itself to itself, and the negative is no longer outside of the Good, but rather it must be contained, posited in the affirmative relation to self, and this is, in fact, no longer the Evil. Therefore the negative, Evil, must now no longer exist outside of the Good. It is just the essential nature of Good to be Evil, whereby of course Evil no longer remains Evil, but as Evil relating itself to itself, annuls its evil character and constitutes itself into Good. Good is that negative relation to itself as its other by which it posits Evil, just as the latter is the movement which posits its negation as negative, that is to say, which annuls it. This double movement is subjectivity.
>
> (Hegel 1974, Vol. 2, p. 90)

This would be difficult to understand if we did not remember the way psychotherapy works. It works, if it works at all, by removing the repression from repressed material. In other words, it demonstrates that something which was rejected as evil does in fact contain truth and goodness. Alvin Mahrer (1989a) perhaps puts it better than anyone when he says that what is hated and feared within us has to be totally owned and owned up to if we are to be whole. The evil, or the seeming evil, has to be taken as our own before it can be transformed. We cannot control what we do not own. And Hegel chimes in at this point with a devastating point about the whole business of human potential, which is so important to us as therapists:

> To say that Man is by nature good amounts substantially to saying that he is potentially Spirit, rationality, that he has been created in the image of God; God is the Good, and Man as Spirit is the reflection of God, he is the good potentially... But when that is said everything is not said; it is just in this potentiality that the element of one-sidedness lies. Man is good potentially, i.e., he is good only in an inward way, good so far as his notion or conception is concerned, and for this very reason not good so far as his actual nature is concerned... It is just in the very fact that Man is only potentially good that the defect of his nature lies.
>
> (Hegel 1974, Vol. 3, p. 46)

These are hard words, but true. We never do become all that we have it within us to be. There are always areas left which have not been worked on, have not been worked out, and which therefore still control us and make us act in compulsive ways. We still give offence when we did not mean to, or let ourselves down when we did not mean to. It is never enough to say: 'Well, I worked on that, and went through immense pain to do so, I deserve some credit.' That is not the way it works. The way it works is to see that it is only the process of overcoming evil, separation, that is good, not the results or the achievements of that process. Hillman put it brilliantly in his statement – 'Symptoms are the gateway to soul.' We need our symptoms, we need our complexes, they are the motor of our goodness. This is immensely paradoxical, as Hegel goes on to say:

> It is therefore not the case that reflection stands in an external relation to evil, but, on the contrary, reflection itself is evil... Spirit is free, and freedom has within itself the essential element of the disunion referred to. It is in this disunion that independent being or Being-for-self originates, and it is in it that evil has its seat; here is the source of the evil, but here also is the point which is the ultimate source of reconciliation. It is at once what produces the disease, and the source of health.
>
> (Hegel 1974, Vol. 3, p. 53)

So when we say, as many of us do, and it has become a cliché by now – 'Trust the process' – we are saying something profoundly important. The process works with disunion, with separation, with what Mahrer (1989a) calls 'disintegrative relationships' – and without these would fall to the ground. Good emerges from evil, and it is this continual or repeated emergence which is the only real key to goodness. And so we are enabled to see that nothing we have done to ourselves or to others is irredeemable. Ordinary thinking, which we have so often to combat as therapists, believes and takes for granted that what is done is done, that we cannot go back into the past and change anything. What we have continually to urge and to demonstrate is that change is possible after all. And Hegel tells us why:

> The characteristic idea in the region of finitude is that each remains what he is; if he has done evil, he is evil; evil is in him as representing this quality. But already in the sphere of morality, and still more in that of religion, Spirit is known to be free, to be affirmative in itself, so that the element of limit in which it gets the length of evil is a nullity for the infinitude of Spirit; Spirit can make what has happened as if it had not happened; the action certainly remains in the memory, but Spirit puts it away.
>
> (Hegel 1974, Vol. 3, p. 96)

This is the answer to those who plague us with the question – 'What happens if the client who comes to you is just evil?' What we are saying all the time is that in our therapeutic context evil is something which seems.

It seems one way, but that is because it has been separated, isolated, denied, hated and feared. If we can work with it, get to know it, see it in all its reality and its ramifications, it can transform into a good form which is full of energy and delight. As Hegel puts in his old-fashioned but supremely accurate language:

> The contradiction is already implicitly solved; evil is known as something which in the Spirit is virtually and absolutely overcome, and in virtue of the fact of its being thus overcome the subject has only to make its will good, and evil, the evil action, disappears.
>
> (Hegel 1974, Vol. 3, p. 130)

So when we are working in psychotherapy, we are all the time working in a spiritual realm where good and evil contend. We do not have to step outside it to deal with such questions: they are implicit in all that we do.

RELATIONSHIP WITH RELIGIONS

If the transpersonal relates to psychology at one end, so to speak, it relates to religion at the other. Here again there are boundary problems to be settled.

Again Wilber can help us. He suggests that religion, too, can be seen as on different levels. He suggests that between the levels of the lower subtle and the higher subtle we get the gods and goddesses of polytheism. They are of the nature of archetypal deity-forms who can be invoked as if from outside and evoked as if from inside. Their deity is often believed to be immanent – that is, to be found in everything, rather than above everything.

Between the levels of the higher subtle and the causal we get the monotheistic gods, who again can be invoked or evoked, but who are more often believed to be transcendent and quite beyond the human. Recent thinking by Matthew Fox and others has of course thrown some doubt on this, but it is still the majority opinion. So God the Father, Allah, Jahweh would all come in here.

Between the levels of the causal and the ultimate we get the idea of the deity as being the Void, the Abyss, the Depth and so forth, beyond any kind of imagination or belief (Wilber 1981b, p. 259).

Well, this puts the various religions in their places, but can we go along with this? My own doubts concern the fact that there appears no place in this account for deity as process, whether in the form of the Holy Trinity of Christianism, which is seen as a perpetual interpenetrating dance (the perichoresis of the hypostases in theology, see Moltmann 1981, pp. 174–5);

whether in the form of the everlasting Tao which is a continual process of becoming (Chen 1989, p. 52); whether in the form of Goddess the Verb (Be-ing) according to Mary Daly (1984); or in some other way. There seems more emphasis in Wilber on substance and unity, even though he tries to say that what he is talking about is not unity, but nonduality.

What seems clear in all this, however, is that if we say that for transpersonal psychotherapy and counselling we do not have to be interested in anything beyond the subtle, we are also saying that we do not have to be interested in religion as such, certainly not in the monotheistic religions which are most easily available in our culture. As individuals we may of course be very interested in such things, but as therapists it is not part of our special field.

CONCLUSION

Steven Hendlin has argued that the best attitude for the transpersonal psychotherapist is 'don't know'. He quotes a Korean Zen master as offering a breathing meditation in which one breathes in for three counts and silently repeats the phrase 'clear mind' and then exhales in seven counts to the phrase 'don't know'. He makes the contemplation of 'don't know' the foundation of his practice and teaching.

> The 'don't know' attitude, based on the realization of impermanence, calls for a faith in the unknown, a faith in... the 'wisdom of insecurity'... Paradox is another form of 'don't know', in that we call something a 'paradox' when we thought we knew and then are thrown back to the insecure 'don't know' shrug of our shoulders when something turns out to be self-contradictory... *Paradox is just 'don't know' in drag.* Our task is to understand that the one who questions is not different from the 'who knows?' question itself. Our lives are the substance and answer to this question. But, I might be wrong. *You never know for sure.*
>
> (Hendlin 1984, p. 12)

Perhaps, with the transpersonal, it is always best to admit in the end that I don't know.

Bibliography

Aaronson, B. and Osmond, H. (1970) *Psychedelics*, Hogarth Press, London.

Abbott, F. (1987) *New men, new minds*, Crossing Press, Freedom.

Achilles Heel can be contacted at 48 Grove Ave, London N10.

Adzema, M. (1985) 'A primal perspective on spirituality', *Journal of Humanistic Psychology*, 25/3, pp. 83–116.

Anthony, R., Ecker, B. and Wilber, K. (eds) (1987) *Spiritual choices*, Paragon House, New York.

Assagioli R. (1967) *Jung and psychosynthesis*, Psychosynthesis Research Foundation, New York.

—— (1975) *Psychosynthesis*, Turnstone Press, Wellingborough.

—— (1991) *Transpersonal development*, Crucible, London.

Avalon, A. (1978) *Shakti and Shakta*, Dover, New York.

Balint, M. (1968) *The basic fault*, Tavistock, London.

Blanck, G. and Blanck, R. (1974) *Ego psychology: Theory and practice*, Columbia University Press, New York.

—— (1979) *Ego psychology II: Psychoanalytic developmental psychology*, Columbia University Press, New York.

Bly, R. (1990) *Iron John: A book about men*, Addison-Wesley, Reading.

Boadella D. (1987) *Lifestreams*, Routledge, London.

Bolen, J.S. (1984) *Goddesses in everywoman: A new psychology of women*, Harper Colophon, New York.

—— (1989) *Gods in everyman: A new psychology of men's lives and loves*, Harper & Row, San Francisco.

Boorstein, S. (1980a) 'Psychotherapy and the transpersonal quest', in S. Boorstein (ed.) *Transpersonal psychotherapy*, Science & Behavior, Palo Alto.

—— (ed.) (1980) *Transpersonal psychotherapy*, Science & Behavior, Palo Alto.

Boss, M. (1963) *Psychoanalysis and daseinanalysis*, Basic Books, New York.

Bower, T. (1977) *A primer of infant development*, W.H. Freeman, San Francisco.

Bradley, B. (1989) *Visions of infancy*, Polity Press, Cambridge.

Bragdon, E. (1990) *The call of spiritual emergency: From personal crisis to personal transformation*, Harper & Row, San Francisco.

Bremner, G. (1988) *Infancy*, Basil Blackwell, Oxford.

Brookes, C. (1980) 'A Jungian view of transpersonal events in psychotherapy', in S. Boorstein (ed.) *Transpersonal psychotherapy*, Science & Behavior, Palo Alto.

Bruner, J. (1960) 'Myth and identity', in H.A. Murray (ed.) *Myth and mythmaking*, Beacon, Boston.

Bushnell, I.W.R. *et al.* (1989) 'Neonatal recognition of the mother's face', *British Journal of Developmental Psychology* 7, 3–15.

Carrington, P. (1980) 'Modern forms of meditation', in S. Boorstein (ed.) *Transpersonal psychotherapy*, Science & Behavior, Palo Alto.

Castillo, G. (1978) *Left-handed teaching*, Holt Rinehart Winston, New York.

Chamberlain, D. (1988) *Babies remember birth*, Ballantine Books, New York.

Chaplin J. (1988) *Feminist counselling in action*, Sage, London.

Chapman, J. (1988) *Tell me who you are*, Self-published, Hanslope.

Chatterjee, M. (1984) *Gandhi's religious thought*, Notre Dame University Press, Notre Dame.

Chen, E.M. (1989) *The Tao Te Ching: A new translation with commentary*, Paragon House, New York.

Chicago, J. (1979) *The Dinner Party: A symbol of our heritage*, Anchor Books, Garden City.

Clark, F.V. (1977) 'Transpersonal perspectives in psychotherapy', *Journal of Humanistic Psychology*, 17 (2), 69–81.

Clarkson, P. (1989) *Gestalt counselling in action*, Sage, London.

Clarkson, P. and Gilbert, M. (1990) 'Transactional analysis', in W. Dryden (ed.) *Individual therapy: A handbook*, Open University Press, Milton Keynes.

Cohen, J.M. and Phipps, J.-F. (1979) *The common experience*, Rider, London.

Colter, M.W. (1988) 'Sexual cross-identity as a fetal response to subliminal parent messages', in P.G. Fedor-Freybergh and M.L.V. Vogel (eds) *Prenatal and perinatal psychology and medicine*, Parthenon, Carnforth.

Connell, B. (1987) *Gender and power: Society, the person and sexual politics*, Polity Press, Cambridge.

Corbin, H. (1981) 'Preface – A letter', in D.L. Miller (ed.) *The new polytheism: Rebirth of the gods and goddesses*, Spring Publications, Dallas.

Coward, H. (1985) *Jung and Eastern thought*, SUNY Press, Albany.

Cox, R. (1987) 'The rich harvest of Abraham Maslow', in A. Maslow, *Motivation and personality* (3rd ed.), Harper & Row, New York.

Czikszentmihalyi, M. (1975) 'Play and intrinsic rewards', *Journal of Humanistic Psychology*, 15(3).

Dalal, F. (1988) 'Jung: A racist', *British Journal of Psychotherapy* 4 (3), 263–81.

Daly, M. (1984) *Pure lust: Elemental feminist philosophy*, The Women's Press, London.

Davis, J., Lockwood, L. and Wright, C. (1991) 'Reasons for not reporting peak experiences', *Journal of Humanistic Psychology*, 31 (1), 86–94.

Deikman, A. (1980) 'Sufism and psychiatry', in S. Boorstein (ed.) *Transpersonal psychotherapy*, Science & Behavior, Palo Alto.

Descamps, M.-A., Cazenave, M. and Filliozat, A.-M. (1990) *Les psychotherapies transpersonelles*, Editions Trismegiste, Lavaur.

Doblin, R. (1991) 'Pahnke's "Good Friday experiment": A long-term follow-up and methodological critique', *The Journal of Transpersonal Psychology*, 23 (1), 1–28.

Domhoff, G.W. (1985) *The mystique of dreams*, University of California Press, Berkeley.

Don, N. (1980) 'The story of Wendy: A case study in multi-modality therapy', in S. Boorstein (ed.) *Transpersonal psychotherapy*, Science & Behavior, Palo Alto.

Donaldson, M. (1978) *Children's minds*, Fontana/Open Books, Glasgow.

Dryden, W. and Ellis, A. (1986) 'Rational-Emotive Therapy (RET)', in Dryden, W. and Golden, W. (eds) *Cognitive-behavioural approaches to psychotherapy*, Harper & Row, London.

Dziurawiec, S. and Ellis, H.D. (1986) 'Neonates' attention to face-like stimuli: Goren, Sarty and Wu revisited', Paper presented at the Annual Conference of the Developmental Psychology Section of the British Psychological Society, Exeter.

Earley, J. (1990) *Inner journeys*, Samuel Weiser, York Beach.

Eisler, R. (1987) *The chalice and the blade*, Harper & Row, San Francisco.

Ellenberger, H. (1970) *The discovery of the unconscious*, Basic Books, New York.

Elliott, J. (1976) *The theory and practice of encounter group leadership*, Explorations Institute, Berkeley.

Emmons, M.L. (1978) *The inner source*, Impact, San Luis Obispo.

Enright, J. (1980) 'Change versus enlightenment', in S. Boorstein (ed.) *Transpersonal psychotherapy*, Science & Behavior, Palo Alto.

Erikson, E.H. (1963) *Childhood and society*, Penguin, Harmondsworth.

Ernst, S. and Goodison, L. (1981) *In our own hands*, The Women's Press, London.

Fabry, J. (1980) 'Use of the transpersonal in logotherapy', in S. Boorstein (ed.) *Transpersonal psychotherapy*, Science & Behavior, Palo Alto.

Faraday, A. (1976) *The dream game*, Harper & Row, New York.

—— (1980) *Dream power*, Berkeley, New York.

Farrar, J. and Farrar, S. (1984) *The witches' way: Principles, rituals and beliefs of modern witchcraft*, Robert Hale, London.

—— (1989) *The witches' god: Lord of the dance*, Robert Hale, London.

Fedor-Freybergh, P.G. and Vogel, M.L.V. (eds) (1988) *Prenatal and perinatal psychology and medicine*, Parthenon, Carnforth.

Fehmi, L. and Selzer, F. (1980) 'Biofeedback and attention training', in S. Boorstein (ed.) *Transpersonal psychotherapy*, Science & Behavior, Palo Alto.

Feinstein, D. and Krippner, S. (1988) *Personal mythology: The psychology of your evolving self*, Tarcher, Los Angeles.

Ferrucci, P. (1982) *What we may be*, Turnstone Press, Wellingborough.

Franklin, M. (1981) 'Play as the creation of imaginary situations: The role of language', in S. Wapner and B. Kaplan (eds) *Toward a holistic developmental psychology*, Lawrence Erlbaum, Hillsdale.

Fransella, F. and Dalton, P. (1990) *Personal construct counselling in action*, Sage, London.

Freud, W.E. (1988) 'The concept of cathexis and its usefulness for prenatal psychology', in P.G. Fedor-Freybergh and M.L.V. Vogel (eds) *Prenatal and Perinatal psychology and medicine*, Parthenon, Carnforth.

Gadon, E. (1989) *The once and future goddess: A symbol for our time*, Harper & Row, San Francisco.

Gale, D. (1990) *What is psychodrama? A personal and practical guide*, Gale Centre, Loughton.

Gallwey, W. (1974) *The inner game of tennis*, Jonathan Cape, London.

Garfield, P. (1976) *Creative dreaming*, Futura, London.

Gedo, J. (1981) *Advances in clinical psychoanalysis*, International Universities Press, New York.

Glouberman, D. (1989) *Life choices and life changes through imagework*, Mandala, London.

Goldberg, P. (1983) *The intuitive edge*, Tarcher, Los Angeles.

Goleman, D. (1977) *The varieties of the meditative experience*, Rider, London.

Goodison, L. (1990) *Moving heaven and earth: Sexuality, spirituality and social change*, The Women's Press, London.

Gordon-Brown, I. and Somers, B. (1988) 'Transpersonal psychotherapy', in J. Rowan and W. Dryden (eds) *Innovative therapy in Britain*, Open University Press, Milton Keynes.

Goren, C. *et al.* (1975) 'Visual following and pattern discrimination of face-like stimuli by newborn infants', *Pediatrics* 56, 544–9.

Graves, R. (1961) *The white goddess*, Faber & Faber, London.

Green, E.E. and Green, A.M. (1986) 'Biofeedback and states of consciousness', in B.B. Wolman and M. Ullman (eds) *Handbook of states of consciousness*, Van Nostrand Reinhold, New York.

Grof, C. and Grof, S. (1990) *The stormy search for the self: A guide to personal growth through transformational crisis*, Tarcher, Los Angeles.

Grof, S. (1979) *Realms of the human unconscious*, Souvenir Press, London.

—— (1985) *Beyond the brain: Birth, death and transcendence in psychotherapy*, SUNY Press, Albany.

—— (1988) *The adventure of self-discovery*, SUNY Press, Albany.

—— (1992) *The holotropic mind*, Harper, San Francisco.

Grof, S. and Grof, C. (eds) (1989) *Spiritual emergency: When personal transformation becomes a crisis*, Tarcher, Los Angeles.

Guest, H. (1989) 'The origins of transpersonal psychology', *British Journal of Psychotherapy*, 6 (1), 62–9.

Guntrip, H. (1961) *Personality structure and human interaction*, Hogarth Press, London.

Hall, N. (1980) *The moon and the virgin*, Harper & Row, New York.

Hammond, J., Hay, D., Moxon, J., Netto, B., Raban, K., Straugheir, G. and Williams, C. (1990) *New methods in RE teaching: An experiential approach*, Oliver & Boyd, Harlow.

Hampden-Turner, C. (1981) *Maps of the mind*, Mitchell Beazley, London.

Hannah, B. (1981) *Encounters with the soul*, Sigo Press, Boston.

Harding, E. (1965) *The I and the not-I*, Bollingen, Princeton.

Harman, W. and Rheingold, H. (1984) *Higher creativity*, Tarcher, Los Angeles.

Haronian, F. (1974) 'The repression of the sublime', *Synthesis*, 1 (1), 51–62.

Hassan, S. (1988) *Combatting cult mind control*, Park Street Press, Rochester.

Havens, R.A. (1982) 'Approaching cosmic consciousness via hypnosis', *Journal of Humanistic Psychology*, 22 (1), 105–16.

Hay, D. (1990) *Religious experience today: Studying the facts*, Mowbray, London.

Heery, M. (1989) 'Inner voice experiences: An exploratory study of thirty cases', *The Journal of Transpersonal Psychology*, 21 (1), 73–82.

Hegel, G.W.F. (1974) *Lectures on the philosophy of religion* (3 vols), Humanities Press, New York.

Hendlin, S.J. (1984) 'Buddhist psychology and beginner's mind', *Voices*, Winter 7–13.

—— (1985) 'The spiritual emergency patient: Concept and example', in (ed.) *Psychotherapy and the religiously committed patient*, Haworth Press.

Hendricks, G. and Fadiman, J. (eds) (1976) *Transpersonal education*, Prentice-Hall, Englewood Cliffs.

Hendricks, G. and Roberts, T.B. (1977) *The second centering book*, Prentice-Hall, Englewood Cliffs.

Hendricks, G. and Wills, R. (1975) *The centering book*, Prentice-Hall, Englewood Cliffs.

Heron J. (1974) *Practical methods in transpersonal psychology*, Human Potential Research Project, Guildford.

—— (1988) *Cosmic psychology*, Endymion Press, London.

Hillman J. (1975) *Re-visioning psychology*, Harper Colophon, New York.

—— (1981) 'Psychology: Monotheistic or Polytheistic?', in D.L. Miller (ed.) *The new polytheism: Rebirth of the gods and goddesses*, Spring Publications, Dallas.

—— (1985) *Anima*, Spring Publications, Dallas.

—— (1990) (ed. T. Moore) *The essential James Hillman*, Routledge, London.

Hillman, J. and Ventura, M. (1992) *We've had a hundred years of psychotherapy and the world's getting worse*, Harper, San Francisco.

Hinshelwood, R. (1989) *A dictionary of Kleinian thought*, Free Association Books, London.

Hoffer, E. (1952) *The true believer*, Secker & Warburg, London.

Horne, J. (1978) *Beyond mysticism*, Wilfred Laurier University Press, Waterloo.

Houston, J. (1982) *The possible human*, Tarcher, Los Angeles.

—— (1986) Interview with Jon Klimo.

—— (1987) *The search for the beloved: Journeys in sacred psychology*, Tarcher, Los Angeles.

Jacobi, J. (1962) *The psychology of C.G. Jung*, Routledge & Kegan Paul, London.

James, W. (1896) *The will to believe and other essays in popular philosophy*, Longmans Green, London.

—— (1901) *The varieties of religious experience*, Collins, London (1974 reprint).

—— (1969) 'Subjective effects of nitrous oxide', in C. Tart (ed.) *Altered states of consciousness*, Wiley, New York.

Janov, A. (1977) *Primal man*, Abacus, London.

—— (1990) *The new primal scream*, Abacus, London.

Johnson, R.A. (1986) *Inner work*, Harper & Row, San Francisco.

Jung, C.G. *Collected works* (esp. Vol. 16), Routledge & Kegan Paul, London.

—— (1973) (ed. G. Adler) *Letters*, Princeton University Press, Princeton.

Kapleau, P. (1967) *The three pillars of Zen*, Beacon, Boston.

Karle, H.W.A. and Boys, J.H. (1987) *Hypnotherapy: A practical handbook*, Free Association Books, London.

Keen, S. (1991) *Fire in the belly: On being a man*, Bantam, New York.

Kernberg, O. (1975) *Borderline conditions and pathological narcissism*, Jason Aronson, New York.

—— (1976) *Object relations theory and clinical psychoanalysis*, Jason Aronson, New York.

Keutzer, C.S. (1982) 'Physics and consciousness', *Journal of Humanistic Psychology* 22 (2), 74–90.

Klimo, J. (1988) *Channeling*, Aquarius, Wellingborough.

Koestenbaum, P. (1976) *Is there an answer to death?*, Prentice-Hall, New York.

Kohlberg, L. (1981) *Essays on moral development*, Vol. 1, Harper & Row, San Francisco.

Kohut, H. (1971) *The analysis of the self*, International Universities Press, New York.

Kopp, S. (1977) *Back to one*, Science & Behavior, Palo Alto.

Korb, M.P., Gorrell, J. and van de Riet, V. (1989) *Gestalt therapy: Practice and theory* (2nd ed.), Pergamon Press, New York.

Kramarae, C. and Treichler, P.A. (eds) (1985) *A feminist dictionary*, Pandora Press, London.

Krishna, G. (1972) *The secret of Yoga*, Turnstone, London.

Lake, F. (1980) *Constricted confusion*, Clinical Theology Association, Oxford.

Lamm, Z. (1984) 'Ideologies in a hierarchical order: A neglected theory', *Science and public policy* February, 40–6.

Lederer, W. (1968) *The fear of women*, Harcourt Brace Jovanovich, New York.

Leonard, G. (1977) *The ultimate athlete*, New York, Avon.

Leuner, H. (1984) *Guided affective imagery*, Thieme-Stratton, New York.

Levin, D.M. (1981) 'Approaches to psychotherapy: Freud, Jung and Tibetan Buddhism', in R.S. Valle and R. von Eckartsberg (eds) *The metaphors of consciousness*, Plenum, New York.

Lipsitt, L. (1969) 'Learning capacities of the human infant', in R.J. Robinson (ed.) *Brain and early behaviour*, Academic Press, London.

Loevinger, J. (1976) *Ego development*, Jossey-Bass, San Francisco.

Love, J. (1976) *The quantum gods*, Compton Russell, Tisbury.

Lowen, A. (1976) *Bioenergetics*, Coventure, London.

Lukoff, D. (1985) 'The diagnosis of mystical experiences with psychotic features', *The Journal of Transpersonal Psychology*, 17 (2), 155–81.

—— (1988) 'Transpersonal perspectives on manic psychosis: creative, visionary and mystical states', *Journal of Transpersonal Psychology*, 20 (2), 111–39.

Mahler, M. *et al.* (1975) *The psychological birth of the human infant*, Basic Books, New York.

Mahrer, A.R. (1983) *Experiential psychotherapy: basic practices*, Brunner/Mazel, New York.

—— (1989) *Experiencing*, University of Ottawa Press, Ottawa.

—— (1989a) *How to do experiential psychotherapy: A manual for practitioners*, University of Ottawa Press, Ottawa.

Manor, O. (1984) *Family work in action*, Tavistock, London.

Maslow, A.H. (1954) *Motivation and personality*, Harper & Bros, New York.

—— (1962) *Toward a psychology of being*, Van Nostrand, New York.

—— (1968) *Toward a psychology of being* (2nd ed.), Van Nostrand, New York.

—— (1970) *Religion, values and peak experiences*, Viking, New York.

—— (1973) *The farther reaches of human nature*, Penguin, Harmondsworth.

—— (1987) *Motivation and personality* (3rd ed.), Harper & Row, New York.

Masterson, J.F. and Rinsley, D.B. (1980) 'The borderline syndrome: The role of the mother in the genesis and psychic structure of the borderline personality', in R.F. Lax *et al.* (eds) *Rapprochement: The critical phase of separation-individuation*, Jason Aronson, New York.

Matthews, J. (ed.) (1991) *Choirs of the god*, Mandala, London.

May, R. (1977) *The meaning of anxiety* (rev. ed.), Norton, New York.

Miller, D.L. (1981) *The new polytheism: Rebirth of the gods and goddesses*, Spring Publications, Dallas.

Mindell, A. (1985) *Working with the dreaming body*, Routledge, London.

Mintz, E.E. (1983) *The psychic thread: Paranormal and transpersonal aspects of psychotherapy*, Human Sciences Press, New York.

Moacanin, R. (1986) *Jung's psychology and Tibetan Buddhism*, Wisdom Publications, London.

Moltmann, J. (1981) *The trinity and the kingdom of God*, SCM Press, London.

Monick, E. (1987) *Phallos: Sacred image of the masculine*, Inner City Books, Toronto.

—— (1991) *Castration and male rage: The phallic wound*, Inner City Books, Toronto.

Moore, R. and Gillette, D. (1990) *King, warrior, magician, lover*, Harper, San Francisco.

Moss, D.M. (1981) 'Transformation of self and world in Johannes Tauler's mysticism', in R.S. Valle and R. von Eckartsberg (eds) *The metaphors of consciousness*, Plenum Press, New York.

Murphy, G. and Ballou, R. (eds) (1960) *William James on psychical research*, Viking, New York.

Murphy, M. (1978) *The psychic side of sports*, Addison-Wesley, Reading.

Naranjo, C. and Ornstein, R.E. (1976) *On the psychology of meditation*, Penguin, Harmondsworth.

Neher, A. (1980) *The psychology of transcendence*, Prentice-Hall, Englewood Cliffs.

Nelson, J.E. (1990) *Madness or transcendence: a new understanding of the crisis and treatment of the mentally ill*, Tarcher, Los Angeles.

Neumann, E. (1963) *The great mother* (2nd ed.), Bollingen, Princeton.

Noble, V. (1991) *Shakti woman*, Harper, San Francisco.

Oden, T. (1972) 'The new pietism', *Journal of Humanistic Psychology*, 12(1).

Pahnke, W.E. (1971) 'Drugs and mysticism', in B. Aaronson and H. Osmond (eds) *Psychedelics: The uses and implications of hallucinogenic drugs*, Hogarth Press, London.

Palazzoli, M.S., Cecchin, G., Prata, G., and Boscolo, L. (1978) *Paradox and counterparadox*, Jason Aronson, New York.

Parfitt, W. (1990) *Walking through walls: Practical esoteric psychology*, Element Books, Shaftesbury.

Pearson, C. (1991) *Awakening the heroes within*, Meristem Publishing, College Park.

Perera, S.B. (1981) *Descent to the goddess*, Inner City Books, Toronto.

Perls, F.S. (1976) *The gestalt approach* and *Eyewitness to therapy*, Bantam Books, New York.

Permantgen, P. (1976) 'What would happen to the American psyche if, along with homerooms, flag saluting and IQ testing, schools had daily dream sharing?', in G. Hendricks and J. Fadiman (eds) *Transpersonal education*, Prentice-Hall, Englewood Cliffs.

Perry, J.W. (1987) *The self in psychotic process*, Spring, Dallas.

—— (1989) *The far side of madness*, Spring, Dallas.

Polster, E. and Polster, M. (1974) *Gestalt therapy integrated*, Vintage Books, New York.

Progoff, I. (1975) *At a journal workshop*, Dialogue House, New York.

Proskauer, M. (1977) 'The therapeutic value of certain breathing techniques', in C.A. Garfield (ed.) *Rediscovery of the body*, Dell, New York.

Rainwater, J. (1981) *You're in charge!*, Turnstone Press, Wellingborough.

Ram Dass, B. (1974) *The only dance there is*, Doubleday, New York.

Ridgway, R. (1987) *The unborn child*, Wildwood House, Aldershot.

Ring, K. (1984) *Heading toward omega*, William Morrow, New York.

Rockman, L. (1984) 'Ritual enactments in primal-encounter groups', *Aesthema* (4), 36–43.

Rogers, C.R. (1990) *A Rogers reader*, Constable, London.

Rowan, J. (undated) 'The ultimate ideology' (unpublished manuscript for The Walsby Society).

—— (1987) *The horned god: Feminism and men as wounding and healing*, Routledge, London.

—— (1988a) *Ordinary ecstasy* (2nd ed.), Routledge, London.

—— (1988b) 'Primal integration', in J. Rowan and W. Dryden (eds) *Innovative therapy in Britain*, Open University Press, Milton Keynes.

—— (1990) *Subpersonalities*, Routledge, London.

—— (1991) 'Encounter groups as a paradigm of integrative psychotherapy', *Journal of integrative and eclectic psychotherapy*, 10 (2), 150–63.

Rowan, J. and Dryden, W. (eds) (1988) *Innovative therapy in Britain*, Open University Press, Milton Keynes.

Rudhyar, D. (1975) *Occult preparations for a new age*, Quest, Wheaton.

—— (1983) *Rhythm of wholeness*, Theosophical Publishing House, Wheaton.

Samuels, A. (1985) *Jung and the post-Jungians*, Routledge, London.

—— (1989) *The plural psyche: Personality, morality and the father*, Routledge, London.

Sand, L. (1984) *Soul directed therapy*, Self-published, Sutton, Surrey.

Schutz, W. (1989) *Joy – 20 years later*, Ten Speed Press, Berkeley.

Segal, L. (1990) *Slow motion*, Virago, London.

Shaffer, J. and Galinsky, M.D. (1989) *Models of group therapy* (2nd ed.), Prentice-Hall, Englewood Cliffs.

Sheldrake, R. (1988) *The presence of the past: Morphic resonance and the habits of nature*, Random House, New York.

Shohet, R. (1985) *Dream sharing*, Turnstone, Wellingborough.

Shorr, J.E. (1983) *Psychotherapy through imagery*, Thieme-Stratton, New York.

Singer, J.L. (1974) *Imagery and daydream methods in psychotherapy and behaviour modification*, Academic Press, New York.

Singer, J. (1990) *Seeing through the visible world*, Unwin Hyman, London.

Sjöö, M. and Mor, B. (1987) *The great cosmic mother: Rediscovering the religion of the earth*, Harper & Row, San Francisco.

Skutch, J. (1986) Interview with Jon Klimo.

Slater, A. (1990) 'Infant development: The origins of competence', *The Psychologist* 3 (3), 109–13.

Small, J. (1982) *Transformers: The therapists of the future*, De Vorss, Marina del Ray.

Smith, H. (1976) *The forgotten truth*, Harper & Row, New York.

Southgate, J. (1983) *Inner and outer group dynamics*, Polytechnic of North London, London (also in *Self and Society*, November/December 1983, 299–325).

Spinelli, E. (1989) *The interpreted world: An introduction to phenomenological psychology*, Sage, London.

Spino, M. (1976) *Beyond jogging*, Celestial Arts, Berkeley.

Spretnak, C. (1982) *The politics of women's spirituality*, Anchor Books, Garden City.

Starhawk (1989) *Dreaming the dark: magic, sex and politics*, Beacon Press, Boston.

—— (1989) *The spiral dance* (2nd ed.), Harper & Row, San Francisco.

Stern, D. (1985) *The interpersonal world of the infant*, Basic Books, New York.

Stewart, B. (1991) *Celebrating the male mysteries*, Arcania, Bath.

Stone, H. and Winkelman, S. (1989) *Embracing our selves: The Voice Dialogue Manual*, New World Library, San Rafael.

Suzuki, R. (1970) *Zen mind, beginner's mind*, Weatherhill, New York.

Tanzer, D.W. (1967) *The psychology of pregnancy and childbirth: An investigation of natural childbirth*, Unpublished doctoral dissertation, Brandeis University.

Tart, C. (1973) 'Scientific foundations for the study of altered states of consciousness', *Journal of Transpersonal Psychology* 3, 93–124.

—— (1975a) *States of consciousness*, Dutton, New York.

—— (ed.) (1975b) *Transpersonal psychologies*, Routledge, London.

Trungpa, C. (1973) *Cutting through spiritual materialism*, Shambhala, Boulder.

Ullman, M. (1989) 'The experiential dream group', in M. Ullman and C. Limmer (eds) *The variety of dream experience*, Crucible, Wellingborough.

Underhill, E. (1961) *Mysticism*, Dutton, New York.

Valassis, B. (1989) Conference presentation, International Primal Association, Appel Farm.

Vaughan F. (1985) *The inward arc: Healing and wholeness in psychotherapy and spirituality*, New Science Library, Boston.

Verny, T. (1982) *The secret life of the unborn child*, Sphere, London.

von Eckartsberg, R. (1981) 'Maps of the mind: The cartography of consciousness', in R.S. Valle and R. von Eckartsberg (eds) *The metaphors of consciousness*, Plenum Press, New York.

Walkenstein, E. (1975) *Shrunk to fit*, Coventure, London.

Walker, B. (1983) *The woman's encyclopedia of myths and secrets*, Harper & Row, San Francisco.

Wallis, R. (1985) 'Betwixt therapy and salvation: The changing form of the human potential movement', in R.K. Jones (ed.) *Sickness and sectarianism*, Gower, Aldershot.

Walsh, R.N. and Vaughan, F. (1980) 'Beyond the ego: Toward transpersonal models of the person and psychotherapy', *Journal of Humanistic Psychology*, 20 (1), 5–31.

Warren-Clarke, L. and Matthews, K. (1990) *The way of Merlin: The male path in Wicca*, Prism Press, Bridport.

Wasdell D. (1990) *The roots of social insanity*, URCHIN, London.

Watkins, J. (1978) *The therapeutic self*, Human Sciences Press, New York.

Watkins M. (1976) *Waking dreams*, Harper Colophon, New York.

—— (1986) *Invisible guests*, The Analytic Press, Hillsdale.

Wehr, D. (1988) *Jung and feminism: Liberating archetypes*, Routledge, London.

Weishaar, M.E. and Beck, A. T. (1986) 'Cognitive therapy', in W. Dryden and W. Golden (eds) *Cognitive-behavioural approaches to psychotherapy*, Harper & Row, London.

Wertheimer, M. (1961) 'Psycho-motor coordination of auditory-visual space at birth', *Science*, 134, 1692.

West, S. (1975) *Psycho-calisthenics*, McDonnell-Winchester, New York.

White, J. (1979) *Kundalini, evolution and enlightenment*, Anchor, New York.

Whitmont, E. (1969) *The symbolic quest*, Princeton University Press, Princeton.

—— (1987) 'Archetypal and personal interaction in the clinical process', in N. Schwartz-Salant and M. Stein (eds) *Archetypal processes in psychotherapy*, Chiron, Wilmette.

Whitmore, D. (1991) *Psychosynthesis counselling in action*, Sage, London.

Wilber, K. (1977) *The spectrum of consciousness*, Quest, Wheaton.

—— (1980) *The atman project*, Quest, Wheaton.

—— (1981a) *No boundary*, Routledge, London.

—— (1981b) *Up from Eden*, Routledge, London.

—— (1982) 'Conversation', in K. Wilber (ed.) *The holographic paradigm and other paradoxes*, Shambhala, Boston.

—— (1983a) *A sociable god*, McGraw-Hill, New York.

—— (1983b) *Eye to eye*, Anchor Books, Garden City.

—— (1986) 'Treatment modalities', in K. Wilber, J. Engler and D. Brown (eds) *Transformations of consciousness*, New Science Library, Boston.

—— (1989) 'Two humanistic psychologies? A response', *Journal of Humanistic Psychology* 29 (2), 230–43.

—— (1991) *Grace and grit: spirituality and healing in the life and death of Treya Killam Wilber*, Shambhala, Boston.

Wilber, K., Engler, J., and Brown, D. (eds) (1986) *Transformations of consciousness*, New Science Library, Boston.

Winnicott, D.W. (1958) *Collected papers: from paediatrics to psychoanalysis*, Tavistock, London.

Wolman, B.B. (1986) 'Protoconscious and Psychopathology', in B.B. Wolman and M. Ullman (eds) *Handbook of states of consciousness*, Van Nostrand Reinhold, New York.

Wong, B.R. and McKeen, J. (1980) 'Transpersonal experience through body approaches', in S. Boorstein (ed.) *Transpersonal psychotherapy*, Science & Behavior, Palo Alto.

Woolger, J.B. and Woolger, R.J. (1990) *The goddess within*, Rider, London.

Woolger, R.J. (1990) *Other lives, other selves: A Jungian psychotherapist discovers past lives*, Crucible, Wellingborough.

Wren-Lewis, J. (1991) 'A reluctant mystic', *Self & Society*, 19 (2), 4–11.

Yalom, I. (1980) *Existential psychotherapy*, Basic Books, New York.

Zinker, J. (1978) *Creative process in gestalt therapy*, Vintage Books, New York.

Name index

Aaronson, B. 42
Abbot, F. 191
Adler, A. 98
Adzema, M. 210
Alderfer, C. 98, 102
Andrews, L. 217
Anthony, R. 9, 21
Assagioli, R. 19, 20, 40–2, 49, 69, 70,
  71, 98, 119, 122, 151, 161
Avalon, A. 189

Bachofen 186
Bailey, A. 219
Balint, M. 103, 123
Ballou, R. 32
Bateson, G. 115
Beck, A. T. 136
Blanck, G. 131, 134
Blanck, R. 131, 134
Bly, R. 186, 188, 190
Boadella, D. 127, 194, 195
Bolen, J. S. 39, 78, 145–6, 185, 190
Boorstein, S. 2, 146–7
Boss, M. 138
Bower, T. 104
Boys, J. H. 19
Bradley, B. 104
Bragdon, E. 103, 139, 140, 141, 204,
  205
Breedlove, L. 205
Bremner, G. 103
Briffault 186
Brookes, C. S. 77, 147–8
Broughton, J. 98
Bruner, J. 65

Buber, M. 98
Bucke, R. M. 48
Burney, C. 64
Bushnell, I. W. R. 104

Cade, M. 3
Carrington, P. 84
Castillo, G. 180
Chamberlain, D. 105, 208
Chaplin, J. 88, 90, 125, 198
Chapman, J. 148–9
Chatterjee, M. 13,
Chen, E. M. 227
Chicago, J. 184
Clark, F. V. 45, 89, 90, 92, 115
Clarkson, P. 55, 135, 138
Cohen, J. M. 7,
Colt, T. 64
Connell, B. 187
Corbin, H. 5, 163
Coward, H. 35
Cox, R. 49
Czikszentmihalyi, M. 211

Dalal, F. 36
Dalton, P. 136
Daly, M. 227
Davis, J. 22
Deikman, A. 84
Descamps, M. A. 10,
Desoille, R. 69, 70, 71
Doblin, R. 25
Domhoff, G. W. 174
Don, N. 76, 90
Donaldson, M. 134

Subject index

He points for me to sit in a chair next to him. Apparently, I am going to talk to the judge through some video-chat-thing. The judge asks me if I am ready for the hearing, and I say that I'm not because I didn't know I was going to have a hearing until I walked into this room. The judge says that happens sometimes, and reschedules the hearing for next month. The officer gets up, and the judge tells him the name of the next inmate to be brought in.

———————

A *month*. The judge said my next hearing won't be for a *month*. Now I regret saying that I wasn't ready for the hearing. Maybe it would've been fine without any preparation and without a lawyer? No, it wouldn't have. But how can I wait another month in jail? Another month away from my family; another month in this red uniform.

In this jail, a red uniform doesn't mean dangerous. It means immigrant. I am in jail for not being a citizen.

BAKING DAY

Mei Davis

M Y BROTHERS, ONLY FIVE AND SIX YEARS OLD, REMEMBER little of Mosul. They do not recall the crowded bazaars. They have no memory of the chockablock market stalls spilling their wares into the streets, heaving bags of pistachios and rice, a patchwork quilt of colorful spices that permeated every inhale. But I am seventeen years old. And I remember far too much.

"The dates, Mama."

"Good, good," she replies. "Put them in the cart."

We stroll down the grocery aisle, lean and tiled with linoleum, and wide enough for Yousif and Rami to run up and down in a game of tag. Instead of the discordant beauty of a hundred people haggling, I hear squeaky wheels and the distant refrains of Christmas classics wafting from hidden speakers.

"Yousif! Rami!" My mother's voice cuts through the quiet store, though the melodic cadence of her native Arabic softens the blow, and the boys toss back half-hearted apologies in English.

"Sorry, Mama!" An English unstrained by an Iraqi accent.

I only use English when I am forced to, which has been often since we first arrived in San Diego three years ago. We stepped off the plane with only our lives and the clothes on our backs, Rami in Mama's arms, Yousif in Papa's. I was grateful then.

I pull more items from the shelves. Flour. Sugar. The shelves are lined with bursts of green, red, and peppermint stripes. Yeast. No Chaldean Christmas would be complete without a day of baking our *klecha*, one of the few traditions that has been neither stolen nor abandoned. A fugitive smile slips onto my face at the thought of sweet, sticky filling, and soft, flaky dough. Nutmeg.

"Safia!" Mama rumbles. "You have your book report due soon?"

If my mother's Arabic is a *dabke* stomp dance, mine is a delicate ballet. "Yes."

Cardamom. Cinnamon.

"Why not invite Amanda over?" She suggests it in the same innocent tone as suggesting another helping of rice, but I don't miss her sidelong look. "She can help us bake the klecha." Fennel seed.

"I don't think she would like it."

Vanilla and walnuts. The bag of nuts crinkles in my hand. In Mosul, I would heft whole handfuls and sift them through my bare fingers into a paper sack, broken bits and rough edges scraping my skin. In Mosul, Asmaa would giggle her way over to my house to join in the baking, and we would devour our walnut klecha the minute they came out of the oven, ignoring my mother's hollow threats. "Slow down, girls, or we'll have none left to give to anyone!" Friends and family would gather into our small, overstuffed kitchen to bake klecha by the pound, more than enough to deliver to all the uncles, aunts, neighbors, friends, and church priests several times over.

"Why wouldn't she like it?" my mother asks.

"I just don't think she would like the klecha," I say. Amanda has never been to our home before.

"Then she can help herself to something else. We'll have plenty of options."

She throws chocolate chips into the cart, pink sprinkles and a plastic jar of green icing. Klecha boasts of a subdued sweetness, and our

baking day has evolved to incorporate two or three more sugary con-
fections to suit my brothers' Americanized taste buds. "Invite her,
Safia. What are you worried for? That she'll say no?"

The question hangs in the air as we move to the checkout line, then
through the automatic doors leading outside. My arms groan under
the weight of the grocery bags. The sun shines. Palm fronds sway, their
spiny trunks wrapped with green wires that will light up like a staircase
of stars once the sun sets.

The streets are free of rubble and strife. I know I should be grateful,
but in the open air of this city, this whole country, I hear nothing but
a mournful kind of hush, the bleak and steady hum of traffic; like
breathing in a dirge. Where are the sweet anthems descending from
the rooftops, church bells melding with the calls to prayer? And how
do I explain to my mother that my biggest fear is not that Amanda
will say no, but that she will say yes?

------◆◆◆◆------

I flip another exhausting page. I squint at the small, block lettering,
and tell myself I should love this book. How many volumes just like
it did I breeze through back in Mosul, consuming hundreds of words
by the hour? Asmaa was always at my side as we dreamed about all the
things we yearned to see but never thought we would, those precious
words living on in our imaginations long after we put the books back
on the shelf. My brain agonizes over these English words, piecing together the ones I don't understand with the ones that I do. I think of
all the things I left behind, clothes and jewelry and best friends. I'm
almost grateful when the doorbell rings.

"I'll get it, Mama." Hamlet will have to wait.

I stare at the doorknob for a moment, swallow once, and open
the door.

"Hey, Safia," Amanda says with a warm smile laced with braces.
She's so different from what I once knew—with her bouncing blonde
hair and bubblegum voice—yet in many ways not different enough. I
wave as her mother drives away, Amanda pokes a curious face through
the door. She notices my slippered feet and the rows of shoes lining
the wall.

AFTERMATH

"How's the book coming along?" she asks, quickly kicking off her flip-flops.

"Don't ask."

"That good?" She grins. "Maybe we can work on it when we're done baking…?"

"Klecha," I say, reminding her of the word.

Mama takes over the scene, striding forward with those hefty arms wide open. "Amanda!" She pares the engulfing embrace back to a version that she's learned doesn't make the average American squirm. "Please, please come inside."

"She's already inside, Mama," I say. The comment jumps out before I can contain it. Amanda giggles into her hands. I regret giving my mother a platform when she turns to Amanda, her hand on her hip.

"You see? You see what I have to put up with?"

"Oh, I know. She's like that all the time with the teachers at school, too," Amanda teases. My mother rounds on me, coiffed eyebrows raised.

"Really?" She taps her chin, looking at me as if we've just met. "Is that true, Safia?"

"Amanda's exaggerating, Mama, you know that."

"Oh really?" Amanda grins. Her face is angelic, the kind that never exaggerates. "I don't think that's what Mrs. Henkel from Honors Chemistry would say."

"And what would Mrs. Henkel say?" my mother asks. She puts an arm around Amanda's shoulders, and they laugh like old friends. The sound of their voices trails down the hallway as my mother points out the landmarks. I follow behind at a distance.

"Bathroom is there, on the right," Mama says. A Christmas tree crammed into a corner and littered sparsely with homemade decorations dominates the living room. "The boys picked it out. Biggest one in the lot. And we are so sorry for the mess. You know how boys can be."

Amanda shrugs. "I don't have any brothers."

"You can have mine," I say. Amanda giggles again. Mama lobs a look. Papa had scooped the boys into the car this morning to get them out of our hair. But they've left the living room looking like a warzone, and we're forced to carve a path to the kitchen through a minefield of

Legos. Regardless, Amanda appears to be impressed when my mother finishes the two-minute tour.

"You have a really nice home, Mrs. Azizi." She flashes a genuine smile. And the way my mother beams at her in return, a mixture of hope and delight, the glow of forging new alliances, severs me that much more from the past, sets me adrift in a sea of cluttered toys, the world I once knew bobbing further and further away.

• • • •

We can't afford one of those fancy standing mixers, so we gather around a large glass mixing bowl that sits like a lone crater on the pink-tiled counter.

"First thing," my mother says, "we make the dough."

"Okay," Amanda says, rubbing her hands together. "So what do we do first?"

My mother spits rapid-fire commands as Amanda and I scurry to keep up. "A tablespoon of yeast. A cup of warm water. Four cups of flour." In goes the butter and oil, my mother's untiring arms mixing and mixing, her lips on constant patrol. "Did Safia tell you about our klecha, Amanda? Traditional Iraqi cookie. We make them for Christmas—very good, very delicious. This recipe was the most famous in our neighborhood. Everyone asked for it. Everyone. But I never told them our secrets, did I, Safia?"

Normally I resist her invitations to sneak back into the past, when we would bake and chatter and go at it like twittering birds. But the yeasty smell of dough perfumed with spices, that fragrant promise of klecha, entices back some of my old humors.

"Never, Mama." I then lean into Amanda and my voice drops to a loud whisper. "Because no one ever really asked for it."

My mother protests loudly. The dough rises with our shared laughter.

"Next," Mama says, "the fillings."

I move to the stove and sautée the dates in a pan coated with melted butter. The air sizzles and crackles with sweetness. At the counter, my mother teaches Amanda the proper ratio of walnuts to spices. Aromas merge and mingle. By the time we finish preparing the fillings, the dough has doubled in size. Anticipation mounts as we grab great, springy handfuls. We wield our rolling pins across the counter till the dough is stretched into thin rectangles, over which we flatten our date filling from one edge to the other in a fine layer.

"It kinda looks like…" Amanda cocks her head and squints. "A pizza."

I can't help but laugh. "What kind of pizzas do *you* eat?" Her fresh eyes are like a new coat of paint on an ancient affair.

"I would eat a date pizza," she says soberly. "I really would." Then her face splits and we are both hunched over, shaking with laughter.

"We are not turning this into a pizza!" my mother declares with all her renowned drama.

She teaches Amanda how to roll the "date pizzas" into long snakes. "One hand on either end. And keep it even!" Then she grabs a sharp knife, swiftly cutting the rolled up pastry into inch thick pieces. Turned on their side they resemble little pinwheels of filling and dough. "Finished! Now lay them on the pan in four neat rows, like this."

We let Amanda do the honors of popping them into the oven. I sit next to her by the oven window to watch them rise and turn golden The two of us bask in the warmth, breathing in the smells as they accumulate, just as Asmaa and I used to do while the first batch baked. Back then, after wolfing most of them down, we would battle our lethargy with a walk through the city, swapping words as we kicked our feet over the Tigris.

"Do you think you'll ever see the ocean?" Asmaa asked me once. We had just finished a book about whales.

"No," I said with an overwrought sigh. "The only place I'll ever get to dunk my toes is in this muddy river."

Not long after, with the smoke and shouting thousands of miles away and the gentle Pacific waves lapping at my ankles, I thought of that precise moment. I thought of Asmaa standing alone on the banks of the confined and stately Tigris that has flowed through my city since antiquity, and I wondered if she would ever see the ocean.

I turn my eyes from the klecha to Amanda. She stares into the oven door with a look of wonder. I stare at her with a look of shame, because I know I should be grateful—for my escape, for my integration into this new and strange society, and for my newfound friendship.

Amanda is a friend who welcomed me on my first day of school and who has never left my side since. She's a friend who mirrors the one that came before, my friend to whom I waved goodbye from the back window of my car, watching her shrinking figure through a wall of tears.

"Safia?" For once my mother's voice sounds soft. "Safia, what's wrong?"

I stand up and wipe my eyes. They are both watching me. But how do I explain to my mother that nothing is wrong? Except that day by day I stand on the sidelines of my life, looking on as everything I once considered irreplaceable is slowly, gently being replaced. I have no answer. So when Mama lays a hand on my shoulder, I cover my face with a hand and run out of the room.

⸻ ❖ ⸻

I hear the creak of the door first, then the soft shuffle of my mother's slippered feet.

"Safia," she says. "Safia. Tell me what's wrong."

"Nothing," I say. I slip further into my bed covers, face hidden.

The bed shifts when she sits. "There was a time, once, when you used to cry for nothing. Sad songs, sad stories. Always a tear in the corner of your eye, I remember. When we left Iraq I wiped Yousif's tears, and Rami's. And even your father's. But your eyes have been dry since we came to this country. I often wonder what has happened to my dreamer, my crier."

"What does it matter to you? Our home is gone. Everything's gone, everyone's gone and you don't even care!"

"You think it does not bother me?" I peek my face out and see tears dripping from her chin, Her voice remains steady. "You think I never want to go back?" She runs her hand down my head, strokes my hair with distant eyes. "I remember—I remind myself that even if we went back, things would not be the same."

"I don't want to go back," I whisper.

"Then what do you want, Safia?"

I comb through my feelings. Through the snarls and tangles, sorrows and loss. "I want to keep a part of it." My whole face is wet when I sit up and look down at my hands, resting in my lap like an open book. "Here, in my palms. I want to be able to take a part of our old life out, hold it, remember it without—" I trail off. Without it being nowhere, and yet everywhere all at once, on every headline, every television screen. Without the last traces being daily scourged away by an unfamiliar culture. Without that terrible gnawing inside that I am growing a new life over the grave of the old.

But I do not know how to explain any of that. My eyes flow with a fresh wave of tears, and I think that maybe I never will. Mama puts her hands on each side of my face, but doesn't say a word. Her rare silence tells me there are things she cannot explain either, and for a moment—this moment—the roiling in my heart subsides.

"Who wipes away your tears, Mama?"

"You do. Your smiles do." She brushes my wet cheeks with her thumbs. "You smile so much when you are with Amanda."

"I know."

"She is waiting for us. She would like to help us finish baking. Will you come?"

I nod. My mother hands me a tissue and I mop my face. I climb out of bed and follow her back into the kitchen where we find Amanda, waiting for us with a pensive look.

"I'm sorry for running off, Amanda."

"Please don't be sorry," she says. I have to smile at her perfect measure of sweetness and tartness, a flavor reminiscent of not so long ago. She gestures to a new batch of klecha still warm on the baking sheet. "I kept moving them along. I hope you don't mind."

"Of course not," my mother says. She shoves us towards the baking trays. "Why don't you girls have some?"

A ruckus erupts at the doorway as Papa returns with the boys. Yousif and Rami tear through the house, clearing away any remaining awkwardness with loud English and louder laughter.

Amanda enthuses over her first taste of klecha. "Officially my new favorite thing!"

The boys pester Mama about when they can decorate sugar cookies. "Mama, we're *starving*!"

I pick up a klecha and take a bite. It's spicy and sweet—a buttery richness and a fragile crunch dissolve on my tongue. It's a complex combination of flavors, a taste of home in the palm of my hand. It's a morsel of comfort, and for that I am grateful.

We Used to Walk These Streets
Photograph by Matthew Barron

ASSIMILATION
Alison McBain

I grew to the sound
of misplaced esses
grandma's American voice
"I says," she said.

My daughters have
brown butter hair
lacking history
of Hiroshima,
desert camps in Utah.

Telling fairy tales to
wide-wondering
faces, fresh
and untethered
from our past

I raise my girls in a world
that looks like them.
I miss the sound
of misplaced esses.

SADRIYA DISTRICT, BAGHDAD

Tracy Davidson

After the blast…an eerie silence…
then the screaming starts.

Smoke clears enough for survivors,
with ringing ears and watering eyes,
to see what their local market has become.

A sea of red and grey — blood and debris
surrounding piles of bodies, parts of bodies,
hunks of burnt flesh. The stench unmistakeable.

Soldiers try to clear the way for ambulances.
Locals clamber over the carnage,
looking for loved ones.

A teenage boy calls for his mother
and sister, slipping and sliding
in the bloody remains of neighbours.

He finds his mother's shopping bag,
the one she made herself from scraps
of material cut up from old baby clothes.
Her hand still clutches it, her face gone.

His wail echoes across the city.

A young American soldier, not much older
than the boy, tries to offer comfort.

The boy turns on him, screams his rage
and frustration, wanting someone
to take it out on. Someone to blame.

The soldier takes it, blinking back tears of his own,
understanding the meaning if not the words.

The boy's voice gives out, he slumps, exhausted,
into the soldier's outstretched arms.

The boy's father comes to take his son, hold him close.
He nods at the soldier, mumbles: "Thank you,"
the limit of his English. The soldier nods back,
looks around at the vision of hell, and thinks: "For what?"

THE MISCARRIAGE
Ingrid Jendrzejewski

I am a battleship, sinking.

When the USS West Virginia went down
at Pearl Harbor, the clean-up crews
could hear tapping from inside the ship.
They knew there were men inside, alive,
but they couldn't reach them,
had no way to save them.

Eventually, the tapping slowed.

After sixteen days, it stopped.

NOW LIVE THROUGH THIS

Written by
ELIZABETH FERNANDEZ

Illustrated by
EMILY SOYNTON

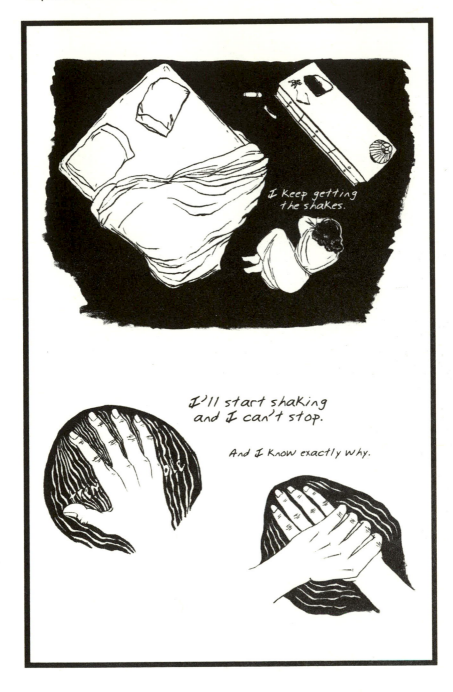

But love
doesn't mean
cowering
while
he shouts
at me.

Love doesn't
mean hurting
somebody the
way he did.